United States
Department
of Agriculture

Forest Service

Rocky Mountain
Research Station

Proceedings
RMRS-P-58
June 2009

National Proceedings: Forest and Conservation Nursery Associations—2008

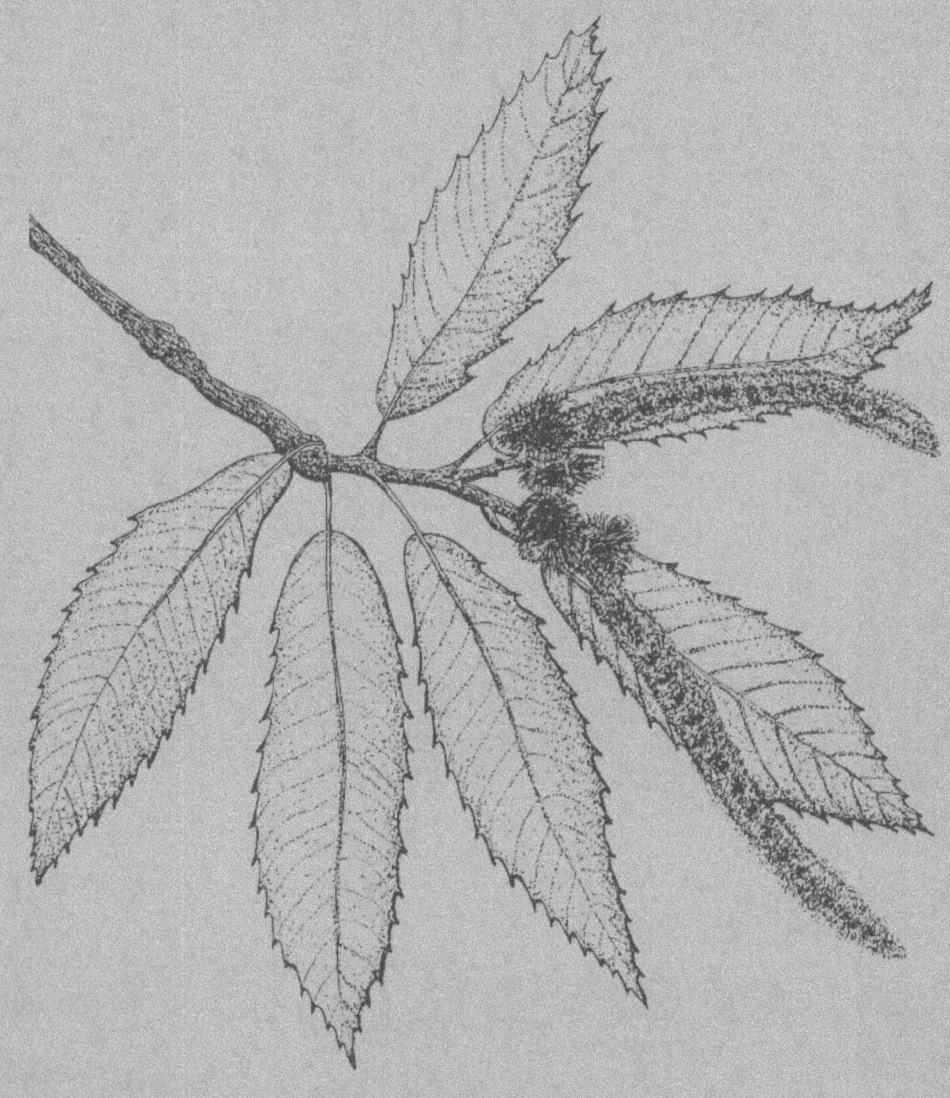

Dumroese, R.K.; Riley, L.E., tech. coords. 2009. **National Proceedings: Forest and Conservation Nursery Associations—2008.** Proc. RMRS-P-58. Fort Collins, CO: U.S. Department of Agriculture, Forest Service, Rocky Mountain Research Station.

Abstract

These proceedings are a compilation of 27 papers that were presented at the regional meetings of the forest and conservation nursery associations in the United States in 2008. The **Western Forest and Conservation Nursery Association** meeting was held at the DoubleTree Hotel in Missoula, Montana, on June 23 to 25. The meeting was hosted by the Montana Conservation Seedling Nursery in Missoula. Subject matter for the technical sessions included energy efficiency and alternative energy in the nursery, alternative growing media components and amendments, and general nursery topics. Afternoon field trips included tours of the Montana Conservation Seedling Nursery and the Confederated Salish and Kootenai tribal forestry nursery outside Ronan, Montana.

The **Southern Forest Nursery Association** meeting was held July 21 to 24 at the Crown Plaza Resort in Asheville, North Carolina. The meeting was hosted by the North Carolina Division of Forest Resources Linville River Nursery. Subject matter for the technical sessions included nursery culture and management, weed management, fumigation alternatives, insect and disease management and resistance programs. Field trips included an afternoon tour of the North Carolina Division of Forest Resources' Linville River Nursery, and an afternoon tour of the Biltmore House grounds, gardens, and winery.

Keywords: bareroot nursery, container nursery, nursery practices, fertilization, pesticides, seeds, reforestation, restoration, tree physiology, hardwood species

Papers were edited to a uniform style; however, authors are responsible for content and accuracy of their papers.

Front cover drawing, American chestnut, by Steven Morrison, College of Natural Resources, Univeristy of Idaho.

National Proceedings:

Forest and Conservation Nursery Associations—2008

Technical Coordinators

R. Kasten Dumroese, Research Plant Physiologist, USDA Forest Service, Rocky Mountain Research Station, 1221 South Main Street, Moscow, ID 83843; Tel: 208.883.2324; FAX: 208.883.2318; E-mail: kdumroese@fs.fed.us.

Lee E. Riley, Supervisory Operations Forester, USDA Forest Service, Dorena Genetics Resource Center, 34963 Shoreview Road, Cottage Grove, OR 97424; Tel: 541.767.5723; FAX: 541.767.5709; E-mail: leriley@fs.fed.us.

Sponsoring Organizations

Montana Conservation Seedling Nursery, Missoula, Montana

North Carolina Division of Forest Resources Linville River Nursery, Crossnore, North Carolina

Acknowledgments

Funding for this publication was provided as a technology transfer service by the USDA Forest Service, State and Private Forestry through the National Reforestation, Nurseries, and Genetic Resources (RNGR) Program. The compilers thank Lane Eskew, Loa Collins, Nancy Chadwick, and Richard Schneider for their assistance in the preparation, printing, and distribution of this publication.

Searchable Internet Database—www.rngr.net

National Nursery Proceedings database includes papers published in the regional nursery proceedings (Western, Intermountain, Northeastern, and Southern) since 1949. The database can be searched by date, author, or keyword and papers are available in portable document format (PDF).

Table of Contents

**No papers received; for more information, contact authors at the addresses provided in the list of attendees.

Western Forest and Conservation Nursery Association Meeting

Missoula, Montana

June 23 to 25, 2008

Ponderosa pine drawing by Lorraine Ashland, College of Natural Resources, University of Idaho.

Growing and Energy Conservation

Eric van Steenis

Eric van Steenis, RPF is with Grotec Equipment Division, Terralink Horticulture Incorporated, 464 Riverside Road, Abbotsford, BC V2S 7M1; Tel: 604.504.2838; E-mail: eric@terralink-horticulture.com.

van Steenis, E. 2009. Growing and energy conservation. In: Dumroese, R.K.; Riley, L.E., tech. coords. 2009. National Proceedings: Forest and Conservation Nursery Associations—2008. Proc. RMRS-P-58. Fort Collins, CO: U.S. Department of Agriculture, Forest Service, Rocky Mountain Research Station: 3–6. Online: http://www.fs.fed.us/rm/pubs/rmrs_p058.html.

Abstract: As energy costs increase, resistance is strong to these costs becoming a larger proportion of production cost. Many options can be considered in this battle. This presentation deals only with altering thermostat settings during initial crop growth stages early in the season. Reducing energy requirements in greenhouse crop production while maintaining quality and on-time delivery is a challenge. Two concepts are discussed with respect to greenhouse heating set points: Q_{10} factors during seed germination and DIF during active growth.

Keywords: greenhouse heating, germination, photosynthesis, Q_{10}

Growing and Energy

A plant is packaged energy. Like any organism, it consumes energy to grow, protect, maintain, and reproduce itself. Within native habitats, plant species evolve to accomplish this within the seasonal time frame, utilizing "free" energy supplied by the sun.

In the nursery, we impose minimum size, time, uniformity, and developmental requirements. Impatience costs money, that is, supplementary energy input in the form of light and heat that is purchased during winter and early spring. Establishment of uniformity early in a crop cycle is perhaps the most energy intensive. If establishing uniformity at lower temperatures is required, then high seed vigor is extremely important because it facilitates seed germination at a wider range of temperatures. Multiple sowing and thinning may be a viable strategy depending on seed cost and availability. Germinating at low temperatures generally results in reduced uniformity that can be partly or wholly re-established at thinning.

Light and heat are the energy forms critical to photosynthesis and "growing." Light drives the photosynthetic process, and heat warms the photosynthetic machinery so it can operate. Heat also encourages convection around plants, thereby replenishing CO_2 supplies and "driving" transpiration. When plants are located outside during the natural growing season, these energy forms are abundantly available and in approximately the correct proportions. In a greenhouse during the winter, however, this is rarely the case. The challenge is to supplement and balance them in such a way that "growth" occurs. Optimum settings are growth-stage dependent.

Heat and Germination

Respiration of stored seed reserves fuels germination. Respiration rate increases with temperature. The goal is fast, uniform, and disease-free germination. Many things can affect germination, but this paper will concentrate on seed temperature. Figure 1 depicts seed response to germination temperature. Given healthy, stratified seeds at appropriate moisture content, a "warm" regime may shorten the germination phase. If approximately 82% germination is the cutoff for switching from a "germination" to "growing" environment, then the "warm" regime allows compression of the germination phase by 5 days (fig. 2).

Does shortening the germination phase pay? Figure 3 depicts the rate, in general, at which energy is supplied to a seedling, and how it accumulates energy over the course of its first growing season. It should be noted that no artificially supplied heat energy results as stored chemical bond energy inside the seedling. The seedling has to capture and store all the energy itself. We cannot "pump it up." The heat energy that we supply helps facilitate the conversion of light to chemical bond energy by warming the production machinery, allowing it to work more quickly and efficiently. A germinating seedling, once showing green, is a small solar panel.

The large up-front fuel expense is due to the inefficient way heat is supplied to germinating seeds. A handful of seeds are distributed into a huge, virtually uninsulated, volume of air termed a greenhouse, which is subsequently heated. Is this worth the cost? Are there other ways to realize the objective? Can we reduce energy use or increase energy use efficiency (figs. 4 or 5)?

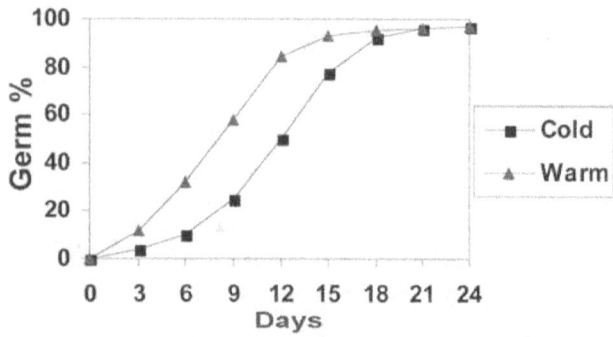

Figure 1. Healthy, stratified seed response to germination temperatures.

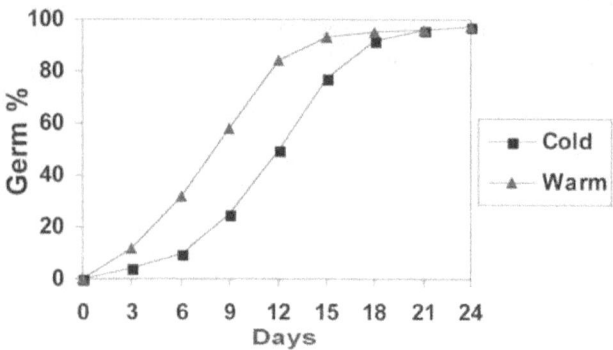

Figure 2. A warmer environment may compress the seed germination phase by 5 days.

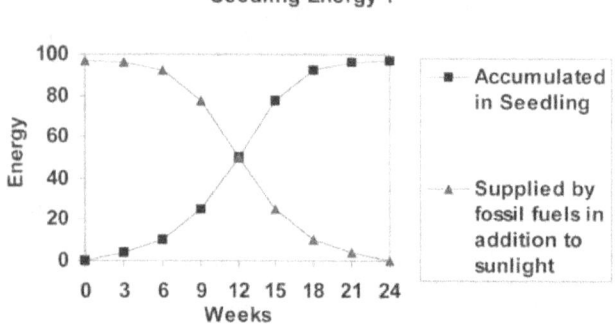

Figure 3. Rate at which energy is artificially supplied to a seedling as compared to accumulated energy in the seedling.

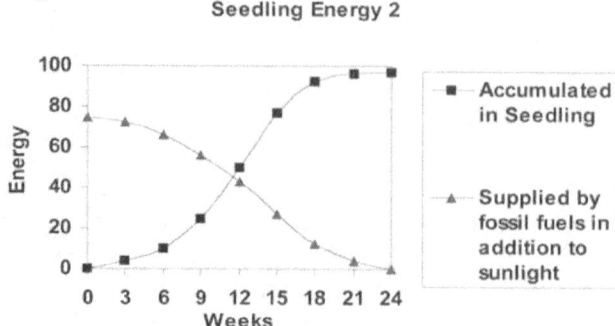

Figure 4. Reduced rate at which energy is artificially supplied to a seedling as compared to accumulated energy in the seedling.

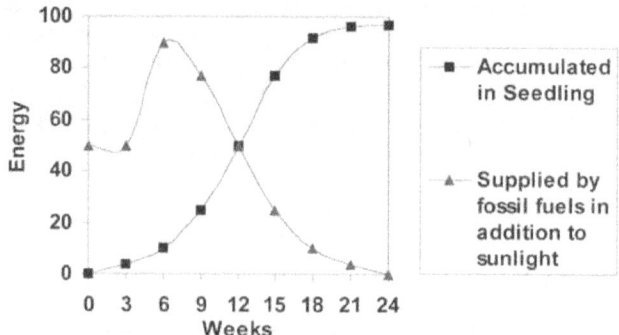

Figure 5. More efficient use of energy in a greenhouse as compared to accumulated energy in the seedling.

Q_{10}

Assume stratification is complete, and moisture, oxygen, and carbohydrate reserves are not limiting. The rate at which biochemical processes proceed within a seed depends on **seed** temperature. The function that describes how the **rate** of a biochemical reaction changes with changing temperature is called the "Q_{10} factor." Over a specified range, it describes how the reaction rate changes per 10 °C (18 °F) interval.

Between 5 and 35 °C (41 and 95 °F) for respiration in plants, the Q_{10} factor is approximately 2. This is an exponential relationship. This means that over the specified temperature range, a 10 °C (18 °F) rise results in a doubling of the respiration rate (fig. 6). From the onset of germination until green is showing, respiration rate equals germination rate.

Practically speaking, raising seed temperature from 5 to 15 °C, 10 to 20 °C, or 15 to 25 °C (41 to 59 °F, 50 to 68 °F, or 59 to 77 °F) in each case doubles respiration rate from the lower temperature. Hence, raising the temperature from 5 to 25 °C (41 to 77 °F) quadruples it! Keep this in mind when choosing germination and growing temperature regimes. At a higher initial temperature, where the respiration/germination rate is initially higher, a certain temperature increase results in a much larger response than at lower temperatures, where initial rates are lower.

Obviously, huge gains in germination speed and uniformity can be made by raising germination temperature ≥25 °C (77 °F). But the question remains: does it pay, especially at high per unit energy costs?

The cost of raising the temperature in a growing facility is a function of the area of the structure, covering heat loss value, inside humidity level, air exchanges per unit time, and outside temperature/wind/precipitation conditions. Greenhouse-heating costs increase in a linear, not exponential, fashion (fig. 7).

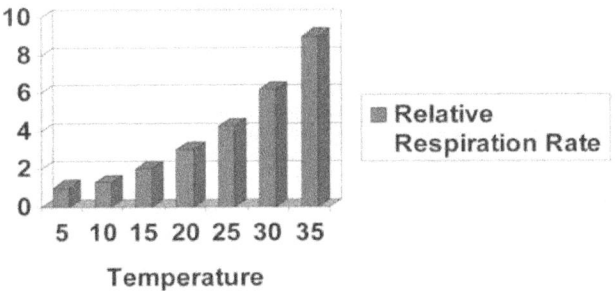

Figure 6. Q_{10} = 2 for plant respiration (5 to 35 °C [41 to 95 °F]).

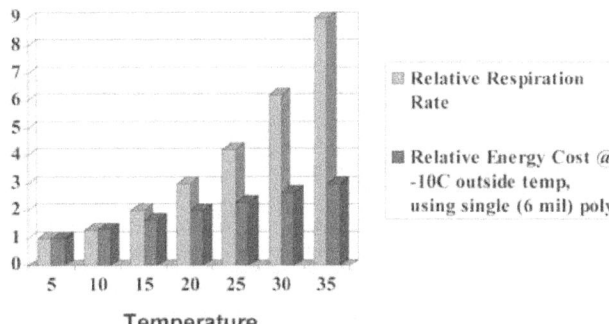

Figure 8. Q_{10} versus greenhouse heating.

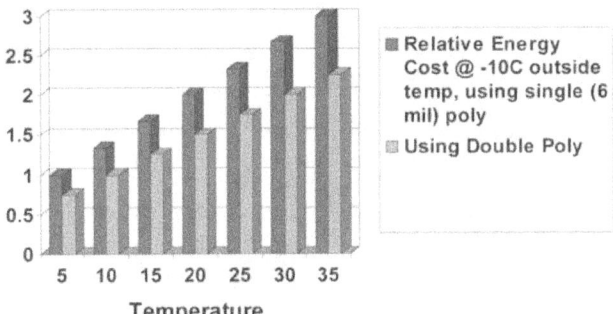

Figure 7. Greenhouse heating is linear.

With each successive increase in greenhouse temperature, the return on the heating investment increases in terms of increased germination speed. In the scenario in figure 8, the first unit of energy is consumed to achieve a greenhouse temperature of 5 °C (41 °F). Respiration (germination) rate is 1. Adding a second unit of energy brings the greenhouse temperature to 20 °C (68 °F) and results in a respiration rate of 3. Adding a third unit of energy brings greenhouse temperature to 35 °C (95 °F) and raises respiration/germination rate to 9 times the rate at 5 °C (41 °F)! In other words, 3 days at 5 °C (41 °F) will give the same germination result as 1 day at 20 °C (68 °F) (that is, seed temperature, not just greenhouse air temperature). Saving 2 days of heating time at 5 °C (41 °F) equals a savings of 33% on the fuel bill to attain the same level of germination.

The bottom line is, it pays to increase germination temperature. In fact, the higher the per-unit energy cost... the more it pays! "You have to spend money to make money."

After Germination _____

Regular growth is an extension of germination. Temperatures that promote growth will promote germination. For many plants, however, optimum germination temperatures are somewhat higher than optimum growing temperatures. This is due to the fact that respiring storage reserves in seeds generate energy requirements for germination type growth, primarily involving reactivation and "unfolding" of previously developed systems and structures. Photosynthesizing organs and "machinery" have maintenance energy requirements that increase exponentially with temperature. This leads to the concept of "net growth," which equals gross photosynthetic production minus respiratory maintenance requirements.

Net Photosynthesis

Energy conversion is the concept. In a greenhouse during winter/spring, with help from stored prehistoric solar energy (natural gas, propane, coal) converted to heat, we make it possible to convert current solar energy (sunlight) to chemical bond energy through the process of photosynthesis. Photosynthesis and energy storage are a result of several factors:

- Photosynthesis (PS) only occurs in the presence of light (and carbon dioxide);
- Net PS = Gross PS – respiration (RS);
- Net PS is positive if PS > RS;
- Net PS is negative if PS < RS;
- 24-hour **net** PS is positive if daytime **net** PS exceeds nighttime respiration losses;
- Annual **net** PS is positive if growing season **net** PS exceeds non-growing season RS losses;
- Once seed reserves are consumed, young plants start out with virtually no stored energy reserves;
- Respiration of stored carbohydrate reserves (energy) drive "growth";
- Net PS has a lower temperature optimum under low light (figs. 9 and 10; note the shape of each line);
- Dark period temperature must allow for reallocation of resources generated during the day (physical growth, maturation and reorganization within the plant) while minimizing respiratory losses (fig. 11);
- Good net PS days can support warmer nights and may require seedlings to process additional photosynthetic products generated during the preceding day;
- Poor net PS days do not require, and cannot support, long and/or warm nights, especially in plants with low stored energy reserves (small, young plants are more vulnerable); and
- A poor net PS day can be bright and very hot, bright and very cold, dull and warm, and so on.

For all aspects of the preceeding discussion, the benefit of **light dependent** temperature control and a **positive** differential between day/night temperatures (DIF) are implied.

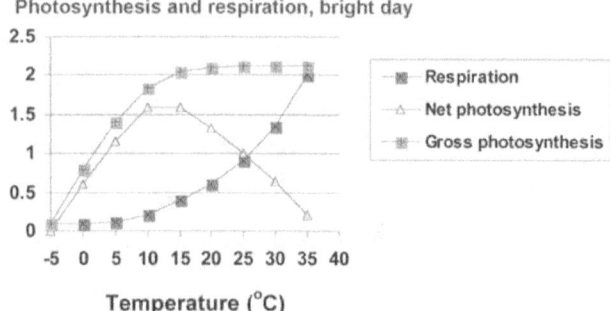

Figure 9. Photosynthesis and respiration on a bright day.

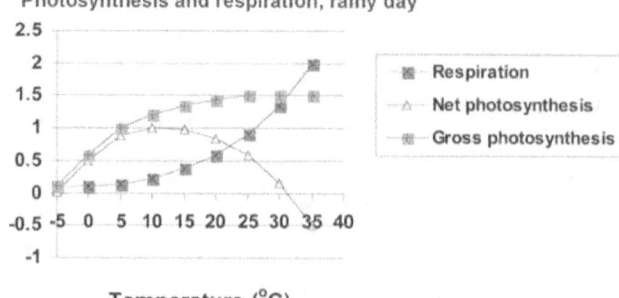

Figure 10. Photosynthesis and respiration on a rainy day.

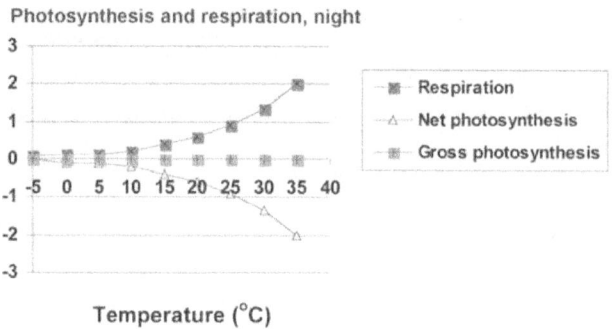

Figure 11. Photosynthesis and respiration at night.

With good solar gain during the day, a positive day/night differential is recommended. The cost/benefit of raising the temperature **above** ambient outside temperature (at night) and/or **above** ambient inside temperature maintained by solar gain (during the day) needs to be kept in mind.

To facilitate rapid **germination**, temperatures from 20 to 25 °C (68 to 77 °F) are recommended. This allows transfer of the germinant from a "**germinating**" to a "**growing**" environment sooner. The germinating environment satisfies the heat sum requirement for seed germination. Respiration of stored seed reserves fuels the process and temperature drives it. A constant day/night temperature is desirable, but not necessary. Maximizing heat sum in the most energy efficient manner is the goal. This can be achieved with variable temperatures. Therefore, heating based on the cost of maintaining a certain temperature change (ΔT) is prudent.

The **growing** environment needs to balance heat with light to maximize net PS during the day. At night, excess heat increases maintenance requirements within the seedling that deplete stored energy reserves. To minimize night-time losses, and thereby maximize the 24-hour net PS gain, a positive DIF is logical.

Summary

- Raising seed temperature during germination pays.
- Excellent forest seedling crops are being produced using night temperatures between 10 to 15 °C (50 to 59 °F) coupled with **light dependent** day temperatures between 15 to <25 °C (59 to <77 °F).
- Lower temperatures require additional attention to humidity conditions. In particular, one needs to closely monitor dew-point temperature in relation to plant temperature to combat diseases and physiological disorders.

Greenhouse Energy Consumption

Eric van Steenis

Eric van Steenis, RPF is with Grotec Equipment Division, Terralink Horticulture Incorporated, 464 Riverside Road, Abbotsford, BC V2S 7M1; Tel: 604.504.2838; E-mail: eric@terralink-horticulture.com.

van Steenis, E. 2009. Greenhouse energy consumption. In: Dumroese, R.K.; Riley, L.E., tech. coords. 2009. National Proceedings: Forest and Conservation Nursery Associations—2008. Proc. RMRS-P-58. Fort Collins, CO: U.S. Department of Agriculture, Forest Service, Rocky Mountain Research Station: 7–9. Online: http://www.fs.fed.us/rm/pubs/rmrs_p058.html.

Keywords: greenhouse heating, Q_{10}, seed germination, humidity

Introduction

Depending on location and luck, natural gas rates have gone from less that CAN\$ 3.00 to more than CAN\$ 20.00/gigajoule (Gj). Natural gas rates are currently around CAN\$ 13.00/Gj, although industry "analysts" predict an increase. A gigajoule is equivalent to the energy released by the combustion of approximately 30 L (8 gal) of gasoline. It is also equivalent to approximately 950,000 BTU, 0.165 barrels of oil, or 278 kilowatt-hours of electricity.

Energy as a proportion of greenhouse crop production cost is rising. This has sparked renewed interest in energy conservation, alternate fuels, different growing facilities, new cropping systems, and so on. This article briefly touches on energy conservation and provides a simple approach for evaluating alternate fuel sources.

Energy Conservation

Awareness of the purpose of energy—what forms are needed, when, and where—is required. Proximity of source to sink is key, because efficiency can be lost during transfer. In greenhouses, the two basic heating system objectives are: (1) to heat the growing plant so it can take advantage of available light during the day and process assimilates at night; and (2) to heat the greenhouse environment to maintain a favorable vapor pressure deficit, facilitating plant transpiration and associated evaporative cooling as well as internal nutrient transport.

Humidity control is a major cost in terms of energy consumption. If replenishing CO_2 is accomplished through venting, this also becomes a major energy cost due to the associated heat loss. Options for management of both may be worth investigating.

During seed germination, humidity (reduction) and CO_2 (injection) are not issues, but proximity of the heat source to seeds is. Germination speed can be approximated using a Q_{10} factor of 2 for plant respiration (van Steenis 2009). Between 5 and 25 °C (41 and 77 °F), germination speed (respiration rate) doubles for every 10 °C (18 °F). This should be weighed against the cost of heating a growing facility. Starting with ambient outside temperatures, one can log heater-running time for each rise in set-point temperature. This information can be used when deciding on heating set points given various outside weather conditions (including both temperature and precipitation). Basically, if a 10 °C (18 °F) rise (between 5 and 25 °C [41 and 77 °F]) can be attained for less than a doubling in fuel consumption, then it is economic to increase temperature (in terms of increased germination speed and subsequent reduced crop cycle time). The added bonus is a more uniform crop. In fact, the higher the price of fuel, the more economic it is!

Common sense heat conservation techniques abound. Sealing cracks, IR trapping and/or anti-condensate polyethylene films, double polyethylene roofs, raising heating pipes higher off the ground, skirting benches, delayed heating until a facility is full, pre-germinating, and so on, are just a few. Literature suggests the biggest gain is from installation of energy curtains. (These have to seal well!) They add an insulating layer of air, reduce total air volume to heat, and limit long-wave radiation loss from the crop. They are more cost effective when installed in gutter-connected greenhouses.

Alternative Fuels

Alternative fuels are intriguing, but it quickly becomes obvious that in order to "easily" take advantage of various options, one needs to be working with a hot water heating system. Unit heaters only lend themselves to natural gas or propane, whereas any fuel can be used to heat a boiler. Some fuels require investment in extra storage, transport, and delivery systems, as well as waste removal. One interesting option is pellet fuel combustion technology, utilizing wood residues and agricultural fibers. Wood pellets in British Columbia and switchgrass pellets in Quebec are two examples.

When evaluating alternatives, consider the capital investment associated with the system technology as well as the fuel price, how the biology of the growing system may change, and don't forget government regulations with respect to waste disposal and air quality. Because the difference in fuel prices determines the payback/economic feasibility, it is imperative that fuels be compared on a dollar per gigajoule or equivalent energy content basis.

Table 1 can be used to calculate the advantages and disadvantages of various fuel types and heat sources in a greenhouse. To use the table, select your current fuel source and price. Move to the left side of the table to obtain the equivalent price per gigajoule. Now choose a new fuel source and its current price to you. How does it compare on a dollar per basis? Realize it currently takes about 2.5 Gj of energy/m² (0.23 Gj/ft²) of growing space to produce a forest seedling crop. Knowing your total greenhouse area quickly gives an indication of how much money the "switch" can "make or break" you. If you are comparing to electricity, it is important to realize that its output (heat) cost equals its input (fuel) cost because it is 100% efficient. In other words, switching from a gas/wood/coal boiler to an electric boiler saves 15% in energy consumed regardless of its price.

An interesting example (from 2001 in British Columbia and expressed in Canadian dollars) is a grower with 2,500 m² (26,900 ft²) of growing area on propane at $ 0.36/L ($ 1.38/gal) using unit heaters (75% efficiency). This rate equals $ 14.50/Gj input cost, which equals $ 14.50/.75, or $ 19.33/Gj (heat) output cost. Electricity is $ 0.058/kWh or $ 16/Gj input **and** output cost. The 2,500 m² x 2.5Gj/ m² x $ 3.33 gives the grower $ 20,812.50 in year 1 if a switch was made to electric element unit heaters or boilers. If wood chips were available at $ 5.00/Gj delivered, the difference in output cost would be $ 19.33 − 5.88 = $ 13.45/Gj or $ 84,062.50 in year 1! This grower installed wood-fired boilers and hot water piping under the benches.

References

van Steenis, E. 2009. Growing and energy conservation. In: Dumroese, R.K.; Riley, L.E., tech. coords. 2009. National proceedings: Forest and Conservation Nursery Associations—2008. Proc. RMRS-P-58. Fort Collins, CO: U.S. Department of Agriculture, Forest Service, Rocky Mountain Research Station: 3–6.

Table 1. Fuel price comparison based on equivalent energy content (CAN$).

Input Price Natural Gas per Gj[1]	Equivalent Input Price Propane per L[2]	Equivalent Input Price #1 fuel oil per L[2]	Equivalent Input Price Bituminous coal per tonne[3] (3.3% mc)	Equivalent Input Price Woodchips per tonne[3] (35% mc)	Equivalent Input Price Wood Pellets per tonne[3] (2% mc)	Equivalent Input Price Electricity per KWhr	Output Price Unit Heater Heat per Gj (75% efficiency)	Output Price Boiler Heat per Gj (85% efficiency)	Output Price Electric Heat per Gj (100% efficiency)
1.00	0.03	0.04	33.00	12.66	18.00	0.00	1.33	1.18	1.00
2.00	0.05	0.08	66.00	25.32	36.00	0.01	2.67	2.35	2.00
3.00	0.08	0.11	99.00	37.98	54.00	0.01	4.00	3.53	3.00
4.00	0.10	0.15	132.00	50.64	72.00	0.01	5.33	4.71	4.00
5.00	0.13	0.19	165.00	63.30	90.00	0.02	6.67	5.88	5.00
6.00	0.15	0.23	198.00	75.96	108.00	0.02	8.00	7.06	6.00
7.00	0.18	0.26	231.00	88.62	126.00	0.03	9.33	8.24	7.00
8.00	0.20	0.30	264.00	101.28	144.00	0.03	10.67	9.41	8.00
9.00	0.23	0.34	297.00	113.94	162.00	0.03	12.00	10.59	9.00
10.00	0.25	0.38	330.00	126.60	180.00	0.04	13.33	11.76	10.00
11.00	0.28	0.41	363.00	139.26	198.00	0.04	14.67	12.94	11.00
12.00	0.30	0.45	396.00	151.92	216.00	0.04	16.00	14.12	12.00
13.00	0.33	0.49	429.00	164.58	234.00	0.05	17.33	15.29	13.00
14.00	0.35	0.53	462.00	177.24	252.00	0.05	18.67	16.47	14.00
15.00	0.38	0.56	495.00	189.90	270.00	0.05	20.00	17.65	15.00
16.00	0.40	0.60	528.00	202.56	288.00	0.06	21.33	18.82	16.00
17.00	0.43	0.64	561.00	215.22	306.00	0.06	22.67	20.00	17.00
18.00	0.45	0.68	594.00	227.88	324.00	0.06	24.00	21.18	18.00
19.00	0.48	0.71	627.00	240.54	342.00	0.07	25.33	22.35	19.00
20.00	0.50	0.75	660.00	253.20	360.00	0.07	26.67	23.53	20.00
21.00	0.53	0.79	693.00	265.86	378.00	0.08	28.00	24.71	21.00
22.00	0.55	0.83	726.00	278.52	396.00	0.08	29.33	25.88	22.00
23.00	0.58	0.86	759.00	291.18	414.00	0.08	30.67	27.06	23.00
24.00	0.60	0.90	792.00	303.84	432.00	0.09	32.00	28.24	24.00
25.00	0.63	0.94	825.00	316.50	450.00	0.09	33.33	29.41	25.00
26.00	0.65	0.98	858.00	329.16	468.00	0.09	34.67	30.59	26.00
27.00	0.68	1.02	891.00	341.82	486.00	0.10	36.00	31.76	27.00
28.00	0.70	1.05	924.00	354.48	504.00	0.10	37.33	32.94	28.00
29.00	0.73	1.09	957.00	367.14	522.00	0.10	38.67	34.12	29.00
30.00	0.75	1.13	990.00	379.80	540.00	0.11	40.00	35.29	30.00
31.00	0.78	1.17	1023.00	392.46	558.00	0.11	41.33	36.47	31.00
32.00	0.80	1.20	1056.00	405.12	576.00	0.12	42.67	37.65	32.00
33.00	0.83	1.24	1089.00	417.78	594.00	0.12	44.00	38.82	33.00
34.00	0.85	1.28	1122.00	430.44	612.00	0.12	45.33	40.00	34.00
35.00	0.88	1.32	1155.00	443.10	630.00	0.13	46.67	41.18	35.00
36.00	0.90	1.35	1188.00	455.76	648.00	0.13	48.00	42.35	36.00
37.00	0.93	1.39	1221.00	468.42	666.00	0.13	49.33	43.53	37.00
38.00	0.95	1.43	1254.00	481.08	684.00	0.14	50.67	44.71	38.00
39.00	0.98	1.47	1287.00	493.74	702.00	0.14	52.00	45.88	39.00
40.00	1.00	1.50	1320.00	506.40	720.00	0.14	53.33	47.06	40.00

[1] Gj = 950 000 BTU
[2] L = 0.26 gal
[3] tonne = 1.1 ton

Improvements for Energy Conservation at the Coeur d'Alene Nursery

Aram Eramian

Aram Eramian is Horticulturist/Bareroot Forester, USDA Forest Service Coeur d'Alene Nursery, 3600 Nursery Road, Coeur d'Alene, ID 83814; Tel: 208.765.7372; E-mail: aeramian@us.fed.us.

Eramian, A. 2009. Improvements for energy conservation at the Coeur d'Alene Nursery. In: Dumroese, R.K.; Riley, L.E., tech. coords. 2009. National Proceedings: Forest and Conservation Nursery Associations—2008. Proc. RMRS-P-58. Fort Collins, CO: U.S. Department of Agriculture, Forest Service, Rocky Mountain Research Station: 10–12. Online: http://www.fs.fed.us/rm/pubs/rmrs_p058.html.

Abstract: In 2002, the USDA Forest Service Coeur d'Alene Nursery in Idaho began to evaluate ways to reduce energy consumption in lighting, refrigeration, and heating and cooling of facility workspace. The primary factor leading up to this was the inefficiency of the nursery's Freon®-based refrigeration system. Energy costs and maintenance of the system were becoming a larger portion of the nursery's operating budget. Through the Bonneville Power Administration (BPA), the nursery used third-party financing, financial incentives, and a design-build contract to accomplish the work with very little capital outlay. Energy consumption has been substantially reduced as a result of the system improvements.

Keywords: water conservation, lighting systems, heating systems

Coeur d'Alene Nursery

The USDA Forest Service Coeur d'Alene Nursery in Idaho was built in 1962 and is administered by the Idaho Panhandle National Forest. The nursery provides plant material in the form of native conifer, shrub, forb, and grass seedlings for reforestation and restoration work within the Northern Region. The nursery maintains 53 ha (130 ac) of seedbeds that can produce 16 million bareroot seedlings, and 17 greenhouses that can grow 4 million container seedlings annually. The nursery will ship approximately 5 million tree seedlings this year to customers in the Northern Region.

Buildings at the nursery include a 306 m² (3,300 ft²) office building, 2,750 m² (29,580 ft²) of additional heated work areas, eight 7 m (22 ft) by 29 m (96 ft) and seven 9 m (30 ft) by 29 m (96 ft) greenhouses, approximately 6,320 m² (68,000 ft²) of shelter house growing space, and 1,950 m² (21,000 ft²) of refrigerated space for seedling cold storage.

Conservation Possibilities

In 2001, maintenance needs (costs) exceeded existing funding levels for refrigeration, lighting, and other mechanical systems. The nursery manager sought financial help from the Region for cooler maintenance. Work was done on the existing refrigeration system to keep it operational, but it was a short-term solution. In 2002, the refrigeration system continued to degrade to the point it was no longer reliable. The work that was done in 2001 increased power consumption rather than reducing it. The nursery manager went back to the Region for assistance with a permanent solution for the coolers. The architect in the Regional Office had been working on energy conservation programs and contacted the Bonneville Power Administration (BPA) to see if any programs were available that could fund some of the maintenance work at the nursery. The BPA was interested in surveying the nursery site because of the amount of power being used annually. In December 2002, a BPA energy manager came to the nursery and conducted a site evaluation. His review identified five areas where improvements could be made to conserve energy: lighting, water conservation, heating, refrigeration, and the building envelope.

Lighting

The nursery space lighting was upgraded under a contract and was funded by an incentive program through BPA. The contractor came to the nursery in the spring of 2003 and assessed the existing interior and exterior lighting systems and developed recommendations for retrofit to more efficient fixtures. Existing fluorescent ballasts and tubes were replaced in the summer and fall of 2003 with more efficient, low-mercury T32 tubes. The replacement of the old fluorescent ballasts also eliminated a polychlorinated biphenyl (PCB) hazard at the facility. In two locations, motion sensors were installed to the light fixtures to efficiently manage power consumption. In the past, lights were continually left on in these locations long after work was completed. Exterior lighting fixtures on buildings were converted from mercury vapor to high-pressure sodium. The retrofit of the lighting system reduced energy consumption to a point where it was noticed by the local utility provider. BPA estimates predicted we would save 200,000 kWh, or US$ 8,850 per year.

Water Conservation

The primary 300-horsepower deep-well turbine pump was evaluated for energy conservation improvements. It was determined, however, that the cost of a variable-frequency drive (VFD) would be very expensive. The breakeven point would have occurred 45 years into the future based on current use rates. Evaluation of past irrigation practices and pump performance curves for the existing pump determined that the system was not being run at optimal levels. Irrigation practices and schedules have been changed to run within optimal pump performance, reducing pump operation hours and thus saving additional energy.

Heating

Heating and cooling systems in office areas have been targeted for upgrading, but at this point have not been completed. Existing electric baseboard heaters and through-the-wall air conditioners will be replaced with heat pumps. BPA estimated the cost savings will be US$ 4,710, or 80,000 kWh per year with this conversion.

Refrigeration

The existing Freon®-based (R401-A) refrigeration system was evaluated by an energy engineering firm in the fall of 2002. The information gathered was used to prepare a prospectus and report for the refrigeration system renovation. The BPA used the report to write a task order that the Northern Region of the Forest Service used to issue a design and build contract in 2003. The terms and schedule of payments for the third party loan that was used to finance the project were included in the task order. Contract design reviews and acceptance of the plans took place in the latter part of 2003.

The demolition of the old system and construction of the new system began in the spring/summer of 2004 after all seedlings for that year were shipped to the field. The contractor was to replace the existing Freon®-based system with an ammonia-to-glycol chiller system. The chiller system included screw compressors equipped with variable frequency drives that reduce power consumption when demand is low. Compact, efficient evaporators were installed inside each of the cooler rooms. All systems are monitored and controlled by a computer, which maximizes system efficiency with the help of variable frequency drives on equipment motors. Warm water produced by the system's condenser is used to defrost the evaporator coils in the cooler rooms, hallways, and loading dock. Construction work on the cooler system was completed in November 2004 in time for storage of fall-lifted bareroot and container seedlings.

Other Items

Water Heaters—Currently 12 electric water heaters are in use in various buildings at the nursery. BPA recommended replacement of these with direct "tankless" water heaters as the older ones fail. No replacements have been made to date. BPA estimates that we would save an additional US$ 509, or 6,400 kWh per year.

Programmable Thermostats—Five programmable thermostats were purchased and installed on existing heaters in various work areas. This has provided more efficient use of the existing heaters by heating work areas only on days that people are scheduled to be working. This has eliminated heaters being left on overnight and on weekends during the peak heating season, saving additional energy. BPA estimated US$ 500 per year in savings with the retrofit.

Payoff of Energy Conservation Efforts

The nursery uses an average of 1.16 million kWh of energy per year since the completion of the lighting and tree cooler renovations. The nursery's historic average energy usage prior to the energy saving improvements was 2.1 million kWh. The largest realized cost savings was the renovation of the tree seedling coolers. Because the main electric meter tracks usage for the entire site, smaller energy conservation work, like replacing thermostats, insulating cracks and holes in building envelops, and turning lights off in areas not being occupied, could not be tracked directly to determine the energy savings. Overall, the measures have reduced energy consumption by about 0.94 million kWh annually since 2005 (fig. 1). In monetary terms at current utility rates, this equates to a cost savings of approximately US$ 56,000 per year. In addition, annual maintenance costs of between US$ 60,000 and US$ 100,000 have been eliminated. An additional 80,000 kWh in energy savings will be gained annually when the heat and cooling renovations for office work areas are completed.

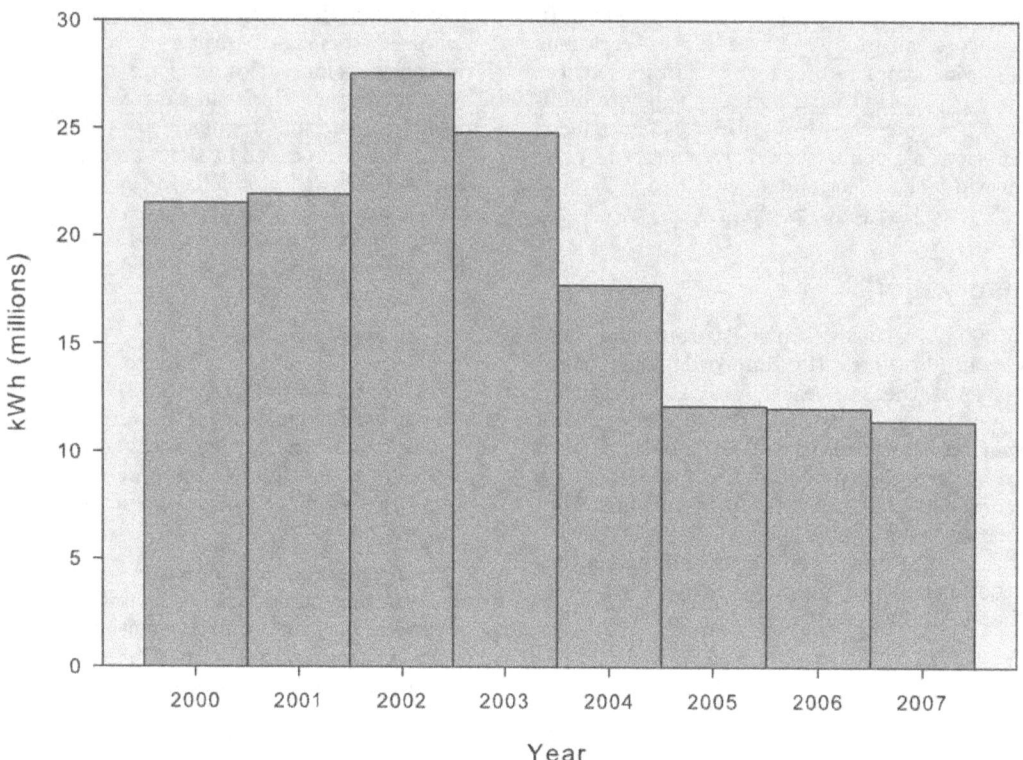

Figure 1. Annual kWh usage for the USDA Forest Service Coeur d'Alene Nursery from 2000 to 2007.

Using a Wood Stove to Heat Greenhouses

Gloria Whitefeather-Spears

Gloria Whitefeather-Spears is Greenhouse Manager for the Red Lake Forestry Greenhouse, PO Box 279, Red Lake, MN 56671; Tel: 218.679.3310; E-mail: gspears@paulbunyon.net.

Whitefeather-Spears, G. 2009. Using a wood stove to heat greenhouses. In: Dumroese, R.K.; Riley, L.E., tech. coords. 2009. National Proceedings: Forest and Conservation Nursery Associations—2008. Proc. RMRS-P-58. Fort Collins, CO: U.S. Department of Agriculture, Forest Service, Rocky Mountain Research Station: 13–16. Online: http://www.fs.fed.us/rm/pubs/rmrs_p058.html.

Abstract: The Red Lake Tribal Forestry Greenhouse in Red Lake, MN, utilizes four types of outdoor furnaces for heating through the fall, winter, and spring. The WoodMaster® is a highly efficient, wood-fired furnace that provides forced-air heat to the greenhouse. The Heatmor™ furnace is an economical wood-fired alternative that can provide lower insurance rates due to the large number of safety features. The Charmaster™ is a combination wood and oil furnace that is used as a backup system when ambient temperatures reach −34 °C (−30 °F). The Lennox™ furnace is an oil-burning furnace that provides a third backup system for the greenhouse.

Keywords: alternative heating systems, alternative fuel, outdoor furnace, in-floor heat, forced-air heat

Why Use an Outdoor Furnace?

Wood-fired outdoor furnaces are becoming popular alternatives to heating greenhouses throughout the winter. Outdoor furnaces have a number of advantages over other sources of heat for both residential and commercial uses.

Cheap Heat

Wood is a renewable resource and, depending on the location of the greenhouse operation, can provide a source of low cost heat throughout the season.

Safety

An outdoor furnace removes the danger of structure fires caused by indoor wood stoves. The usual installation distances for most furnaces range from 15 to 45 m (50 to 150 ft), but this distance can be doubled if desired or necessary. Safer outdoor units may also result in lower insurance rates.

Convenience

The wood-burning furnace can be situated beside the woodpile, eliminating the need to haul wood from the pile to the furnace. An injection air furnace burns any type and quality of wood, wet or dry, and unsplit in lengths of 90 to 140 cm (36 to 54 in). The large capacity firebox can achieve burn times averaging 23 hours or more per fill.

Cost Savings

Outdoor furnaces can easily heat most residential and commercial buildings, shops, garages, motels, factories, and restaurants. One furnace can heat multiple buildings.

Uses and Installation of Outdoor Furnaces

Outdoor furnaces can provide a source of heat for a multiplicity of items and structures, including water heaters, clothes dryers, pools and hot tubs, sidewalks, and driveways. They can be installed as forced air heating, in-floor heating, as a unit heater, to supplement existing boiler heating, or to provide heat for hot water baseboards. This discussion will predominantly focus on forced air and in-floor heating.

WATER TO AIR HEAT EXCHANGER APPLICATION

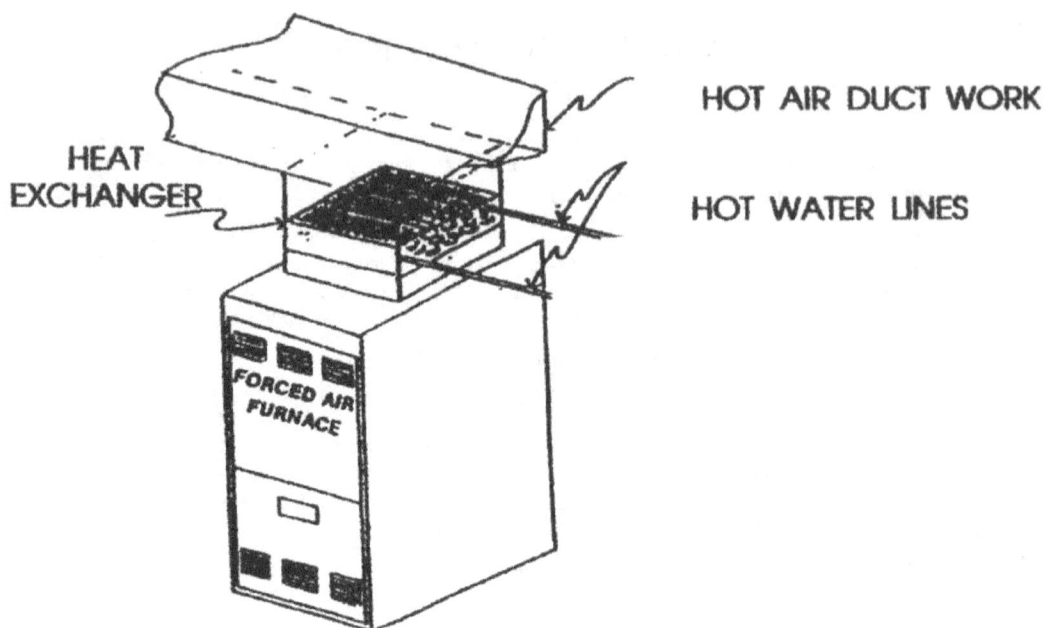

HEAT
EXCHANGER

HOT AIR DUCT WORK

HOT WATER LINES

FORCED AIR
FURNACE

Figure 1. The heat exchanger works on the same principle as a car heater. Air is blown across the heat exchanger, taking the heat from the water and blowing it through the existing duct work.

Forced Air Heating

A water-to-air heat exchanger (fig. 1) can be installed in the ductwork directly above an existing furnace (referred to as the plenum). Hot water constantly circulates through the exchanger. The hot water line coming from the hot water tube enters the bottom fitting of the heat exchanger and exits the top fitting, and then returns to the furnace. If the plenum is too large or too small, it must be altered to fit the heat exchanger properly.

The blower, controlled by a thermostat, blows air across the heat exchanger coil and transfers the heat through the house. A more even heat is provided with this system. Any existing furnace can stay in place as a back up. In most cases, the heat exchanger is placed in a horizontal position, keeping all four sides level. The air must be forced through the heat exchanger evenly.

In-Floor Heating

An in-floor heating system (fig. 2) can be installed by placing hot water pipes in the floor at the time the slab is poured. Water circulates through the tubing and heats the concrete, which radiates and heats the building. Valves control the water flow in each loop. Manual control valves are used between manifolds for temperature control, and electric zone valves are used for more even heat. Thermostats are used to individually control the heat in any part of the building.

Types of Outdoor Furnaces _____

The Red Lake Tribal Nursery currently uses four different types of outdoor furnaces for heating greenhouses through the fall, winter, and spring.

WoodMaster®

WoodMaster® (Red Lake Falls, MN) produces four types of furnaces varying in size and type of steel used. The main features of the furnace used at Red Lake Tribal Nursery are reviewed below.

Forced Air—The furnace warms water to its optimal heating temperature, which is constantly maintained by automatic controls.

High Efficiency—A circulation pump continuously circulates the heated water to provide proper heat distribution and ensure that the desired temperature is maintained.

Adaptability—The versatile design of the WoodMaster® makes it compatible with most existing heating systems. The installation is easy and allows the furnace to be used as a primary heat source or in conjunction with an existing heating system.

Durability—The welds on every stove are air tested for safety and performance. Total in-house manufacturing guarantees that each unit leaves the factory in showroom condition backed by a 10-year limited warranty.

IN-FLOOR HEAT APPLICATION

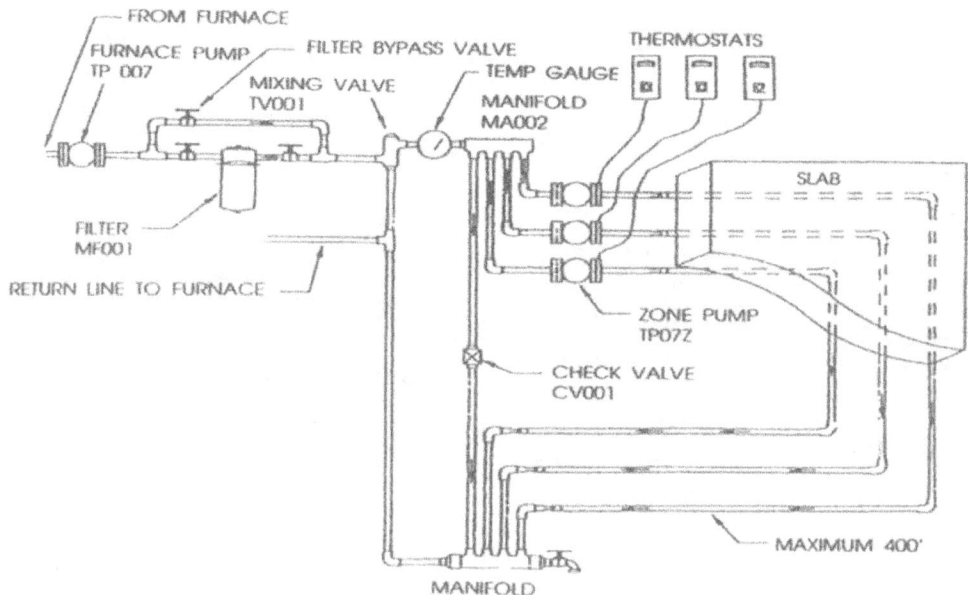

Figure 2. Water flow diagram for in-floor heat.

Insulation—High efficiency, noncombustible insulation prevents any chance of fire. A red warning light located to the front of the furnace warns when water is needed. The large water capacity at the top of the fire drum reduces water evaporation. Even under heavy burning conditions only 8 to 19 L (2 to 5 gal) are needed per year.

The WoodMaster® furnace used at Red Lake as a water capacity of 1,900 L (500 gal), and is rated at 140,000 BTUs.

Heatmor™

A Heatmor™ furnace (Warroad, MN) is manufactured from stainless steel with a low chrome/nickel content and high corrosion resistance. The outer insulated door eliminates heat loss to the environment, and the firebrick-lined firebox allows a hotter, more complete burn. Due to an injection air system, the burn cycle in this furnace is very hot and brief. Less wood is consumed, less creosote is formed in the chimney, and even the wettest wood burns easily.

Safety—The Heatmor™ furnace is safe, with little to no fire danger from the furnace. The outside door lock prevents access from small children, and lessens the chance of tampering. An automatic high-limit switch shuts off the forced draft. Additional safety features include a low water indicator, safety pressure relief system, adjustable water temperature, pressure release overflow, and an anti-flashback door safety latch.

Economical—The Heatmor™ furnace provides the ability to heat outbuildings, multi-dwellings, and any other domestic heating needs.

Convenient—Chimney flues provide easy access for general maintenance. The burn cycle can last up to 12 to 24 hours, and the ash auger provides an easy ash removal system. In addition, the furnace comes completely wired.

Lower Insurance Rates—Several other safety features are provided by the Heatmor™ furnace, including the insulated door handle, inner door safety latch, and an atmospheric pressure system. In addition, the system has been lab tested by both PFS Corporation (Cottage Grove, WI) and CSA International (Chicago, IL) and approved to UL standards. The outer insulated door will not expose a hot door to personnel working around the furnace. These safety features may result in lower insurance premiums.

The Heatmor™ furnace system in use at Red Lake has a water capacity of 570 L (150 gal), and is rated at 100,000 BTUs.

Charmaster™

The Charmaster™ furnace is a forced air and water-to-air heat exchanger, and is a combination wood and oil furnace. Wood is the primary fuel source at Red Lake, with oil as the backup system. Either #1 or #2 fuel oil can be used in this system. The Charmaster™ stove is much smaller than the other systems used at Red Lake.

Plenum—The super large heat exchanger cuts chimney heat loss. This feature can cut wood consumption up to 50% or more.

Zone Pumps and Blowers—Zone pumps circulate water from the pipes to the heat exchanger when thermostats call for heat in various areas. The furnace blowers distribute the hot air throughout the greenhouses. Honeywell thermostats activate the zone pumps and furnace blowers simultaneously.

The Charmaster™ furnace is used when outside temperatures drop to –34 °C (–30 °F). There is no water storage system, as the water is fed through circulating pipes. The furnace is rated at 140,000 BTUs.

Lennox™

The Lennox™ furnace (Richardson, TX) is an oil-burning furnace that provides a third backup system for the greenhouse. This system burns #1 or #2 heating oil. Like the Heatmor™, the Lennox™ furnace is constructed of stainless steel, and resembles most home furnaces.

Annual Maintenance _____

At the Red Lakes Tribal Forestry Greenhouses, annual maintenance on all wood- and oil-burning furnaces is important prior to seasonal use.

Off-Season

Fireboxes in wood-burning furnaces are protected during the summer by placing chimney caps over the chimney when not in use.

Pre-Season Inspection/Care

All furnace pumps are inspected prior to use to determine if they are working properly. Boilers are tested periodically by local dealers, and fuel filters are changed. As cooler weather approaches, the systems are fired-up and allowed to burn for 7 days. At this time, prescribed, annual boiler treatments are added to the boilers.

Seasonal Use

Ash augers are used often during the heating season (as required). Ash is removed and made available to local people for processing hominy corn. Water levels are maintained at proper levels and furnaces are checked daily or during every shift. When furnaces are not in use, water is left in the stoves to protect boilers from rusting and corrosion. Any required service work is done by a qualified service technician.

The content of this paper reflects the views of the authors, who are responsible for he facts and accuracy of the information presented herein.

Geothermal Energy for Greenhouses

Jacky Friedman

Jacky Friedman is Nursery Manager, IFA Nurseries, Incorporated, 1205 S Spring Street, Klamath Falls, OR 97601; Tel: 541.850.0952; E-mail: jfisher@ifanurseries.com.

Friedman, J. 2009. Geothermal energy for greenhouses. In: Dumroese, R.K.; Riley, L.E., tech. coords. 2009. National Proceedings: Forest and Conservation Nursery Associations—2008. Proc. RMRS-P-58. Fort Collins, CO: U.S. Department of Agriculture, Forest Service, Rocky Mountain Research Station: 17–19. Online: http://www.fs.fed.us/rm/pubs/rmrs_p058.html.

Keywords: alternative energy, heating systems

Geothermal energy is heat (thermal) derived from the earth (geo). The heat flows along a geothermal gradient from the center of the earth to the surface. Most of the heat arrives at the surface of the earth at temperatures too low for much use. However, plate tectonics ensure that some of the heat is concentrated at temperatures and depths favorable for its commercial extraction (fig. 1). The water may circulate to a depth of at least 4,270 m (14,000 ft). It is then heated and moves upward along fault zones and fractures.

Geothermal energy use in greenhouses is not a new concept. Bananas are grown in greenhouses in Iceland using geothermal energy.

Geothermal Energy Use in Klamath Falls

Klamath Falls, in southern Oregon, is located approximately 1,300 m (4,300 ft) above sea level (fig. 2). The Klamath Basin occupies the northwest corner of the Basin and Range Geological Province. This Province stretches south as far as Mexico and east to Utah. The north-south running ranges that separate the broad, flat basins are actually the fault lines between two separate blocks—one that has been pushed up (horst) and another that has been pushed down (graben). Extensive geological mapping of the Klamath Basin has found hundreds of these fault lines.

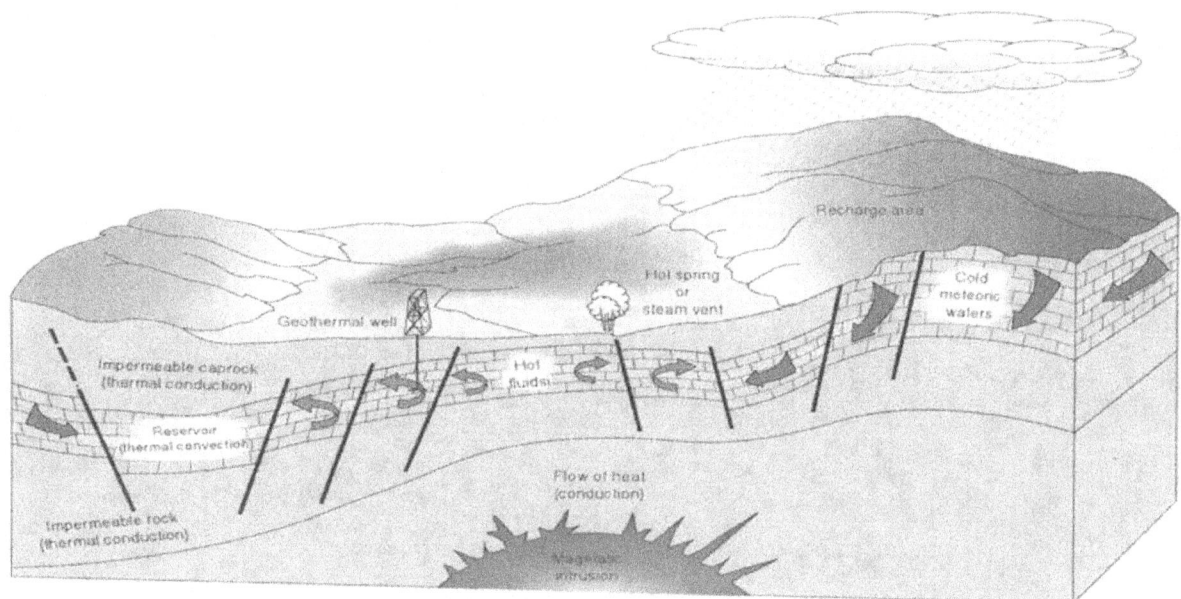

Figure 1. Plate tectonics allow geothermal heat to flow along a gradient from the center of the earth to the surface.

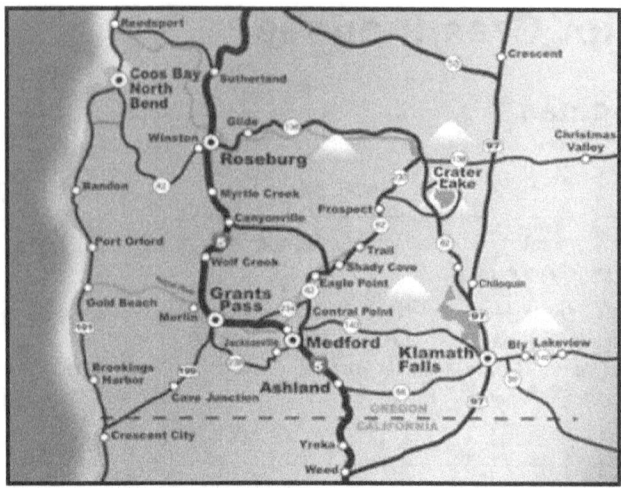

Figure 2. Klamath Falls is located in southwest Oregon in the northwest corner of the Basin and Range Geological Province.

The hot water in the Klamath basin probably originates as seepage from the Cascade Range to the west, Crater Lake to the north and, in part, from seepage from Upper Klamath Lake. The City of Klamath Falls is in a Known Geothermal Resource Area (KGRA). Records show native Indians utilizing the hot water for over 10,000 years, and the early settlers believed the "hot springs" would heal their ailments.

In 1982, the City of Klamath Falls constructed a "district heating system" (DHS) to provide the geothermal resource to the downtown area. The DHS was originally designed for a thermal capacity of 20 million BTU/hour. In 1992, however, only 25% of the DHS was being utilized, and a marketing effort began to attract new users.

The DHS currently provides geothermal energy for heating purposes to the Klamath Falls waste water treatment plant, approximately 37,160 m^2 (400,000 ft^2) of city

buildings, some of the schools, the library, U.S. Post Office, 9,750 m^2 (105,000 ft^2) of heated sidewalks, 350 private homes, and a new development, including a hotel and individual businesses.

Klamath Falls has two main systems. The "closed loop" system is typically used with private homes. The "open loop" system is used for much of the downtown area, in which any water removed from the aquifer must be replaced. All open loop systems have a production well and an injection well (fig. 3). The production well pumps are vertical line shaft pumps, oil lubricated, with variable speed drives. Only one production well is used at a time depending on the demand for heat.

Approximately 1,340 m (4,400 ft) of 20-cm (8-in) steel pipes convey the geothermal flow from the production wells to the heat exchanger. The geothermal flow is then injected back into the aquifer via the injection well.

The geothermal flow goes through the heat exchanger and the heat is transferred to a secondary system. The heat exchanger transfers 10,000 BTU/hour. The secondary water system uses municipal water. The hot water is pumped through a loop of pipeline around the downtown area of Klamath Falls. Each user of the system has a heat exchanger, and the heat is then transferred to their individual tertiary system.

The DHS is designed to deliver heating energy. The water flow is merely a means to convey the energy. The capacity to deliver heat is limited both by the flow capacity of the system and what the customer does with the heating water before sending it back. The heat delivered by the water depends on both the flow and the temperature change of the water. Flow is essentially fixed by the hardware selected in the design—pumps, pipes, control valves, heat exchangers, and so on. Any significant increase in flow requires larger equipment and increased power.

Recent improvements to the district heating system have increased the maximum capacity of the system to 36 million BTU/hour. The geothermal energy is currently available yearly from September to July.

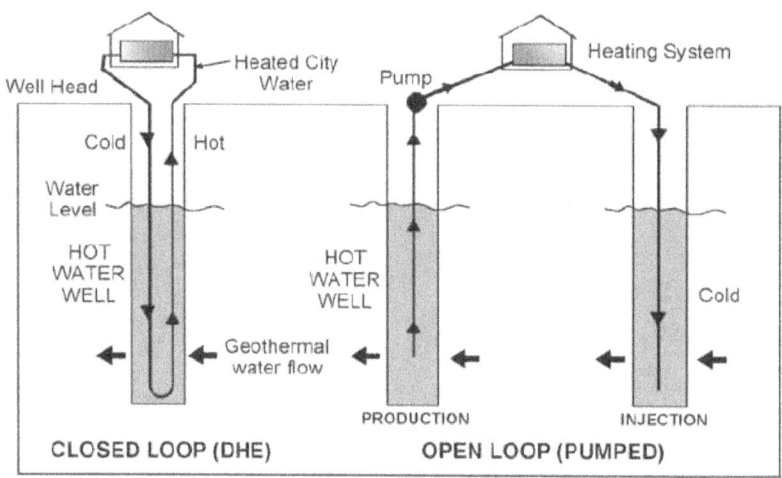

Figure 3. Two systems, "closed loop" and "open loop," are used in the various geothermal heating systems in Klamath Falls, OR.

IFA Nursery, Incorporated Geothermal Use _____

In 2001, IFA Nurseries, Incorporated (IFA) commenced the building of a new state-of-the-art greenhouse facility in Klamath Falls. The nursery now has 16,260 m² (175,000 ft²) of greenhouse space for growing seedlings for reforestation. The location was chosen for various reasons, but one incentive was the use of the DHS.

IFA's hot water supply from the city reaches our heat exchanger at about 83 °C (182 °F), and the supply temperature to our tertiary loop is about 82 °C (180 °F) (fig. 4). A computerized system monitors greenhouse temperatures and heat demand, and, in turn, an automatic valve opens the city supply line to allow flow through the heat exchanger. Valves located on the unit heaters at the greenhouses also open and close as the demand for heat fluctuates. Hot water flows into the forced air units on the unit heaters and warm air is forced through ducting and under-bench convection tubing. In addition to heating the greenhouse, we heat our main operations building and offices.

Several factors should be taken into account when looking at the economics of such a project. IFA chose to locate in Klamath Falls for several positive reasons, and the geothermal energy was just one of them. Users of the DHS are charged per Therm (100,000 BTU). The City-metered geothermal rate is set at 80% of the current commercial natural gas rate, with a rate increase of no more than 10% per year.

IFA saves a considerable amount of money on energy costs by using geothermal energy versus natural gas. The initial start-up costs of such a project are high, with much specialized and high-cost equipment required. A level of expertise was required in this project and we are grateful for the expertise at Oregon Institute of Technology Geothermal Heat Center for their assistance throughout the project. IFA received the Governors Award in Oregon in 2001 for best environmental construction for the project in Klamath Falls.

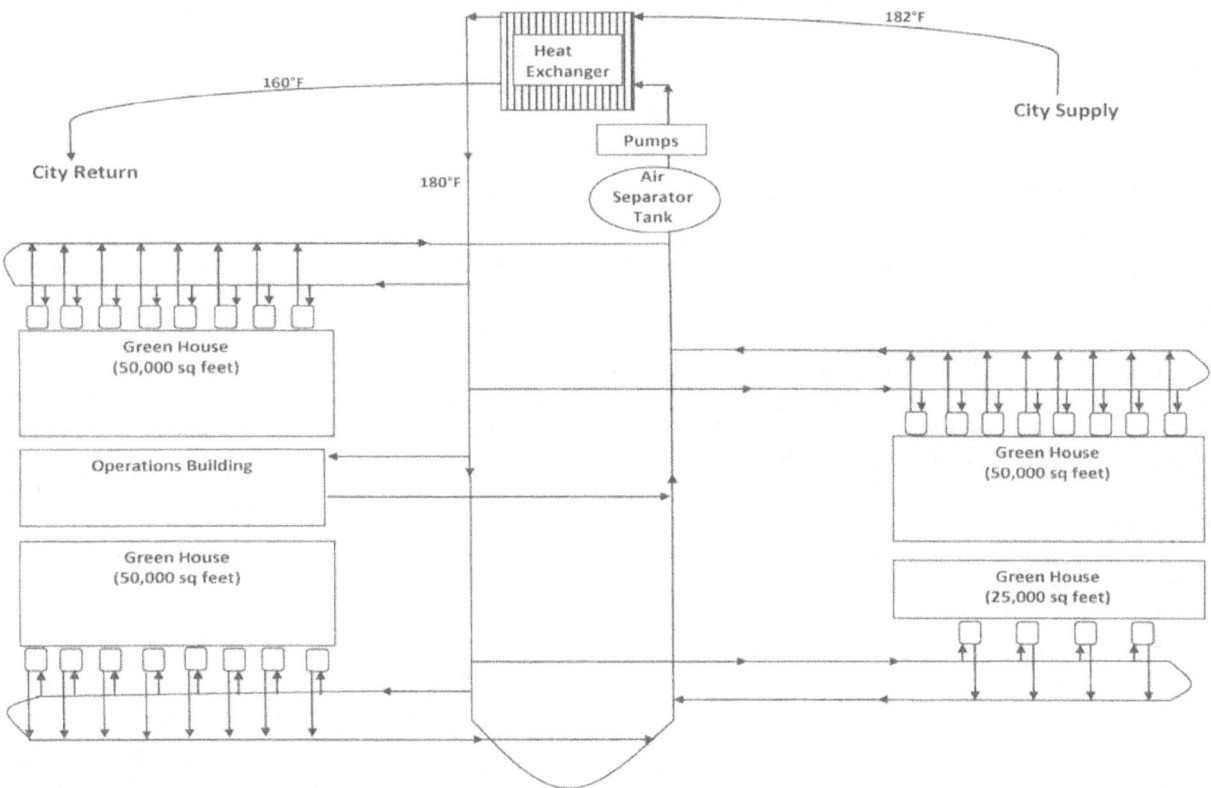

Figure 4. Tertiary heating loop for greenhouses and operations building at IFA Nurseries, Incorporated in Klamath Falls, OR.

Using Waste Oil to Heat a Greenhouse

Marla Schwartz

Marla Schwartz, and her husband Jim, are Owners of Northwoods Nursery, Incorporated, PO Box 149, Elk River, ID; Tel: 208.826.3408; E-mail: marlas@idahovandals.com.

Schwartz, M. 2009. Using waste oil to heat a greenhouse. In: Dumroese, R.K.; Riley, L.E., tech. coords. 2009. National Proceedings: Forest and Conservation Nursery Associations—2008. Proc. RMRS-P-58. Fort Collins, CO: U.S. Department of Agriculture, Forest Service, Rocky Mountain Research Station: 20–21. Online: http://www.fs.fed.us/rm/pubs/rmrs_p058.html.

Keywords: alternative fuel, wood-burning stove, oil-burning stove, heat exchange

History

During the winter of 1990, Northwoods Nursery (Elk River, ID) purchased a wood-burning system to heat the current greenhouses. This system burned slabs of wood to heat water that was then pumped into the greenhouses.

The winter of 1990 was extremely harsh, requiring non-stop operation of the heating system. In order to keep seedlings in the greenhouse from freezing, the burner required stoking every 30 minutes for 24 hours per day, 7 days per week. If the system was allowed to go out, there was no method available to restart the burner, and all water pipes would freeze very quickly.

The point learned during that period was to research options before buying a heating system for greenhouses.

Current System

Due to the problems encountered with the wood-burning system, Northwoods Nursery converted from wood to a waste oil system. At that time, waste oil was a great alternative due to the cost, that is, free. Loggers were dumping waste oil on roads and in creeks, and would therefore make it available to the nursery as a disposal alternative. But change happens.

During the past year, waste oil has become a commodity. The nursery has started to use stove oil, used cooking oil, waste oil, or whatever anyone provides that will burn in the stove. In the current burner, the oil enters through an injector (similar to a jet engine), and shoots heat into a baffling system. Water is heated in a large aluminum tank and then pumped out to heat the greenhouses (figs. 1 and 2). The water needs to be treated to prevent corrosion.

All pipes carrying heated water are insulated with Styrofoam™, although a low cost alternative could be old Styroblock™ containers. All fittings are placed above ground for easy access and maintenance.

Cautions

Waste oil must be kept warm prior to use. The nursery currently keeps the oil in a tank in the burner room so that the oil will remain liquid.

Precautions must be taken with ash resulting from burning a combination of waste oil and oil from unknown sources. Because oil from diesel engines may contain heavy metals, ash from this type of waste oil cannot be used with food products or fertilizer applications.

Figure 1. Waste oil burner in use to heat greenhouses at the Northwoods Nursery.

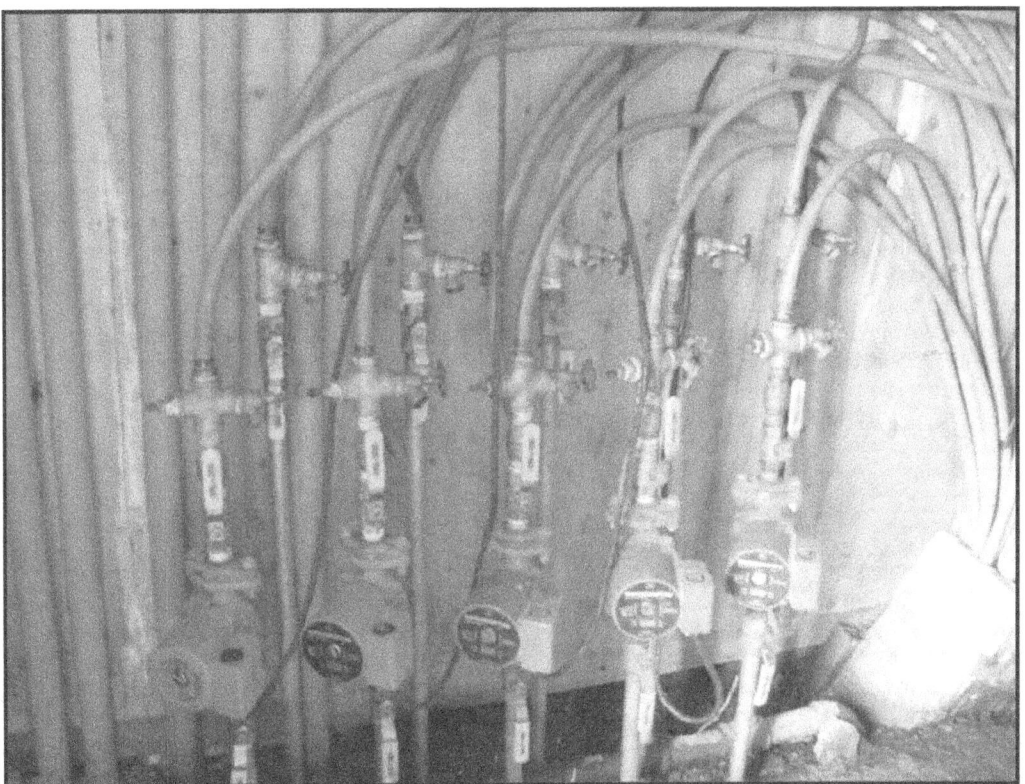

Figure 2. Pumping system for hot water distr bution to heat greenhouses.

Biodiesel from Waste Cooking Oil for Heating, Lighting, or Running Diesel Engines

Rico O. Cruz

Rico O. Cruz is Program Manager, Laboratory and Biological Services Program, Department of Science and Engineering, Confederated Tribes of the Umatilla Indian Reservation, PO Box 638, Pendleton, OR 97801; Tel: 541.276.0105; E-mail: ricocruz@ctuir.com.

Cruz, R.O. 2009. Biodiesel from waste cooking oil for heating, lighting, or running diesel engines. In: Dumroese, R.K.; Riley, L.E., tech. coords. 2009. National proceedings: Forest and Conservation Nursery Associations—2008. Proc. RMRS-P-58. Fort Collins, CO: U.S. Department of Agriculture, Forest Service, Rocky Mountain Research Station: 22–25. Online: http://www.fs.fed.us/rm/pubs/rmrs_p058.html.

Abstract: Biodiesel and its byproducts and blends can be used as alternative fuel in diesel engines and for heating, cooking, and lighting. A simple process of biodiesel production can utilize waste cooking oil as the main feedstock to the transesterification and cruzesterification processes. I currently make my own biodiesel for applications related to my nursery and greenhouse operations, which helps me reduce costs under the current circumstances of high fuel costs.

Keywords: fossil fuel, diesel, renewable fuels, biofuel, esters, triglycerides, glycerin

Introduction

In my opinion, the dynamics of environmental degradation and the increasing demand for energy require humans to find alternative sources of energy. I see our world beset with four major energy-related problems: (1) fossil fuel is running out; (2) a reduction in fossil fuel would harm the world economy; (3) fossil fuel is one of the central aspects to wars and rebellions; and (4) the earth is getting warmer due, in part, to the increase of carbon dioxide in our atmosphere. Not using renewable energy is expensive. For example, the United States gives the fossil fuel industry US$ 5 billion in tax money annually (Tickell and Tickell 1999), spends US$ 50 billion to maintain its military presence in the Middle East (Ramsey 1998), and has spent, as of 11 June 2008, US$ 528 billion on the war in Iraq (National Priorities Project 2008). Environmental costs are high too. It seems to me that everyone is talking about climate change, and for good reason. Carbon dioxide levels in the atmosphere, mostly from burning fossil fuels, increased from 280 ppb in 1750 to 360 ppb in 2000 (Consumer Reports 1996). While CO_2 does not directly affect health, synergistic effects are obvious, and lowering CO_2 emissions from fossil fuels would reduce air pollutants, such as smog-producing ozone and particulate matter.

Solutions

One solution to environmental degradation and the energy crisis is development of renewable and clean sustainable forms of fuels or energy sources. The supply of renewable energy (for example, ethanol, biogas/biomass, biodiesel, photovoltaics, wind, geothermal, and hydropower) is almost infinite. Compared with the limited availability of fossil fuels, biofuels are constantly grown and replenished. Fossil fuels took at least 40 million years to form, while biofuels can be produced in 3 months (fig. 1). Renewable fuels are carbon neutral, strengthen the economy by creating jobs and infrastructure, and reduce the petroleum deficit. For example, the United States could decrease its annual trade deficit by more than US$ 53 billion and create 1.43 million jobs in biofuels and supporting services by producing 100% of its fuel domestically (Campbell 1997). The U.S. ethanol industry alone adds US$ 51 billion to the economy; allows farm income to increase by US$ 2.2 billion; creates 5,800 direct jobs and 50,000 indirect service jobs; generates US$ 555 million federal taxes; and reduces the trade deficit by US$ 1.3 billion (Urbanchuk 1996).

Using renewable energy makes sense to me. In my opinion, our energy vision should seek harmony with culture and ancestral teachings. Our ancestors have taught respect for Mother Earth, that is, to live in harmony and respect what she has provided, to not take without giving, to not use and abuse without consideration of the holistic impact of our actions to future generations of our people. Our ancestors have taught us to conduct our life in a respectful, sustainable manner, walking lightly on the earth.

A PERSPECTIVE

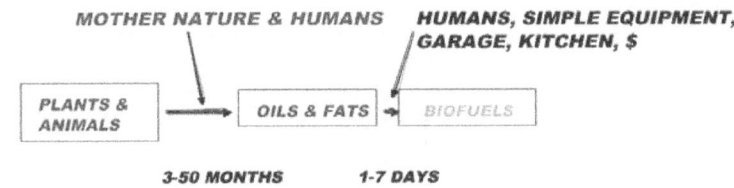

FOSSIL FUELS

RENEWABLE FUELS

Figure 1. A perspective on fossil fuels and renewable fuels.

I feel that many businesses and energy technologies of today do not hold this as a primary guiding philosophy. I am using renewable biodiesel in my nursery and personal life in order to live more in harmony with Mother Earth.

Biodiesel

Dr. Rudolf Diesel developed the first diesel engine prototype in 1893, and demonstrated its use with renewable peanut oil (biodiesel) at the World Exhibition in Paris in 1900. Although it took another 80 years for interest in biodiesel to return, I see worldwide interest in biodiesel increasing. Biodiesel is physically and chemically similar to petroleum diesel fuel, and can, therefore, be used as substitute for fueling diesel engines without engine modifications. Biodiesel is environmentally and user-friendly for several reasons: (1) when burned or used as fuel in engines, significant reductions in emissions can be attained (fig. 2); (2) no sulfur or lead is produced; (3) emissions may not contribute to acid rain production; (4) it is safer to use because its flash point, or fire point, is about 200 °C (400 °F); (5) it is miscible and readily mixes with petroleum products and alcohol so it can be blended with petroleum products and alcohol at any percentage; and (6) it recycles carbon dioxide. Biodiesel has a zero net balance of CO_2 emissions because plants need CO_2 for growth and development. Studies indicate that for every liter of vegetable oil produced, the crop uses at least 2.7 kg (6 lb) of CO_2. Using biofuels is almost a win-win situation (fig. 3), depending on what feedstock is used. Although it takes at least 40 million years for nature to convert organic matter into crude oil that can then be processed into petroleum products (fig. 4), I am producing biodiesel in as little as 3 months. I have been promoting biodiesel as an alternative fuel since 1995 in the Phillipines, Uganda, Azerbaijan, Russia, Canada, Bulgaria, United States, and Paraguay.

EMMISSIONS REDUCTION (DIESEL EMISSIONS BASE)

CO_2 = 78-100% (NET, PLANTS USE CO_2 FOR GROWTH)
SO_2 = 100% (NO SULFUR ADDED)
SOOT, PARTICULATES = 40-60%
CO, HC = 10-50%
PAHs: (phenanthren = 97%; benzofloroanthen = 56%; benzapyren = 71%; aldehydes and aromatic compounds = 13%)
NOx = PLUS/MINUS 5-10% (ENGINE'S AGE, DESIGN, TUNING)

Figure 2. Emissions reduction using diesel emissions as base.

Production

In the early 1990s I was involved with demonstrating and piloting biodiesel; this novel work was part of my post-doctoral investigation on biofuels (Cruz 1992; Peterson and others 1992). Biodiesel is produced through a process called transesterification, which is basically a chemical reaction of a triglyceride with an alcohol in the presence of a catalyst to produce fatty acid esters (commonly termed biodiesel) and glycerin (fig. 5). Our projects, however, embraced a simple, short fuel-making process, termed cruzesterification (fig. 6). This process uses simple equipment, no heat application, and no fuel washing (fig. 7), along with waste or used cooking oil from area restaurants, food service institutions, and households, to make small batches of biodiesel.

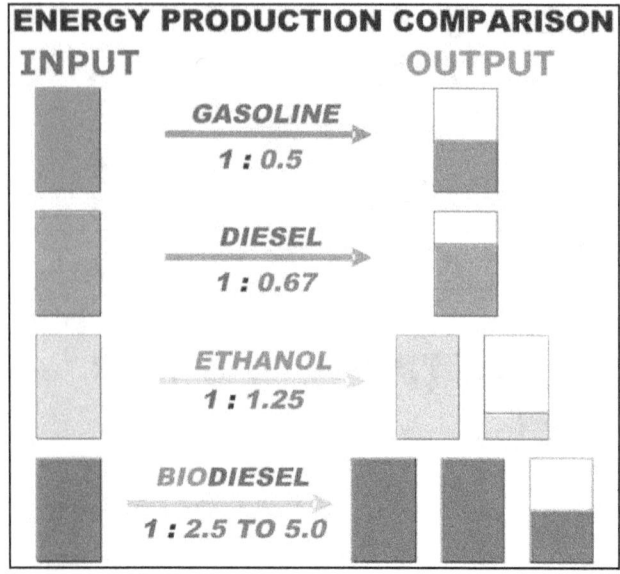

Figure 3. A comparison of energy input/output of biofuels and petroleum fuels.

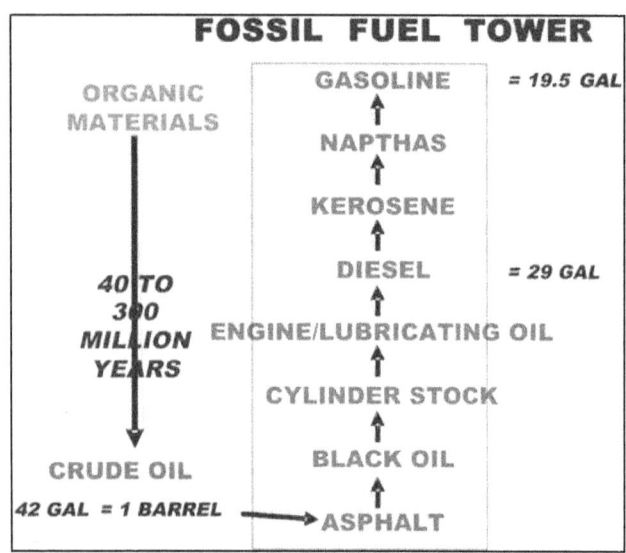

Figure 4. Process flow of petroleum products.

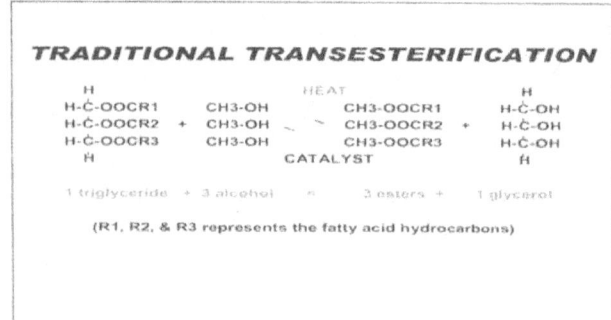

Figure 5. Traditional transesterification process.

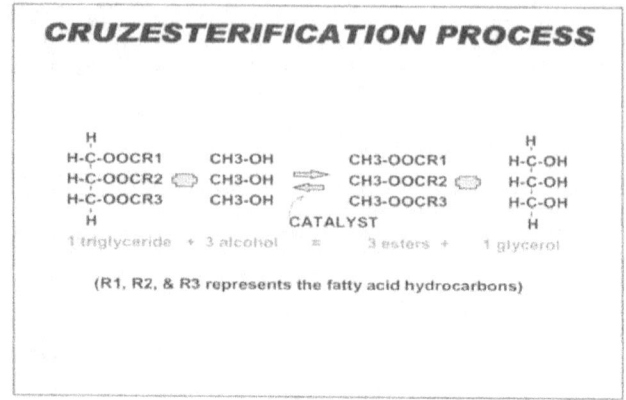

Figure 6. The cruzesterification process.

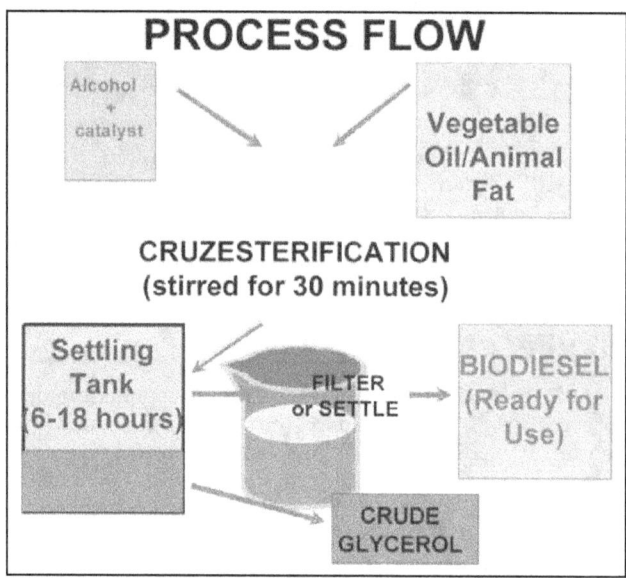

Figure 7. Simple biodiesel process flow.

Essentially, cruzesterification employs used (usually less than 3 months old in storage) cooking oil or yellow grease that has been filtered or screened to eliminate any water or food morsels. Any amount of water in the oil and alcohol will prevent and stop the reaction. I prefer young used oil or grease because the older the oil, the more free fatty acid (FFA) it contains, which competes with the potassium hydroxide catalyst. At too high a level, FFA stops the chemical reaction. The process of making biodiesel requires taking several precautions, including the use of non-rubber gloves, eye protection, and a breathing mask or respirator, and completing all mixing in a well-ventilated area, at an ambient temperature ≥13 °C (55 °F), and at least 18 m (20 yd) from sources of open flames or embers, including cigarettes. My recipe for making biodiesel is easy. Please contact me for complete details. I am happy to share my technique.

Figure 8. A demonstration vehicle used by the author.

Biodiesel Application in Engines

I use biodiesel for work and personal use. I have used biodiesel in an old Ford Bronco with a Toyota engine (100% biodiesel), a 2005 Volkswagen New Beetle (5% to 100% biodiesel), and, because some times I need to get away from the nursery, in the 10HP engine on my boat (100% biodiesel). I drive my Beetle up to 1,290 km (800 mi) per week (fig. 8).

Recommendations and Outlook __

In my opinion, making your own fuel for use in nursery/greenhouse operations is a good strategy to minimize environmental degradation problems, minimize global warming/greenhouse gases, and improve cost effectiveness in day-to-day operations. As fuel for engines, biodiesel or blends can be used in tractors, backhoes, bulldozers, mowers, pumps, trucks, cars, back-up or main generator sets, any 2-stroke engines as additive, and other equipment that have diesel engines. Biodiesel can substitute as heating oil for heating a greenhouse during winter operations and lighting whenever

needed. It can also be used for cooking or for sterilizing planting media and laboratory glasswares/gadgets.

For more information on biodiesel system plans, processors/kits, multi-fuel heater plan, supplies, gadgets, equipment, chemicals, test kits, accessories, How-To books/DVDs, one-on-one training/consulting work, and ASTM specifications, the following resources are available online:

> www.utahbiodieselsupply.com
> www.biodieselamerica.org
> www.journeytoforever.org
> www.ecoenergyinternational.com
> www.biodiesel.org
> www.homebiodieselkits.com

References

Campbell CJ. 1997. The coming oil crisis. Essex (Great Britain): Multi Science Publishing Company and Petroconsultants, SA.

Campbell CJ. 1998. Running out of gas. The National Interest 51(Spring):47-55.

Consumer Reports. 1996. Turning up the heat. Consumer Reports, September. p 38-44.

Cruz RO. 1992. Process development and evaluation of rapeseed biodiesel: a progress report. Moscow (ID): University of Idaho, Agricultural Engineering Department.

National Priorities Project. 2008. The cost of war. URL: http://www.nationalpriorities.com (accessed 11 Jun 2008).

Peterson CL, Reece DK, Cruz RO, Thompson J. 1992. Comparison of ethyl and methyl esters of vegetable oil as a diesel fuel substitute: liquid fuels from renewable resources. In: Alternative Energy Conference, ASAE International Winter Meeting; 1992 December; Nashville, TN. St Joseph (MI): American Society of Agricultural Engineers. p 99-110.

Ramsey C. 1998. Challenge to genocide: let Iraq live. New York (NY): International Action Center.

Tickell J, Tickell K. 1999. From the fryer to the fuel tank. Sarasota (FL): Green Teach Publishing.

Urbanchuk J. 1996. Ethanol: fueling an economic engine: macro-economic and fiscal impacts of ethanol production under the 1996 Farm Bill. Washington (DC): Renewable Fuels Association.

Growing Media Alternatives for Forest and Native Plant Nurseries

Thomas D. Landis and Nancy Morgan

Thomas D. Landis is Retired Nursery Specialist, USDA Forest Service, and currently Consultant, 3248 Sycamore Way, Medford, OR 97504; Tel: 541.858.6166; E-mail: nurseries@aol.com. **Nancy Morgan** is Technical Specialist with Sun Gro Horticulture, 1904 NE 20th Avenue, Canby, OR 97013; Tel: 503.266.5814; E-mail: nancym@sungro.com.

Landis, T.D.; Morgan, N. 2009. Growing media alternatives for forest and native plant nurseries. In: Dumroese, R.K.; Riley, L.E., tech. coords. 2009. National Proceedings: Forest and Conservation Nursery Associations—2008. Proc. RMRS-P-58. Fort Collins, CO: U.S. Department of Agriculture, Forest Service, Rocky Mountain Research Station: 26–31. Online: http://www.fs.fed.us/rm/pubs/rmrs_p058.html.

Keywords: Sphagnum peat moss, vermiculite, compost, carbon-to-nitrogen ratio, coir, rice hulls, bark

Introduction

The choice of growing medium, along with container type, is one of the critical decisions that must be made when starting a nursery. The first growing medium was called "compost" and was developed in the 1930s at the John Innes Horticultural Institute in Great Britain. It consisted of a loam soil that was amended with peat moss, sand, and fertilizers (Bunt 1988). Soil was heavy and variable, however, so it was difficult to achieve consistency from batch to batch. In the 1950s, researchers at the University of California developed the first true artificial growing media using a series of mixtures of fine sand, peat moss, and fertilizers (Matkin and Chandler 1957). The Cornell "Peat-Lite" mixes, the predecessors of modern growing media, were developed at Cornell University in the 1960s using various combinations of peat moss, vermiculite, and perlite (Mastalerz 1977). Following the publication of the first comprehensive manual for growing forest tree seedlings, a growing medium of 50% Sphagnum peat moss and 50% coarse vermiculite became the basic standard (Tinus and McDonald 1979).

In recent years, a number of factors, including variability in the quality and availability of components, have caused container growers to consider new materials.

1. The cost of Sphagnum peat moss, vermiculite, and other components are becoming increasingly expensive (table 1). Fuel for extraction, processing, and transportation is a major factor in these increasing costs, especially for nurseries far from the source. Diesel fuel costs have almost doubled in the past 3 years (fig. 1), and there's no sign of them going down anytime soon.

2. Some growers have health concerns about the traditional media components of vermiculite and perlite. The WR Grace mine in Libby, MT contained a unique type of vermiculite that had asbestos as a co-mineral. Although it closed in 1990, and other asbestos-free vermiculite sources are now being used, many growers still have concerns. A recent report on a series of tests of vermiculite sources by the National Institute of Occupational Safety and Health stated: "The use of commercial vermiculite horticulture products presents no significant asbestos exposure risk to commercial greenhouse or home horticulture users" (Vermiculite Association 2005). Perlite dust can be an irritant to eyes and lungs, but the Occupational Safety and

Table 1. The cost of growing media has increased significantly in the past 4 years.[a]

Component or Additive	Price Increase (%)
Sphagnum peat moss	45
Vermiculite	38
Perlite	28
Sawdust	30
Composted bark	24
Wetting agent	8

[a]Courtesy of Sun Gro Horticulture.

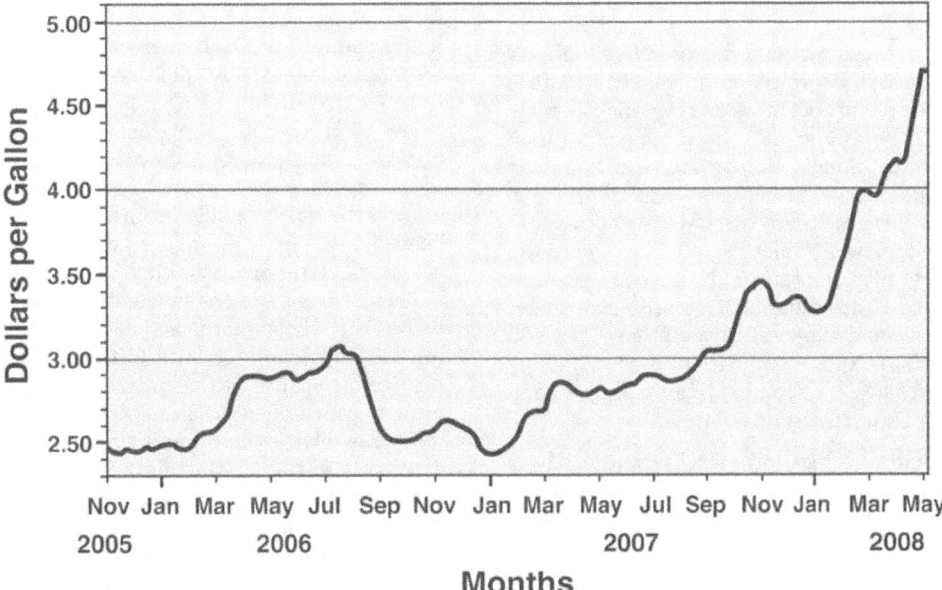

Figure 1. Much of the increasing costs of growing media is from fuel costs, and diesel costs have almost doubled in the past 3 years.

Health Administration (OSHA) considers it a nuisance dust. A Material Safety Data Sheet from a perlite supplier states that: "although there are no published reports of adverse health effects from exposure to perlite dust, dust levels should be maintained below the OSHA Permissible Exposure Limit for perlite and respirators used when airborne dust is present" (EaglePicher Filtration and Minerals 2004). Still, many growers would like alternatives to vermiculite and perlite.

3. Growers would like to use environmentally friendly growing media. Peat moss has been the most popular component over the past several decades, but growers have concerns about the destructive and non-sustainable harvesting of peat (Rainbow 2004). For instance, the European Union has issued directives to reduce the use of peat in growing media, and encouraged research with composted organic wastes (Bragg and others 2006).

Changing to a new growing medium will, however, require adjusting irrigation, fertilization, and other cultural procedures—sometimes drastically.

Characteristics of a Growing Medium

The ideal growing medium for forest and native plant nurseries should have the following characteristics.

Physical

Any medium consists of the solid material and the pores between them. The total pore space is expressed as a percentage, and can be divided into large pores ("macropores")

that provide for gaseous exchange and root growth, and small pores ("micropores") that control the water-holding capacity.

Chemical

The important chemical properties of a growing medium include pH and electrical conductivity (EC). Media particles also contain mineral nutrients, and electrical charges on their surfaces hold nutrients applied as fertilizer.

Biological

Growing media can harbor pathogenic fungi and bacteria. "Suppressive" media contains beneficial microorganisms that can reduce the chances for disease.

Economic

Availability is a major cost factor. Local materials are usually the most cost effective.

Alternative Media Components

Substrates containing only organic components often lose macroporosity over time. Decomposition of organics creates an overabundance of small particles that hold excessive water and reduce air porosity. A mixture of organic and inorganic components, such as pumice or perlite, can help maintain the percentage of large pores later in the growing season (Bilderback and others 2005).

Organics

Because of the increased cost and decreased availability of Sphagnum peat moss, numerous organic substitutes have been studied. Some types of peat moss and organic composts have been found to be antagonistic to pathogenic fungi. The least-decomposed "blonde" Sphagnum peat has been shown to suppress damping-off fungi, such as *Pythium* spp. (Wolffhechel 1988). Organic composts have also proven to have suppressive properties (Nameth 2002). Those composts with a high carbon-to-nitrogen ratio (C:N) have proven most effective (Hoitink and Cooperband 2008). Early trials found that composted bark could suppress Phytophthora root rot, and pine bark can also be inoculated with bacteria (*Bacillus* spp.) and fungi (*Trichoderma* spp.) to enhance suppression of root disease organisms (Castillo 2004).

Composts—"Compost," like "organic," is one of those words that is generally assumed to be beneficial, and more research has been done with composts in growing media than with any other component. It is difficult, however, to draw conclusions because of the wide variety of raw organics used for composting. Chemical and physical analyses of four common composts used in growing media illustrate this variation (table 2).

As can be seen, soluble salt levels were excessive for both total salts (as measured by electrical conductivity) and sodium, which can cause serious problems with germinating seeds and young plants. Leaching these composts with fresh water before use can effectively lower soluble salts below damaging levels (Carrion and others 2006). The pH of these composts is slightly alkaline and was, therefore, not considered a limiting factor (Miller 2004).

Wastes used for composting are often high in nitrogen and phosphorus, especially those containing animal manure; note that the turkey litter is 10 times above recommended rates. The C:N is one of the most important characteristics to measure in both raw materials and finished compost. The C:N is a good indicator of whether nitrogen will be limiting or excessive; the higher the C:N, the higher the risk of nitrogen being unavailable to plants. The carbon in easily decomposed compounds, such as sugars and cellulose, are quickly used as an energy source by soil microorganisms, which also need nitrogen for growth and reproduction. Because this nitrogen is stored in their cells, it is unavailable

for plant uptake. As carbon sources become depleted, the high populations of soil microorganisms gradually die and nitrogen is released for plant growth. When C:N is greater than 15:1, available nitrogen is immobilized. As ratios drop below 15:1, however, nitrogen becomes available for plant uptake. Some composts have C:N ratios as low as 10:1, indicating they are a ready source of available soil nitrogen and are therefore considered fertilizers. A major problem has been the variation in nitrogen drawdown between batches of compost (Handreck 2005).

Wood wastes, such as sawdust, have very high C:N (400:1 to 1300:1). These materials are often composted with manure or supplemented with fertilizer to supply the needed nitrogen. Because of the inherent differences in chemical properties between different woods, however, the suitability of sawdust as an organic growing media component is extremely variable. Mastalerz (1977) stated that sawdust from incense-cedar (*Libocedrus decurrens*), walnuts (*Juglans* spp.), or redwood (*Sequoia sempervirens*) is known to have direct phytotoxic effects, and sawdust from western redcedar (*Thuja plicata*) is toxic to many horticultural plants. In the Pacific Northwest, raw Douglas-fir (*Pseudotsuga menziesii*) sawdust has successfully been used to grow conifer seedlings when it comprised 30% or less of the medium (for example, Sun Gro® Forestry Mix #3 [Sun Gro Horticulture, Canby, OR]). For example, Western Forest Systems, Incorporated of Lewiston, ID, has been utilizing a 30:70 sawdust:peat growing medium for 10 years without major cultural problems, although large wood splinters or chips need to be removed by hand during container filling and seeding. Still, the new medium has resulted in a cost savings of more than 40% (Schaefer 2009).

The C:N of tree bark can be considerably lower than sawdust (70:1 to 500:1), and has become a preferred material for horticultural composts. Composed pine bark (CPB) has become the standard growing media component for horticultural nurseries, especially in the southern United States where the cost of Sphagnum peat moss is prohibitive (Pokorny 1979). At a reforestation nursery in northern Mexico, pine bark is composted on-site and inoculated with benefical microorganisms. Not only do seedlings grow well in CPB, but the bark was found to suppress root-rot fungi and the use of fungicides was reduced (Castillo 2004). Fresh and aged bark

Table 2. Chemical and physical analysis of raw materials commonly used in growing media composts (modified from Chong 2003; Chong and Purvis 2006).

Characteristic tested	Ideal range	Mushroom waste	Turkey litter	Municipal waste	Paper Mill sludge
pH	5.5 to 6.5	8.2	8.7	8.4	7.2
Electrical Conductivity[a] (ds/m)	<1.0	4.0	4.1	3.0	1.2
Ammonium nitrogen (ppm)	<10	15	103	4	37
Nitrate nitrogen (ppm)	100 to 200	89	232	0.02	0.02
Phosphorus (ppm)	6 to 9	6	27	2	8
Sodium (ppm)	0 to 50	511	501	139	387
Total Porosity (%)	> 50	71	73	66	72
Aeration Porosity (%)	15 to 30	40	45	32	40
Water-holding Porosity (%)	25 to 35	31	28	34	31

[a] EC measured as dilution of 1 part substrate:2 parts water.

of Douglas-fir is being widely used as a major component of growing media in the Pacific Northwest (Altland 2006). Bark of other tree species may also prove useful, but tests should be conducted before operational use.

The physical properties of the waste materials in table 2 were generally good, as all measures of porosity met or exceeded the ideal ranges. This varies considerably, however, with the raw material used for composting. When composted green waste was mixed with peat moss in ratios from 10% to 50%, total porosity and water-holding capacity were reduced (Prasad and Maher 2001). Some municipal wastes containing tree leaves and lawn clippings have particles so small that they can seriously reduce aeration porosity (McCloud 1994). Composts should be screened to remove excessive fine particles before use; the percentage of fines passing through a 100-mesh screen should not exceed 15% of the total volume (Miller 2004).

One recent trial in Finland compared the growth of Norway spruce (*Picea abies*) in the traditional medium of 100% sphagnum peat moss versus mixes of peat with composted nursery waste. The nursery waste compost consisted of cull container and bareroot seedlings and weeds that had been composted for 4 years and then filtered through a 4-mm screen. At harvest, the seedlings grown in the compost-amended medium were smaller than those grown in pure peat moss (fig. 2). Survival after outplanting was comparable, but seedlings grown in the compost-amended medium were still significantly shorter after 4 years. The authors concluded that changes in irrigation and fertilization could correct for these growth differences (Veijalainen and others 2007).

Compost-based media should be tried with other native plants. In Florida, a variety of native plants grown in biosolid:yard waste compost were as large or larger than those grown in a peat-based growing medium (Wilson and Stoffella 2006).

Coconut Coir—Coir is a waste material made from the fiber in the shell of coconuts. During the late 1980s, a method was developed to process coconut husks by grinding, washing, screening, and grading. Because it is only found in tropical areas, however, its main cost is transportation.

Coir is being used as a substitute for peat moss because it has a high lignin content, decomposes slowly, wets easily, and holds water. The pH of coir is ideal, ranging from 5.8 to 6.5, but the EC can be high if the husks have been stored in salt water. In this case, the product needs to be thoroughly leached with fresh water, although reputable suppliers will have already done this. Coir has a moderate CEC of 39 to 60 meq/l (less than peat moss), and can adsorb mineral nutrients (Newman 2007). Coir improves the aeration and wettability of peat media, and is an excellent root medium. Few trials have been done with forest and native plants, although Rose and Haase (2000) found that Douglas-fir seedlings in a coir-based medium were significantly smaller than those grown in peat moss.

Composted Rice Hulls—Several nurseries have used rice hulls in place of composted pine bark. Rice hulls are the sheath of the rice grain and a waste product of rice processing. The hulls are run through a hammer mill with 0.5-cm (0.2-in) screens, and then composted in piles for at least 18 months. The pH of the finished product ranges from 5.4 to 5.7, with a total porosity around 30%. Media containing rice hulls were less conducive to fungus gnats (Laiche and Nash 1990; Lovelace and Kuczmarski 1994).

Fresh Rice Hulls—In a forest nursery in Greece (Tsakaldimi 2006), uncomposted rice hulls in a 1:3 mixture with peat were an effective substitute for perlite for growing Aleppo pine (*Pinus halepensis*) seedlings (fig. 3). In another study with the same species, a growing medium of 70% Sphagnum peat moss and 30% fresh rice hulls produced quality pine seedlings that performed well after outplanting (Marianthi 2006).

Inorganics

Growers have also been looking for alternatives to traditional inorganic components, especially vermiculite and perlite.

Pumice—Pumice is a natural volcanic material that is readily abundant in Oregon and other areas in the western United States. Pumice has been used as a substitute for perlite in growing media because it resists compaction and has minimal water-holding capacity. Chemical analysis has shown that pumice is chemically inert, with a slightly alkaline pH and low salt content; due to its negligible CEC, pumice contributes little to plant nutrition. Particle size will

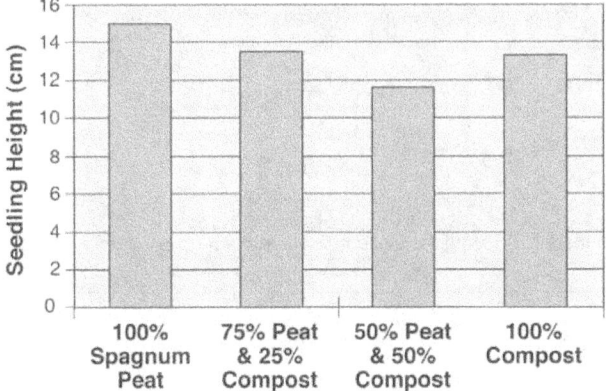

Figure 2. Conifer seedlings grown in composted nursery waste were smaller than those from the traditional 100% peat medium, but had good survival after outplanting (modified from Ve jalainen and others 2007).

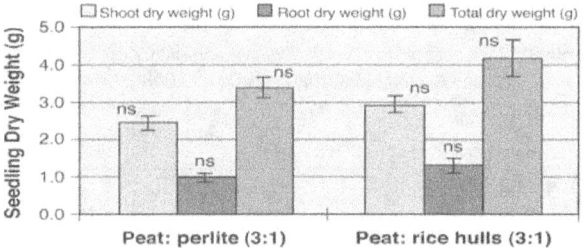

Figure 3. Fresh rice hulls were found to be a good substitute for perlite when mixed 1:3 with peat moss (modified from Tsakaldimi 2006).

determine physical properties, especially porosity. The total porosity of #6 grade pumice from Bend, OR, was 52%, and was almost equally divided between aeration and water-holding porosity. Horticultural nurseries incorporate up to 33% pumice into their bark-based growing media with good results (Buamscha and Altland 2005). Pumice has not been widely used in forest or native plant nurseries, but should prove to be a good way to increase porosity.

The Return of Steam Pasteurization

Steam pasteurization is a tried-and-true method to eliminate pathogenic fungi and bacteria from growing media. The standard recommendation is to heat the medium to 60 to 82 °C (140 to 177 °F) for a minimum of 30 minutes (Bunt 1988). Although it has been used for more than 50 years, pasteurization is not common nowadays. This may change with the discovery that the virulent new fungal pathogen known as sudden oak death, or ramorum blight (*Phytophthora ramorum*), has been shown to survive in growing media as resistant sporangia or chlamydospores (Linderman and Davis 2006). Although this pathogen is only found naturally in coastal California and Oregon, it has been shown to affect a wide variety of host plants, and transportation of infected growing medium could be catastrophic. Recent research has shown that steam pasteurization can effectively eliminate *P. ramorum* and other root rot fungi from growing media by heating at 50 °C (122 °F) or higher for 30 minutes (table 3).

Summary

Nurseries are looking for alternatives to many of the traditional growing media components, such as Sphagnum peat moss, vermiculite, and perlite. Because transportation costs are a major factor in the cost of growing media, growers should consider more local components, including composts, coconut coir, fresh or composted rice hulls, and pumice. A growing medium affects many aspects of nursery culture, and changing to a new growing medium will require adjusting irrigation, fertilization, and other cultural procedures. It is always best, therefore, to test any new growing medium before full operational use.

References

Altland J. 2006. Douglas fir bark: a complicated but competent substrate. Digger 50(6):23-30.

Bilderback TE, Warren SL, Owen JS, Albano JP. 2005. Healthy substrates need physicals too! HortTechnology 15:747-751.

Bragg N, Brocklehurst T F, Smith AC, Bhat M, Waldron KW. 2006. The development of sustainable growing media components from composted specific bio-waste streams. International Plant Propagators' Society Combined Proceedings 55:256-258.

Buamscha G, Altland J. 2005. Pumice and the Oregon nursery industry. Digger 49(6):18, 20-21, 23, 25-27.

Bunt AC. 1988. Media and mixes for container-grown plants. Boston (MA): Unwin Hyman. 309 p.

Carrion C, Abad M, Fornes F, Noguera V, Maquieira A, Puchades R. 2006. Leaching of composts from agricultural wastes to prepare nursery potting media. Acta Horticulturae 697:117-124.

Castillo JV. 2004. Inoculating composted pine bark with beneficial organisms to make a disease suppressive compost for container production in Mexican forest nurseries. Native Plants Journal 5(2):181-185.

Chong C. 2003. Use of waste and compost in propagation: challenges and constraints. International Plant Propagators' Society Combined Proceedings 52:410-414.

Chong C, Purvis P. 2006. Use of paper-mill sludges and municipal compost in nursery substrates. International Plant Propagators' Society Combined Proceedings 55:428-432.

EaglePicher Filtration and Minerals. 2004. Material safety data sheet for celatom perlite. URL: http://www.epcorp.com/NR/rdonlyres/6787FEDB-4BEF-4ACD-85A6-7AB94AFB8C62/0/PerliteallGrades.pdf (accessed 10 Jul 2008).

Handreck K. 2005. Media properties. International Plant Propagators' Society Combined Proceedings 54:75-77.

Hoitink HAJ, Cooperband L. 2008. Compost use for plant disease suppression. In: Rynk R, van de Kamp M, Willson GB, Singley ME, Richard TL, Kolega JJ, editors. On-farm composting handbook. Ithaca (NY): Natural Resource, Agriculture, and Engineering Service. NRAES-54. 186 p.

Laiche AJ Jr, Nash VE. 1990. Evaluation of composted rice hulls and a lightweight clay aggregate as components of container-plant growth media. Journal of Environmental Horticulture 8(1):14-18.

Linderman RG, Davis EA. 2006. Survival of *Phytophthora ramorum* compared to other species of Phytophthora in potting media components, compost, and soil. HortTechnology 16(3):502-507.

Linderman RG, Davis EA. 2008. Eradication of *Phytophthora ramorum* and other pathogens from potting medium or soil by treatment with aerated steam or fumigation with metam sodium. HortTechnology 18(1):106-110.

Lovelace W, Kuczmarski D. 1994. The use of composted rice hulls in rooting and potting media. International Plant Propagators' Society Combined Proceedings 42:449-450.

Marianthi T. 2007. Kenaf (*Hibiscus cannabinus* L.) core and rice hulls as components of container media for growing *Pinus halepensis* M. seedlings. Bioresource Technology 97:1631-1639.

Table 3. Steam pasteurization is effective against fungal pathogens in growing media, including the virulent new pathogen *Phytophthora ramorum* (modified from Linderman and Davis 2008).

Fungal pathogen	Unheated	Temperature[a] treatments for 30 minutes				
		45 (113)[a]	50 (122)	55 (131)	60 (140)	65 (149)
Cylindrocarpon scoparium	97	56	0	0	0	0
Phytophthora ramorum - Isolate A	77	0	0	0	0	0
Phytophthora ramorum - Isolate B	85	7	0	0	0	0
Pythium irregulare	98	23	0	0	0	0

[a] °C (°F).

Mastalerz JW. 1977. The greenhouse environment. New York (NY): John Wiley and Sons. 629 p.

Matkin OA, Chandler PA. 1957. The U.C.-type soil mixes. In: Baker KF, editor. The U.C. system for producing healthy container-grown plants. Parramatta (Australia): Australian Nurserymen's Association. Extension Service Manual 23. p 68-85.

McCloud TL. 1994. Composting leaves for potting mix. International Plant Propagators' Society Combined Proceedings 42:447-448.

Miller M. 2004. Using compost successfully in propagation systems. International Plant Propagators' Society Combined Proceedings 53:412-415.

Nameth ST. 2002. Disease-suppressive media could help you save money. Greenhouse Management and Production 22(6):67-69.

Newman J. 2007. Core facts about coir. Greenhouse Management and Production 27(2):57.

Pokorny FA. 1979. Pine bark container media—an overview. International Plant Propagators' Society Combined Proceedings 29:484-495.

Prasad M, Maher MJ. 2001. The use of composted green waste (CGW) as a growing medium component. Acta Horticulturae 549:107-113.

Rainbow A. 2004. The peatering out project. International Plant Propagators' Society Combined Proceedings 53:177-182.

Rose R, Haase DL. 2000. The use of coir as a containerized growing medium for Douglas-fir seedlings. Native Plants Journal 1:107-111.

Schaefer JK. 2009. Growing reforestation conifer stock: Utilizing peat/sawdust medium. In: Dumroese, R.K.; Riley, L.E., tech. coords. 2009. National proceedings: Forest and Conservation Nursery Associations—2008. Proc. RMRS-P-58. Fort Collins, CO: U.S. Department of Agriculture, Forest Service, Rocky Mountain Research Station: 35-36.

Swanson BT. 1989. Critical physical properties of container media. American Nurseryman 169(11):59-63.

Tinus RW, McDonald SF. 1979. How to grow tree seedlings in containers in greenhouses. Fort Collins (CO): USDA Forest Service, Rocky Mountain Forest and Range Experiment Station. General Technical Report RM-60. 256 p.

Tsakaldimi M. 2006. Use of inorganic and organic solid wastes for container-seedling production. In: Protection and restoration of the environment VII. Selected proceedings of the seventh biennial protection and restoration of the environment international conference. Journal of Hazardous Materials 136(1). 8 p.

Veijalainen A-M, Juntunen M-L, Heiskanen J, Lilja A. 2007. Growing Picea abies container seedlings in peat and composted forest-nursery waste mixtures for forest regeneration. Scandinavian Journal of Forest Research 22:390-397.

Vermiculite Association. 2005. Statement by the Vermiculite Association on the recently released government studies of vermiculite and the potential asbestos exposure. URL: http://www.vermiculite.org/pdf/TVA-statement-010505.pdf (accessed 10 Jul 2008).

Wilson SB, Stoffella PJ. 2006. Using compost for container production of ornamental wetland and flatwood species native to Florida. Native Plants Journal 7(3):293-300.

Wolffhechel H. 1988. The suppressiveness of sphagnum peat to Pythium spp. Acta Horticulturae 221:217-222.

Comparing Growth of Ponderosa Pine in Two Growing Media

R. Kasten Dumroese

R. Kasten Dumroese is the National Nursery Specialist with the USDA Forest Service, Rocky Mountain Research Station, 1221 South Main Street, Moscow, ID 83843; Tel: 208.883.2324; E-mail: kdumroese@fs.fed.us.

Dumroese, R.K. 2009. Comparing growth of ponderosa pine in two growing media. In: Dumroese, R.K.; Riley, L.E., tech. coords. 2009. National Proceedings: Forest and Conservation Nursery Associations—2008. Proc. RMRS-P-58. Fort Collins, CO: U.S. Department of Agriculture, Forest Service, Rocky Mountain Research Station: 32–34. Online: http://www.fs.fed.us/rm/pubs/rmrs_p058.html.

Abstract: I compared growth of container ponderosa pine (*Pinus ponderosa*) seedlings grown in a 1:1 (v:v) Sphagnum peat moss:coarse vermiculite medium (P:V) and a 7:3 (v:v) Sphagnum peat moss:Douglas-fir sawdust medium (P:S) at three different irrigation regimes. By using exponential fertilization techniques, I was able to supply seedlings with similar amounts of fertilizer over time even though irrigation frequency differed. Although I noted a reduced growth rate in P:S seedlings, final morphology was, for the most part, similar to their P:V cohorts. When given similar rates of fertilizer, seedlings grown at reduced irrigation frequencies were fairly similar to those given robust amounts of irrigation, indicating that growers may be able to reduce irrigation frequency without a loss of stock quality.

Keywords: container seedlings, alternative growing media

Introduction

Traditionally, container forest nurseries in the Pacific Northwest grew small conifer seedlings for reforestation in a 1:1 (v:v) Sphagnum peat moss:vermiculite growing medium. Sphagnum peat moss served as the principal water holding matrix while still providing high porosity, and the light-weight vermiculite added water-holding capacity as well as high cation exchange capacity (Landis and others 1990). Sawdust is now being offered as replacement for vermiculite, with the standard Sphagnum peat moss:vermiculite mix being modified to a 7:3 (v:v) Sphagnum peat moss:Douglas-fir sawdust mix. Potential advantages of sawdust-amended medium include a more stable supply than vermiculite and reduced costs. Nursery managers in the northern Rocky Mountains were concerned that using a 100% organic medium may result in lower porosity (poorer aeration) that could cause increased root disease expression (Landis and others 1989), particularly of root rot caused by *Cylindrocarpon* spp. and *Phytopthora* spp. (Dumroese and James 2005), and that high carbon (C):nitrogen (N) in the non-composted sawdust might lead to nutrient deficiencies and reduced growth (Landis and others 1990).

Using a typical reforestation species, one fertilization level, and three moisture regimes, my objective was to compare growth when seedlings were grown in conventionally used Sphagnum peat moss:vermiculite or Douglas-fir sawdust-amended media.

Materials and Methods

This study was done at the University of Idaho Center for Forest Nursery and Seedling Research in Moscow. The media, a 1:1 (v:v) Sphagnum peat moss:coarse vermiculite (P:V) and a 7:3 (v:v) Sphagnum peat moss:Douglas-fir sawdust (P:S) were supplied by SunGro Horticulture (Hubbard, OR). Sawdust was fresh (non-decomposed), so the medium was amended at the company with Nitroform® (38% N; Nu-Gro Technologies, Grand Rapids, MI) at a rate of 0.44 kg/m^3 to reduce problems with N availability caused by high C:N. Except for vermiculite, sawdust, and Nitroform®, the media were similar (table 1). At the nursery, media were mechanically added to 160/90 (315B) Styroblock® containers commonly used in reforestation (volume = 90 ml [5.5 in^3]; depth = 15 cm [6 in]; diameter = 3 cm [1.2 in]; density = 756/m^2 [71/ft^2]). Ponderosa pine (*Pinus ponderosa*) seeds were sown the first week of March; seedlings were grown inside the university greenhouse following the basic environmental conditions reported in Wenny and Dumroese (1987).

My treatments included the two media and three irrigation regimes (90%, 75%, 60%) applied in a completely randomized design. Treatments were replicated four times and each block container served as a replicate. After watering sown containers to field capacity and waiting about an hour, I weighed each container. Containers were irrigated when actual container weight was 90%, 75%, or 60% of container field capacity weight. Once germination was complete (3 weeks after planting), seedlings

Table 1. Media characteristics as supplied by manufacturer.

Ingredients	Peat moss:vermiculite (P:V)	Peat moss:sawdust (P:S)
	Canadian Sphagnum peat moss	Canadian Sphagnum peat moss
	Coarse vermiculite	Douglas-fir sawdust
		Nitroform® 0.44 kg/m³
pH	3.8 to 4.2	3.5 to 3.9
Soluble salts	0.06 to 0.08 mmho/cm	0.1 to 0.15 mmho/cm
Bulk density	0.2 g/cm³	0.2 g/cm³
Nutrient	— ppm —	— ppm —
N	5 to 10	5 to 10
P	1 to 5	1 to 5
K	5 to 10	1 to 5
Ca	5 to 10	5 to 10
Mg	1 to 6	1 to 5

were fertilized each time they were irrigated (fertigation). I modified the basic nursery regime of Wenny and Dumroese (1987) so seedlings in each treatment combination received 40 mg N applied exponentially during the growing season following the general methods of Timmer and Aidelbaum (1996). By using the exponential fertilizer equations, I could assume a daily fertilizer application frequency and calculate a daily fertilizer amount. For each subsequent fertigation event, the necessary amount of fertilizer (cumulative daily amounts since the prior irrigation) was diluted in the calculated amount of water required to recharge the medium to field capacity weight. When fertigated, containers were placed into a metal tray and watered from above with a watering can. Excess water that accumulated in the tray was collected and reapplied. Thus, I was able to give each treatment an equivalent amount of fertilizer per unit of time.

Every 6 weeks after germination was complete, I systematically collected 20 seedlings from each replicate and measured height (top of medium to tip of growing point or terminal bud), root-collar diameter (RCD) 5 mm above the medium, and shoot and root biomass after drying at 60 °C (140 °F) to constant weight.

Using the general linear model (PROC GLM; SAS Institute Incorporated, Cary, NC), my model statements for seedling parameters included irrigation regime, medium, and the interaction (alpha = 0.05). When $P \leq 0.05$, means were separated using Tukey's HSD.

Results

In general and for all irrigation regimes combined, seedling morphology was similar in both media. P:S yielded seedlings with 5% more RCD—this 0.16 mm increase was statistically significant ($P = 0.02$) although perhaps not biologically so. Seedlings growing in P:S also had significantly higher root ($P = 0.005$) and shoot N ($P = 0.0002$) concentrations, about 9% and 18% more, respectively.

Irrigation regime had surprisingly few effects on seedling growth. For both media combined, seedlings grown at a 60% block weight had significantly ($P = 0.001$) less height growth (about 1.5 cm [0.6 in] less than those grown at 75% and 2.5 cm [1 in] less than those at 90%). Shoot biomass,

however, was borderline for significance ($P = 0.052$), with the 60% and 75% treatments having 12% less biomass than the 90% treatment. Root N concentration was 13% less in the 60% treatment, significantly ($P = 0.01$) less than seedlings receiving more frequent irrigation.

Root biomass was the only parameter affected ($P = 0.001$) by a medium x irrigation interaction. Seedlings grown at a 60% irrigation regime in both media had a higher mean root biomass than those grown at 75%. Regardless of medium across all irrigation frequencies, seedling heights and RCDs followed similar trends throughout the growing season (fig. 1), although height growth in the P:S medium was significantly less than that of the P:V medium for a portion of the rapid growth phase.

Irrigation frequency was significantly reduced by target container weight ($P = 0.0001$), but not by medium ($P = 0.12$). To maintain 90% target container weight, irrigation was required every 2.1 days, significantly more than the 4.6 days for 75% target container weight that was significantly more than the 7.8 days for 60% target container weight. Irrigating at these frequencies maintained containers at 89%, 76%, and 61% target container weight, respectively.

Discussion

At the onset of the production cycle, the P:S had a higher C:N than the P:V medium. In general, when C:N >20:1, microorganisms use the available N for growth and reproduction, making it unavailable for immediate use by plants. As the carbon sources are depleted, the microorganisms gradually die, and the N stored in their cells is released back into the system. At this point, the N becomes available for plant use (see Landis and Morgan 2009). To circumvent this decrease in early growth caused by N limitation (immobilization) due to high C:N, Nitroform® was added to the P:S medium. Even so, I noted a decrease in the early growth rate in the P:S compared to the P:V medium (fig. 1). Toward the end of the growing season, however, seedling growth in P:S "caught up" to that of seedlings in P:V, probably because the N in the Nitroform® was being released through the death of the microorganisms. The P:S and P:V seedlings were fertilized with 40 mg N, but the P:S seedlings had access to more N

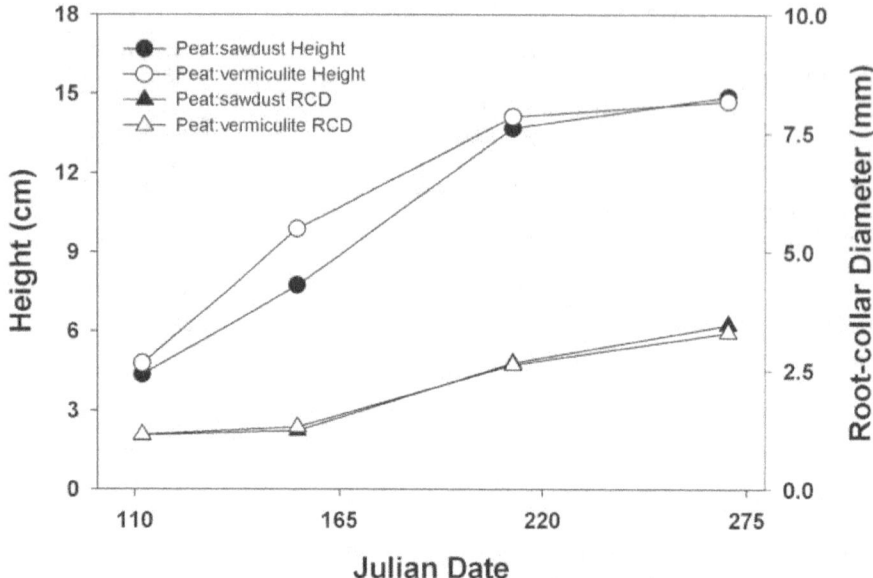

Figure 1. Height and root-collar diameter growth of ponderosa pine seedlings growing in 1:1 (v:v) Sphagnum peat moss:coarse vermiculite (P:V) or a 7:3 (v:v) Sphagnum peat moss:Douglas-fir sawdust (P:S) medium, pooled across irrigation treatments. Julian date 110 was April 19, about 6 weeks after sowing, and Julian date 275 is October 1.

because of the additional Nitroform®, leading to the higher N concentrations in roots and shoots of seedlings grown in P:S.

Seedlings grown under the 90% and 75% block weight regimes were similar in morphology, indicating that final seedling parameters need not be sacrificed by reduced irrigation frequency, provided that similar amounts of N are applied. Growers may be able to better schedule irrigation frequency (and potentially redistribute employee work loads) by irrigating when seedlings reach lower block weights. Reduced irrigation frequency could also mitigate expression of foliar diseases.

The reduced early growth I observed concurs with observations by Justin (2009) and those reported by Davis and others (2009), but similarity in final seedling size between the two media concurs with observations by Schaefer (2009). I detected no real differences in water-holding capacity (based on frequency of containers achieving target dry-down block weights), which agrees with Schaefer (2009).

It appears that the P:S medium is an appropriate replacement for P:V. For best results, growers must track seedling growth, compare growth rates with target curves, and adjust fertility to keep the crop growing properly—the same process any good grower uses routinely.

References _____

Davis AS, Eggleston K, Pinto JR, Dumroese RK. 2009. Evaluation of three growing media substrates for Western larch seedling production at thte USDA Forest Service Coeur d'Alene Nursery. In: Dumroese, R.K.; Riley, L.E., tech. coords. 2009. National Proceedings: Forest and Conservation Nursery Associations—2008.

Proc. RMRS-P-58. Fort Collins, CO: U.S. Department of Agriculture, Forest Service, Rocky Mountain Research Station:37–41.

Dumroese RK, James RL. 2005. Root diseases in bareroot and container nurseries of the Pacific Northwest: epidemiology, management, and effects on outplanting performance. New Forests 30:185–202.

Justin J. 2009. Growing media trials at the Montana Conservation Seedling Nursery. In: Dumroese, R.K.; Riley, L.E., tech. coords. 2009. National proceedings: Forest and Conservation Nursery Associations—2008. Proc. RMRS-P-58. Fort Collins, CO: U.S. Department of Agriculture, Forest Service, Rocky Mountain Research Station:42–43.

Landis TD, Tinus RW, McDonald SE, Barnett JP. 1989. The container tree nursery manual. Volume 5, the biological component. Washington (DC): USDA Forest Service. Agricultural Handbook. 674.

Landis TD, Tinus RW, McDonald SE, Barnett JP. 1990. The container tree nursery manual. Volume 2, containers and growing media. Washington (DC): USDA Forest Service. Agricultural Handbook. 674.

Landis TD, Morgan N. 2009. Growing media alternatives for forest and native plant nurseries. In: Dumroese, R.K.; Riley, L.E., tech. coords. 2009. National proceedings: Forest and Conservation Nursery Associations—2008. Proc. RMRS-P-58. Fort Collins, CO: U.S. Department of Agriculture, Forest Service, Rocky Mountain Research Station:26–31.

Schaefer JK. 2009. Growing reforestation conifer stock: UtiliΩing peat/sawdust medium. In: Dumroese, R.K.; Riley, L.E., tech. coords. 2009. National proceedings: Forest and Conservation Nursery Associations—2008. Proc. RMRS-P-58. Fort Collins, CO: U.S. Department of Agriculture, Forest Service, Rocky Mountain Research Station:35-36.

Timmer VR, Aidelbaum AS. 1996. Manual for exponential nutrient loading of seedlings to improve outplanting performance on competitive forest sites. Sault Ste Marie (ON): Canadian Forest Service. NODA/NFP Tech. Rep. TR-25. 24 p.

Wenny DL, Dumroese RK. 1987. A growing regime for containerized ponderosa pine seedlings. Moscow (ID): University of Idaho, Idaho Forest, Wildlife, and Range Experiment Station. Bulletin 43.

Growing Reforestation Conifer Stock: Utilizing Peat/Sawdust Medium

Janice K. Schaefer

Janice K. Schaefer is Owner/Manager at Western Forest Systems Incorporated, 1509 Ripon Avenue, Lewiston, ID 83501; Tel: 208-743-0147; E-mail: schaeferjk@clearwire.net.

Schaefer, J.K. 2009. Growing reforestation conifer stock: utilizing peat/sawdust medium. In: Dumroese, R.K.; Riley, L.E., tech. coords. 2009. National Proceedings: Forest and Conservation Nursery Associations—2008. Proc. RMRS-P-58. Fort Collins, CO: U.S. Department of Agriculture, Forest Service, Rocky Mountain Research Station: 35–36. Online: http://www.fs.fed.us/rm/pubs/rmrs_p058.html.

Keywords: container seedlings, alternative growing media

Western Forest Systems, Incorporated (WFS) (Lewiston, ID) has been utilizing a peat/sawdust blended mix as our growing medium for the past 10 years. Our decision to change from a peat/vermiculite blend to a peat/Douglas-fir (*Pseudotsuga menziesii*) sawdust blend involved worker health and safety issues, seedling culture, seedling production, and economic impact.

WFS began making a concerted effort to find an alternative to 50:50 peat:vermiculite (v:v) forestry blend when vermiculite was found to be contaminated with tremolite and actinolite, both of which are very toxic forms of asbestos. The U.S. Environmental Protection Agency (EPA) in Region 10 showed some vermiculite products contained asbestos. Consumers have no way of knowing which vermiculite products are contaminated (EPA 2000). Verification of testing of the vermiculite in the product being purchased by WFS was never granted or a hard copy received.

WFS began a slow transition to 70:30 peat:sawdust forestry mix on ponderosa pine (*Pinus ponderosa*). Transition to this mix was made for all pine species, while tests began on western larch (*Larix occidentalis*), Douglas-fir, and true fir species (*Abies* spp.). The transition took approximately 5 years to complete.

No major cultural ramifications were noted by changing from 50:50 peat:vermiculite to 70:30 peat:sawdust soilless mix. Similar soil mix challenges occurred with occasional pathogen detection of *Pythium* spp. and *Fusarium* spp. WFS purchases growing media in 0.08 m³ (2.8 ft³) bags, and testing is always done prior to sowing. Growth regimes have not changed significantly, although the peat:sawdust mix may retain more water volume. Annual historical data shows block weights to be slightly heavier (from 1% to 5%) with this mix, but plant tissue and media analysis do not show any significant differences.

Production challenges occur when utilizing our Gleason flat filler. Large debris in the peat:sawdust mix is an issue. WFS used Styroblock™ systems ranging in size from 65 cm³ (4 in³ [313B]) to 330 cm³ (20 in³ [615A]). Large Douglas-fir bark splinters make it difficult to fill the smaller cavity openings in the 313B Styroblock™ cells. As cavity diameters increase, the problem decreases. The filler needs to be cleaned more often to remove "dams" of splinters from the block hopper area. The employee removing filled blocks from the machine must clear splinters and remove large sticks prior to blocks reaching the return auger. Splinters also jam in the dibble plate, causing blocks to occasionally stick to the plate. To reach ideal cell compaction, the filler vibration settings had to be increased when the mix was changed from peat:vermiculite to the peat:sawdust mix.

Nurseries are not immune to the current economic issues in agriculture production. Forestry blends containing vermiculite have elevated in price at a faster rate than other blends. According to our supplier, this is driven by increased transportation costs and fluctuations in vermiculite supply. Vermiculite is currently being shipped to the United States from South Africa. Costs to transport media from suppliers to our greenhouse have increased by 33% from the first quarter of 2007 to the first quarter of 2008, plus an additional US$ 100 for State of Idaho fuel surcharge. Table 1 shows the cost per seedling changes over a 10-year time frame. All data are specific to our nursery in Lewiston, ID.

We attempted to address as many variables as possible in order to increase the success of our transition.

Table 1. Comparison of 50:50 peat:vermiculite mix to 70:30 peat:sawdust mix.

Crop year	Cost/ft³* (US$)		Cost/10,000 ft³* (US$)		Cost/seedling (US$) for	
	peat:vermiculite	peat:sawdust	peat:vermiculite	peat:sawdust	peat:vermiculite	peat:sawdust
1998	2.40	1.35	24,000	13,500	0.001	0.005
2003	3.16	1.82	31,600	18,200	0.011	0.007
2008	4.07	2.34	40,700	23,400	0.015	0.008

*1 ft³ = 0.03 m³

Reference _____

[EPA] U.S. Environmental Protection Agency. 2008. Sampling and
analysis of consumer garden products that contain vermiculite.
URL: http://yosemite.epa.gov/r10/owcm.nsf/asbestos/vermiculite-
home (accessed 15 Aug 2008).

Evaluation of Three Growing Media Substrates for Western Larch Seedling Production at the USDA Forest Service Coeur d'Alene Nursery

Anthony S. Davis, Kent Eggleston, Jeremy R. Pinto, R. Kasten Dumroese

Anthony S. Davis is Assistant Professor of Native Plant Regeneration and Silviculture and Director of the Center for Forest Nursery and Seedling Research, College of Natural Resources, University of Idaho, PO Box 441133, Moscow ID 83844-1133; Tel: 208.885.7211; E-mail: asdavis@uidaho.edu. **Kent Eggleston** is Horticulturist/Forester, USDA Forest Service Coeur d'Alene Nursery, 3600 Nursery Road, Coeur d'Alene, ID 83814; E-mail: keggleston@us.fed.us. **Jeremy R. Pinto** is Botanist and Tribal Nursery Coordinator, USDA Forest Service, Rocky Mountain Research Station, 1221 South Main Street, Moscow, ID 83843; E-mail: jpinto@fs.fed.us. **R. Kasten Dumroese** is National Nursery Specialist, USDA Forest Service, Rocky Mountain Research Station, 1221 South Main Street, Moscow, ID 83843; E-mail: kdumroese@fs.fed.us.

Davis, A.S.; Eggleston, K.; Pinto, J.R.; Dumroese, R.K. 2009. Evaluation of three growing media substrates for western larch seedling production at the USDA Forest Service Coeur d'Alene Nursery. In: Dumroese, R.K.; Riley, L.E., tech. coords. 2009. National Proceedings: Forest and Conservation Nursery Associations—2008. Proc. RMRS-P-58. Fort Collins, CO: U.S. Department of Agriculture, Forest Service, Rocky Mountain Research Station: 37–41. Online: http://www.fs.fed.us/rm/pubs/rmrs_p058.html.

Abstract: In response to concerns regarding growing media substrate costs, and the impact of growing media on seedling quality, we evaluated three peat-based growing media substrates at the USDA Forest Service Coeur d'Alene Nursery in Idaho. Current medium consists of 80:20 peat:fresh Douglas-fir sawdust (v:v). Two other substrates, 75:25 peat:fine screened Douglas-fir bark (v:v) and 100% peat were explored as alternatives. Although sawdust and bark are currently sold at less than half the cost of peat, making them interesting alternatives from a financial basis, we found that western larch seedlings performed best when grown in either the 100% peat medium or the peat:bark medium.

Keywords: sawdust, Douglas-fir bark, peat, growth rate, nitrogen immobilization

Introduction

Most container forest tree seedlings produced in the Inland Northwest of the United States are grown using a Sphagnum peat-based substrate. Given the high cost of peat moss, and environmental concerns regarding its production, amendments are considered a viable way to reduce overall peat consumption. Sawdust, pine bark, and coconut coir can be used as organic amendments, while perlite, sand, and vermiculite are often incorporated as inorganic components of growing media mixes (Landis and others 1990).

Growing medium is known to affect plant performance in bareroot and container nursery production (Rose and Haase 2000; Davis and others 2006; Salifu and others 2006). With that in mind, and realizing the increasing costs of growing media, the USDA Forest Service Coeur d'Alene Nursery in Idaho has been interested in finding an alternative growing substrate. The nursery had previously shifted from a 100% peat substrate to a substrate consisting of 80:20 peat:sawdust by volume to reduce costs. Decreased growth, however, was observed with this mix. To offset this problem, fertilizer rates were increased. While this provided some relief from the high cost of peat, it did not identify the most effective method of producing seedlings, and left production costs vulnerable to fluctuations in fertilizer costs. Because sawdust and bark are each currently about 40% of the cost of peat, they represent economically viable alternatives to 100% peat. Thus, our study objectives were to: (1) determine the influence of growing medium on western larch (*Larix occidentalis*) seedling morphology; and (2) assess the physical and chemical properties of three common growing media used for container seedling production.

Materials and Methods _____

We tested three growing media: (1) 80:20 (v:v) Sphagnum peat:fresh Douglas-fir (*Pseudotsuga menziesii*) sawdust (current medium at Coeur d'Alene); (2) 100% peat; and (3) 75:25 (v:v) Sphagnum peat:finely screened (≤0.95 cm particle size; Buamscha and others 2007) Douglas-fir bark. Western larch seeds of a single source were sown on 4 February 2008 into Styroblock™ (Beaver Plastics, Acheson, Alberta, Canada) 160/90 (315B) containers, each filled with one of three media types. Each Styroblock™ represented one replication, and as media mixes were replicated six times, this led to a total of 18 Styroblock™ containers (3 treatments x 6 replications). Seedlings were fertigated when block weights reached 80% of their weight at field capacity (see table 1 for fertilizer composition), which corresponded to approximately twice weekly during rapid growth.

On 18 May 2008 (105 days after sowing), we randomly selected five seedlings from each container for evaluation of height, root-collar diameter, and shoot and root dry weight. We also determined the bulk density, cation exchange capacity (CEC), and carbon-to-nitrogen ratio (C:N) of each medium.

We analyzed data using analysis of variance (ANOVA) for a randomized complete block design to identify differences among treatments for seedling height, root-collar diameter, and root volume, as well as soil physical and chemical properties. To minimize the possibility of making a Type II error, a significance level of $\alpha = 0.05$ was selected for analysis of treatment differences using Tukey's mean separation test. For seedling parameters, the experimental unit was each group of 30 seedlings from a treatment replication, and the observational unit was each individual seedling. SAS® software (SAS Institute, Cary, NC) was used for all data analyses.

Results and Discussion _____

Media Properties

Bulk density was lowest in 100% peat, and was 29% and 58% higher in the peat:sawdust (80:20) and peat:bark (75:25) mixes, respectively (fig. 1). This result was expected given the inherently higher bulk densities of bark and sawdust compared to peat (Landis and others 1990). Despite being statistically significant, we believe these differences have little biological significance; our bulk density values were below the point (<20%) at which one would expect to see

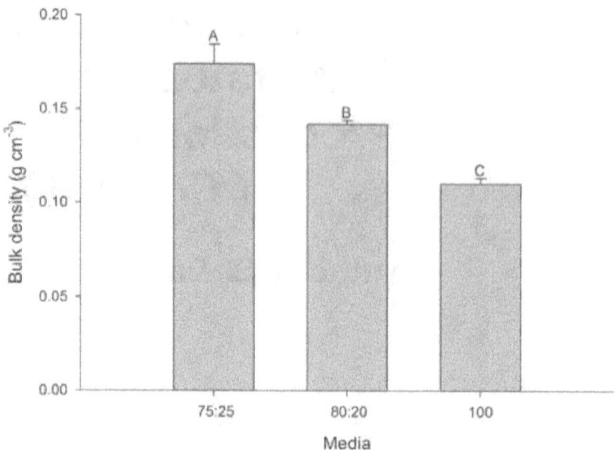

Figure 1. Bulk density of three media mixes (75:25 = 75% peat, 25% fine screened Douglas-fir bark by volume; 80:20 = 80% peat, 20% fresh Douglas-fir sawdust by volume; 100 = 100% peat). Different letters indicate significant differences at $\alpha = 0.05$.

reduced or irregular root growth (Heilmen 1981; Seigel-Issem and others 2005). CEC was highest in 100% peat, and 30% and 27% lower in the peat:sawdust and peat:bark mixes, respectively (fig. 2). This, too, was expected, given that pine bark has about one-third the CEC of peat (Landis and others 1990). C:N was lowest in 100% peat, and was 58% and 36% higher in the peat:sawdust and peat:bark mixes, as was expected given the known high C:N of sawdust (Kanamori and Yasuda 1979; Davis and others 2007). The significant differences observed in C:N, however, may have biological implications. Kanamori and Yasuda (1979) found that peat moss and softwood bark immobilized very little applied nitrogen, whereas sawdust immobilized much more. Decreased nitrogen availability due to immobilization could lead to reduced seedling growth.

Seedling Morphology

Seedling height and root-collar diameter in 100% peat and the peat:bark mixture were significantly greater than those grown in peat:sawdust (figs. 3 and 4). Peat:sawdust seedlings were smaller than those called for in the seedling specifications at Coeur d'Alene Nursery. We believe these differences in seedling morphology were due to the microbial immobilization of nitrogen driven by the aforementioned high C:N that occurs in sawdust, which corresponds with the conclusions of Haynes and Goh (1977). In the peat:sawdust medium, it is possible that the immobilized nitrogen will be remineralized later in the growing season and available to seedlings (Kanamori and Yasuda 1979). From a grower's perspective, this unpredictable (Buamscha and others 2008) addition of nitrogen may lead to unacceptable changes in seedling characteristics later in the growing season (that is, lammas growth or foliage more susceptible to blight caused by *Botrytis* spp.). Perhaps more importantly, the less than optimum growth of seedlings early in the growing season indicates reduced efficiency of resources (greenhouse heat, water, fertilizer, and labor), which translates into higher costs.

Table 1. Fertilizer properties used for seedlings grown in this study.

Nutrient	Application rate (ppm)
Nitrogen	230
Phosphorus	23
Potassium	96
Magnesium	40
Calcium	89
Sulfur	45

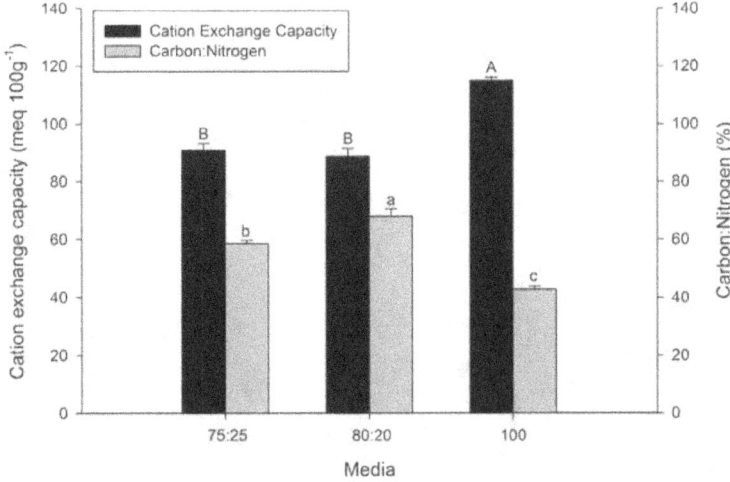

Figure 2. Cation exchange capacity and carbon-to-nitrogen ratio (C:N) of three media mixes (75:25 = 75% peat, 25% fine screened Douglas-fir bark by volume; 80:20 = 80% peat, 20% fresh Douglas-fir sawdust by volume; 100 = 100% peat). Different letters indicate significant differences at α = 0.05.

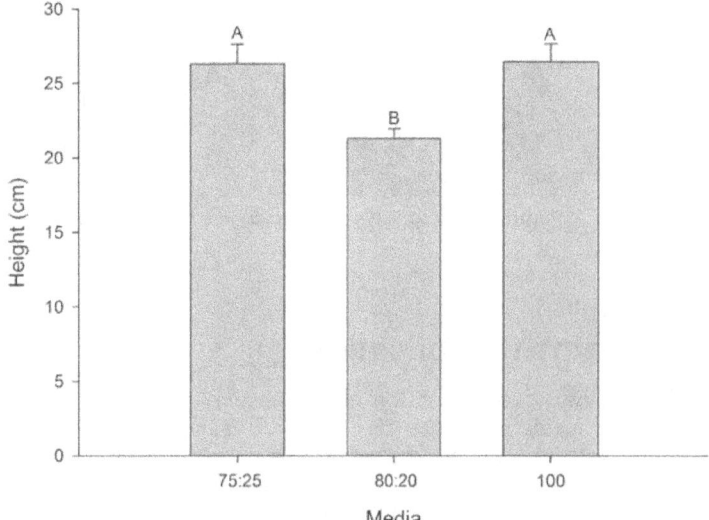

Figure 3. Height of western larch seedlings grown for 105 days in three media mixes (75:25 = 75% peat, 25% fine screened Douglas-fir bark by volume; 80:20 = 80% peat, 20% fresh Douglas-fir sawdust by volume; 100 = 100% peat). Different letters indicate significant differences at α = 0.05.

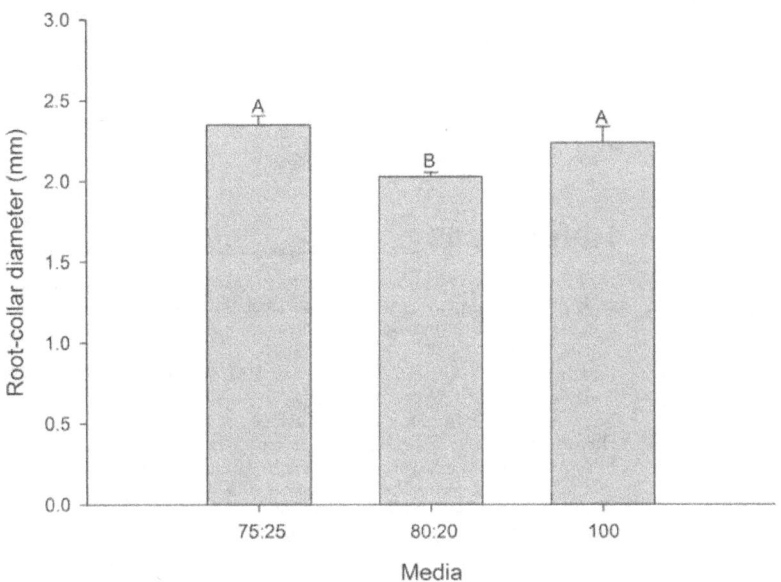

Figure 4. Root-collar diameter of western larch seedlings grown for 105 days in media mixes (75:25 = 75% peat, 25% fine screened Douglas-fir bark by volume; 80:20 = 80% peat, 20% fresh Douglas-fir sawdust by volume; 100 = 100% peat). Different letters indicate significant differences at α = 0.05.

Figure 5. Photograph of trial allowing for ocular assessment of variability in seedling morphology.

Management Implications

We clearly observed variability in seedling quality caused by growing media substrate (fig. 5). Seedlings grown in peat:sawdust did not meet the criteria desired for lifting, whereas those grown in the other substrates did. Examining substrate cost under current economic conditions and subsequent seedling performance, we feel that using the 75:25 peat:bark mixture at the Coeur d'Alene Nursery is a prudent choice (table 2). Continuous evaluation of growing media and fertilization protocols under different economic conditions is an important component of producing quality, cost effective seedlings. As growers seek alternatives, however, we urge them to use caution and test changes to regimes on small batches of seedlings rather than an entire crop. The disadvantage, however, is that the results of any operational studies can be easily compromised by poor study design or execution. We encourage growers to consult with nursery specialists and read Dumroese and Wenny (2003) to ensure their tests provide meaningful results.

Acknowledgments

This project was supported through funding provided by the USDA Forest Service Coeur d'Alene Nursery, the University of Idaho Center for Forest Nursery and Seedling Research, and the USDA Forest Service Reforestation, Nurseries, and Genetic Resources team. Wade Pruett (Phillips Soil Products), Heather Gang (University of Idaho Center for Forest Nursery and Seedling Research), and Amy Ross-Davis provided additional support.

References

Buamscha MG, Altland JE, Horneck DA, Sullivan DM, Cassidy J. 2007. Chemical and physical properties of Douglas-fir bark relevant to the production of container plants. HortScience 42: 1281-1286.

Buamscha MG, Altland JE, Sullivan DM, Horneck DA, McQueen JPG. 2008. Nitrogen availability in fresh and aged Douglas-fir bark. HortTechnology 18:619-623.

Davis AS, Jacobs DF, Wightman KE, Birge ZD. 2006. Organic matter added to bareroot nursery beds influences soil properties and morphology of *Fraxinus pennsylvanica* and *Quercus rubra* seedlings. New Forests 31:293-303.

Davis AS, Jacobs DF, Wightman KE. 2007. Organic matter amendment of fallow forest tree seedling nursery soils influences soil

Table 2. Summary of findings pertaining to selecting a growing medium for use at the USDA Forest Service Coeur d'Alene Nursery. (Costs as of June 2008.)

Growing medium	Cost (US$/ yd)	Seedling morphology	Medium C:N
100% peat	38.00	Meets specifications	Low
80:20 peat:sawdust	33.40	Below specifications	High
75:25 peat:bark	32.25	Meets specifications	Medium

properties and biomass of a sorghum cover crop. Tree Planters' Notes 52:2-6.

Dumroese RK, Wenny DL. 2003. Installing a practical research project and interpreting research results. Tree Planters' Notes 50(1):18-22.

Haynes RJ, Goh KM. 1977. Evaluation of potting media for commercial nursery production of container-grown plants. New Zealand Journal of Agricultural Research 20:371-381.

Heilman P. 1981. Root penetration of Douglas-fir seedlings into compacted soil. Forest Science 27:660-666.

Kanamori T, Yasuda T. 1979. Immobilization, mineralization and the availability of the fertilizer nitrogen during the decomposition of the organic matters applied to the soil. Plant and Soil 52:219-227.

Landis TD, Tinus RW, McDonald SE, Barnett JP. 1990. The container tree nursery manual. Volume 2, containers and growing media. Washington (DC): USDA Forest Service. Agriculture Handbook 674. 88 p.

Rose R, Haase DL. 2000. The use of coir as a containerized growing medium for Douglas-fir seedlings. Native Plants Journal 1:107-111.

Salifu KF, Nicodemus MA, Jacobs DF, Davis AS. 2006. Evaluating chemical indices of media for nursery production of *Quercus rubra* seedlings. HortScience 41:1342-1346.

Siegel-Issem CM, Burger JA, Powers RF, Ponder F, Patterson SC. 2005. Seedling root growth as a function of soil density and water content. Soil Science Society of America Journal 69:215-226.

Growing Media Trials at the Montana Conservation Seedling Nursery

John Justin

John Justin is Nursery Manager, Montana Department of Natural Resouces Conservation Seedling Nursery, 2705 Spurgin Road, Missoula, MT 59804; Tel: 406.542.4327; E-mail: jjustin@state.mt.us.

Justin J. 2009. Growing media trials at the Montana Conservation Seedling Nursery. In: Dumroese, R.K.; Riley, L.E., tech. coords. 2009. National Proceedings: Forest and Conservation Nursery Associations—2008. Proc. RMRS-P-58. Fort Collins, CO: U.S. Department of Agriculture, Forest Service, Rocky Mountain Research Station: 42–43. Online: http://www.fs.fed.us/rm/pubs/rmrs_p058.html.

Keywords: Sphagnum peat moss, vermiculite, Douglas-fir sawdust, compost

Introduction

The Montana Conservation Seedling Nursery (MCSN) in Missoula produces 750,000 container seedlings annually in containers ranging in size from 66 cm³ (4 in³) up to 61 L (16 gal) pots. The MCSN is a production facility with no research funding. When we encounter a promising idea for improving our seedlings or the efficiency of nursery operations, we rarely perform detailed tests. Our standard is a "quick and dirty test." If initial results are promising and we can eliminate anticipated risks, we quickly go operational with the change.

Growing media is one of the largest material costs in container seedling production. Frequent price increases have motivated the MCSN to evaluate numerous growing media options. Because we do not have the ability to custom mix on site, we are limited to testing what is commercially available. For years, our standard mix consisted of 50% Sphagnum peat and 50% coarse vermiculite. This mix worked well for all our conifer production. As our species and container size options diversified, and peat and vermiculite prices increased, we began to look at other options. Our goals were to reduce growing media costs and to find the best medium for each species we produced. We evaluated the following factors when testing growing media:

- Cost including shipping;
- Texture and drainage;
- Wetting and drying characteristics;
- Plant response in the media; and
- Species suitable for the media.

Media Testing

The MCSN evaluated the following growing media mixes over the last 6 years:

- 50% Sphagnum peat, 50% coarse vermiculite (50:50 peat:vermiculite);
- 70% Sphagnum peat, 30% coarse vermiculite (70:30 peat:vermiculite);
- 75% Sphagnum peat, 25% coarse vermiculite (75:25 peat:vermiculite);
- 70% Sphagnum peat, 30% Douglas-fir sawdust, nitroform (70:30 peat:sawdust); and
- EKO Compost™ Outdoor Planting Mix (EKO Compost; Missoula, MT).

50:50 Peat:Vermiculite Mix

Advantages, Disadvantages, Current Status—The 50:50 mix has been our standard tried and true medium, so no surprises were found with the results. The medium wets and dries well, and is excellent for conifers and small containers. However, the medium dries too rapidly in deciduous production, and is too light in large containers. The 50:50 peat:vermiculite medium is excellent for growing conifers, but has become costly due to the rising cost of vermiculite and transportation costs. Use of this mix was discontinued in 2005.

70:30 and 75:25 Peat:Vermiculite Mixes

Advantages, Disadvantages, Current Status—Use of either the 70:30 or 75:25 peat:vermiculite mixes would result in a cost savings of approximately 7%. We observed no discernable changes in plant performance. These media wet and dry well, although they dry too rapidly in deciduous production, and are too light for large containers. The mixes were excellent for conifers and small containers, but both 70:30 and 75:25 peat:vermiculite mixes are costly. The 70:30 peat:vermiculite medium was used in 2005 and 2006 for all production. The 75:25 peat:vermiculite medium is currently used for all containers under 1.6 L (100 in³), and some conifer species in larger containers.

70:30 Peat:Sawdust Mix

Advantages, Disadvantages, Current Status—The 70:30 peat:sawdust mix is lower in cost, will reduce excessive growth in deciduous species, but will require changes in our fertilization program. It has caused slow growth and stunting in many conifer species, and it dries very rapidly, requiring an increase in irrigation frequency. We tested the 70:30 peat:sawdust medium on a small scale on numerous species from 2002 to 2004. We found no suitable use for this medium in our operations. Stunting and unacceptable shoot size variation was common in all conifer species. The mix was useful for reducing growth rates in fast-growing deciduous plants, but the quick drying characteristics of the medium resulted in increased irrigation costs.

EKO Compost™

Advantages, Disadvantages, Current Status—EKO Compost™ consists of composted organic matter, Sphagnum peat moss, and pumice. The cost of this medium is approximately 50% less than all other mixes. It is available locally and easy to order. The compost is very coarse, but holds water well in large containers. Unfortunately, the medium does not fill small containers well due to its coarseness, and there is a risk of contaminants and variability in the compost component. The large cost savings with this medium makes it very attractive. We use this medium in all large containers over 1.6 L (100 in³) in volume, and for hardwoods grown in 1.6 L (100 in³) containers. We have not tested the EKO Compost™ medium in smaller containers because of concerns with disease and drainage, especially for conifers.

Conclusions

The Montana Conservation Seedling Nursery currently uses a growing medium of 75% Sphagnum peat moss and 25% coarse vermiculite for all seedling production in containers smaller than 1.6 L (100 in³) in volume. We use EKO Compost™ Outdoor Planting Mix for containers with a volume of 1.6 L (100 in³) or greater, except for selected conifer species. Growing medium with a sawdust component has not worked in our operation, and no further testing is planned. Future testing will focus on using 100% Sphagnum peat moss in our small container sizes.

The content of this paper reflects the views of the authors, who are responsible for the facts and accuracy of the information presented herein.

Influence of Container Size on Wyoming Big Sagebrush Seedling Morphology and Cold Hardiness

Kayla R. Herriman, Anthony S. Davis,
R. Kasten Dumroese

Kayla R. Herriman is Graduate Research Assistant, Center for Forest Nursery and Seedling Research, College of Natural Resources, University of Idaho, Moscow ID 83844-1133; E-mail: kayla.traver@vandals.uidaho.edu. **Anthony S. Davis** is Assistant Professor of Native Plant Regeneration and Silviculture and Director of the Center for Forest Nursery and Seedling Research, College of Natural Resources, University of Idaho, Moscow ID 83844-1133; E-mail: asdavis@uidaho.edu. **R. Kasten Dumroese** is National Nursery Specialist, USDA Forest Service, Rocky Mountain Research Station, Moscow ID 83843; E-mail: kdumroese@fs.fed.us.

Herriman, K.R.; Davis, A.S.; Dumroese, R.K. 2009. Influence of container size on Wyoming big sagebrush seedling morphology and cold hardiness. In: Dumroese, R.K.; Riley, L.E., tech. coords. 2009. National Proceedings: Forest and Conservation Nursery Associations—2008. Proc. RMRS-P-00. Fort Collins, CO: U.S. Department of Agriculture, Forest Service, Rocky Mountain Research Station: 44–47.Online: http://www.fs.fed.us/rm/pubs/rmrs_p000.html.

Abstract: Wyoming big sagebrush (*Artemisia tridentata*) is a key component of sagebrush steppe ecosystems and is a dominant shrub throughout the western United States. Our objective was to identify the effect of container size on plant morphology of Wyoming big sagebrush. We used three different stocktypes (45/340 ml [20 in³], 60/250 ml [15 in³], 112/105 ml [6.4 in³]) of 1-year old seedlings to examine seedling quality in regards to cold hardiness, height, root-collar diameter, dry mass, root volume, shoot volume, and root:shoot. Cold hardiness was measured four times in the fall and once in the spring. All other measurements were taken in the spring. Cold hardiness was not affected by container size. Plant height, root-collar diameter, and dry mass increased with container size. Shoot volume increased with container size, and root volume of seedlings from the two largest container sizes was greater than that of seedlings grown in 112/105 ml (6.4 in³). Our results indicate the strong effect that container size has on plant morphology. This information provides us with a greater ability to develop target plants for use in restoring a particular site.

Keywords: seedling, nursery, stocktype, outplanting

Introduction

Throughout much of the western United States, Wyoming big sagebrush (*Artemisia tridentata*) is a signature species, serving an important ecological role in sagebrush steppe ecosystems (Meyer and Monson 1992; McIver and Starr 2001; Lambrecht and others 2007). Sagebrush is critical habitat for wildlife, including sage grouse (*Centrocercus urophasianus*) and pronghorn (*Antilocapra americana*) (Yoakum 1982; Rosentreter 2005). These ecosystems have been degraded by fire, noxious weeds, and land use patterns. Many of these ecosystems were exhausted by livestock grazing pressure between 1870 and 1900. Due to the many years of grazing and the low resilience of these ecosystems, exotic annual grasses, such as cheatgrass (*Bromus tectorum*), and noxious weeds were able to establish (Mack and Thompson 1982; Young and others 1987; Monsen and McArthur 1995; McIver and Starr 2001).

Restoration of sagebrush ecosystems has only recently increased in practice and has predominately focused on direct seeding (Hou and Romo 1998; Chambers 2000; Pierson and others 2007). Seedling establishment is paramount to restoration success. Once established, seedlings have shown relatively high rates of survival. Schuman and Belden (2002) found that after 8 years, 59% of seedlings survived. Kiger and others (1987) found long-term survival rates of 33% after 11 years. Direct seeding has shown success in long-term survival, as well as in seed-increase gardens (Welch 1997). In regards to outplanting, nursery-grown sagebrush seedlings could be a more effective method of restoring sagebrush ecosystems, especially with the influence of cost and seed availability (Beyers 2004).

The initial cost of nursery-grown seedlings is higher than that of direct seeding, mainly due to the cost of nursery production and costs associated with shipping plants. Container seedlings may, however, have greater establishment success in harsh site conditions, particularly where repeated direct-seeding operations are required to obtain desired results. Thus, the initial cost of growing, handling, and planting container seedlings may yield more desirable results (better plant establishment and growth) and be more cost effective over time than repeated, or perhaps even single, direct-seeding events (Clements and Young 2000). Sagebrush produces seeds within 3 to 5 years following establishment (Lysne 2005), indicating that surviving plants rapidly become a viable seed source, and able to further colonize the site. Our study objective was to identify the effect of container size on plant morphology of Wyoming big sagebrush so that appropriate target plant specifications can be developed for restoration of degraded sites.

Materials and Methods

Plant Materials

Seedlings were started inside a greenhouse at the Rocky Mountain Research Station in Moscow, ID. Seeds (Humboldt and Elko Counties, Nevada sources) were sown 17 May 2007 into three sizes of Styroblock™ (Beaver Plastics, Acheson, Alberta, Canada) containers: (45/340 ml [20 in³], 615A; 60/250 ml [15 in³], 515A; 112/105 ml [6.4 in³], 415B) (table 1). Thinning and transplanting was conducted on 6 June 2007 to ensure that all cells were filled with a single germinant. Fertilizer was initially applied with irrigation at 100 ppm nitrogen and switched to 25 ppm nitrogen on 4 June 2007 for the rest of the growing season. Seedlings were moved to the University of Idaho Center for Forest Nursery and Seedling Research (Moscow) on 26 October 2007 for hardening and overwintering. Seedlings were outplanted 14 and 15 March 2008 in southern Idaho to examine subsequent field performance.

Plant Morphology Assessment

Height and root-collar diameter were measured on all 480 seedlings of each stocktype following lifting from containers. Root and shoot volume were also measured at this time on a subsample of 40 seedlings of each stocktype using the water displacement method (Burdett 1979). A further subset of 10 seedlings from each stocktype was destructively harvested to determine seedling dry mass following oven-drying at 70 °C (158 °F) for >72 hours.

Cold Hardiness Assessment

Seedlings were tested on four dates in 2007 (5 November, 19 November, 5 December, and 20 December) and once in 2008 (19 March). At each date, cold hardiness was determined via freeze-induced electrolyte leakage (FIEL; Flint and others 1967). Tissue samples from 25 seedlings were randomly selected and five samples were used at each test date. Tissue was cut into 1-cm (0.4-in) lengths and divided into five replicates; one segment of plant was placed into a vial containing 2.5 ml (0.08 oz) of deionized water and a grain of sand to help promote nucleation and decrease surface tension. At each test date, five test temperatures (2 [control], –10, –20, –30, and –40 °C [36, 14, –4, –22, –40 °F) were used. In addition to FIEL, chilling hours were recorded beginning 1 September 2007 using iButton Thermachron® temperature sensors (Maxim/Dallas SemiConductors, Dallas, TX).

Data Analysis

We used SAS® software (SAS Institute Incorporated, Cary, NC) for analysis of variance (ANOVA) to identify differences among treatments. Treatment means were separated using Tukey's honest significant difference (HSD) test ($\alpha = 0.05$). SigmaPlot® (SYSTAT, San Jose, CA) and Microsoft Excel® (Microsoft Corporation, Seattle, WA) were used to calculate LT50s.

Results and Discussion

Plant Morphology

All sagebrush seedling parameters were significantly affected by container size (fig. 1, table 2), which we anticipated given the greater growing space among containers and subsequent resource allocation (Pinto 2005; Dominguez-Lerena and others 2006). Mean height, root-collar diameter, shoot volume, and dry mass for roots and shoots all significantly increased (P < 0.0001) as container size increased. Root volume showed no significant difference (P = 0.0054) between the two largest stocktypes, 45/340 ml (20 in³) and 60/250 ml (15 in³), although they were significantly different from the smallest stocktype, 112/105 ml (6.4 in³). This could be attributed to the fact that, for one growing season under this growing regime, Wyoming big sagebrush could not adequately fill the cavity of a 45/340 ml (20 in³) cell.

Cold Hardiness

Chilling hours accumulated by 5 November 2007 were 65 days at 5 °C (41 °F) and 237 days at 10 °C (50 °F). By the end of data recording, chilling hours at 5 and 10 °C (41 and 50 °F) had accumulated to 677 and 1,217 days, respectively. Stocktype had no effect on cold hardiness measured by the FIEL method and verified using the whole plant freeze test

Table 1. Specifications for containers used.

Beaver Plastics Styroblock™ type		Top diameter		Depth		Volume		Seedling density per	
		mm	in	mm	in	cm³	in³	m²	ft²
112/105 ml (6.4 in³)	415B	36	1.4	148	5.8	108	6.6	530	49
60/250 ml (15 in³)	515A	51	2.0	151	6.0	250	15.3	284	26
45/340 ml (20 in³)	615A	59	2.3	151	6.0	336	10.5	213	20

Figure 1. Wyoming big sagebrush grown in three different sizes of Styroblock™ containers.

Table 2. Influence of stocktype on Wyoming big sagebrush morphology, presented as mean, Tukey grouping, and standard error (SE). Different letters indicate significance within a column at $\alpha = 0.05$.

| Stocktype | Height (cm) | Root-collar diameter (mm) | Volume (cm³) | | Dry mass (g) | |
			Shoot	Root	Shoot	Root
45/340 ml (20 in³)	18.67 a (0.21)	3.05 a (0.03)	13.85 a (0.65)	11.73 a (0.65)	2.28 a (0.15)	1.50 a (0.10)
60/250 ml (15 in³)	15.86 b (0.18)	2.68 b (0.02)	9.62 b (0.42)	11.17 a (0.60)	1.46 b (0.09)	1.09 b (0.08)
112/105 ml (6.4 in³)	10.41 c (0.11)	2.04 c (0.02)	5.35 c (0.17)	5.85 b (0.23)	0.96 c (0.11)	0.66 c (0.05)

(data not shown). Despite the relatively low number of chilling hours, which typically induce cold hardiness (Christersson 1978; Kozlowski and Pallardy 2002), at the time FIEL measurement began, all three stocktypes had LT_{50} values below −30 °C (−22 °F) (table 3). This level of cold hardiness held for all fall measurements. When lifted on 19 March 2008, LT_{50} values indicated that seedling cold hardiness had decreased to between −10 and −20 °C (14 and −4 °F), which is logical, as dehardening usually occurs due to the influence of rising temperatures and change in day length (Kozlowski and Pallardy 2002). A minimal threshold of cold hardiness at outplanting may be necessary, as Lambrecht and others (2007) found that a single episodic freezing treatment on big sagebrush seedlings resulted in an arresting of growth and negatively affected photosynthetic tissues.

Conclusion and Future Directions

Wyoming big sagebrush seedling morphology was clearly influenced by container size, with plant size increasing as container size increased. Cold hardiness was unaffected by container size, but values at the end of the growing season (November/December) were higher (plants were hardier) than prior to lifting (March). Further examination of the cold hardiness cycle of sagebrush will provide insight to growers attempting to maximize storage and coordinate outplanting with times of higher stress resistance, for which cold hardiness is often a surrogate measure (Burr 1990).

For coal mine restoration, the limited availability and increasing cost of native plants seeds has raised the question as to whether outplanting seedlings is a feasible alternative to direct seeding for meeting desired shrub densities (Schuman and others 2005). This same question could be asked for sites impacted by other factors, such as fire. The demand for native shrub seeds over the past decade in the western United States has been high due to the millions of hectares of native rangelands in need of rehabilitation following wildfire (Schuman and others 2005). Direct seeding is perceived to have a greater seed:seedling efficiency. However, more thorough, long-term studies to examine the costs and benefits of direct seeding versus outplanting have not yet been completed (Kleinman and Richmond 2000; Schuman and others 2005).

Seedlings grown during this study were outplanted on sites in southern Idaho and will be tracked to evaluate the influence of container size on field performance of container-grown Wyoming big sagebrush. Future studies should compare the costs of direct seeding and planting of container seedlings with regard to meeting restoration objectives.

Table 3. Cold hardiness (LT$_{50}$) according to stocktype across five measurement dates; < −40 °C (−40 °F) indicates that LT$_{50}$ was below −40 °C and beyond the scope of measurement.

Stocktype	LT$_{50}$ (°C) by Measurement date				
	5-Nov	19-Nov	5-Dec	20-Dec	19-Mar
45/340 ml (20 in³)	−37	< −40	< −40	< −40	−11
60/250 ml (15 in³)	< −40	< −40	−40	< −40	−13
112/105 ml (6.4 in³)	−35	< −40	< −40	< −40	−16

°F = (°C*9/5)+32

Acknowledgments

This study was funded by the Great Basin Native Plant Selection and Increase Project and the University of Idaho Center for Forest Nursery and Seedling Research. Field and technical support was provided by Amy Ross-Davis, Heather Gang, Rob Keefe, Jeremy Pinto, Nathan Robertson, Nancy Shaw, Karen Sjoquist, and Maggie Ward.

References

Beyers JL. 2004. Postfire seeding for erosion control: effectiveness and impacts on native plant communities. Conservation Biology 18(4):947-956.

Burdett AN. 1979. A non destructive method for measuring the volume of intact plants. Canadian Journal of Forest Research 9(1):120-122.

Burr KE. 1990. The target seedling concept: bud dormancy and cold-hardiness. In: Rose R, Campbell SJ, Landis TD, editors. Proceedings, Western Forest Nursery Association; 1990 August 13-17; Roseburg, OR. Fort Collins (CO): USDA Forest Service, Rocky Mountain Forest and Range Experiment Station. General Technical Report RM-200. p 79-90.

Chambers JC. 2000. Seed movements and seedling fates in disturbed sagebrush steppe ecosystems: implications for restoration. Ecological Applications 10(5):1400-1413.

Clements CD, Young JA. 2000. Antelope bitterbrush seedling transplant survival. Rangelands 22(1):15-17.

Christersson L. 1978. The influence of photoperiod and temperature on the development of frost hardiness in seedlings of *Pinus sylvestris* and *Picea abies*. Physiologia Plantarum 44:288-294.

Dominguez-Lerena S, Herrero Sierra N, Carrasco Manzano I, Ocana Bueno L, Penuelas Rubira JL, Mexal JG. 2006. Container characteristics influence *Pinus pinea* seedling development in the nursery and field. Forest Ecology and Management 221(1-3): 63-71.

Flint HL, Boyce BR, Beattie DJ. 1967. Index of injury: a useful expression of freezing injury to plant tissues as determined by the electrolytic method. Canadian Journal of Plant Science 17:229-230.

Hou J, Romo JT. 1998. Seed weight and germination time affect growth of 2 shrubs. Journal of Range Management 51:699-703.

Kiger JA, Berg WA, Herron JT, Phillips CM, Atkinson RG. 1987. Shrub establishment in the mountain shrub zone. In: Proceedings of the 4th biennial symposium on surface mining and reclamation of the Great Plains, American Society for Surface Mining and Reclamation; 1987 March 16-20; Billings, MT. Bozeman (MT): Montana State University, Reclamation Research Unit. Report 87-04. p L-3-1-6.

Kleinman LH, Richmond TC. 2000. Sagebrush and mine reclamation: What's needed from here? In: Billings land reclamation symposium, striving for restoration, fostering technology, and policy for reestablishing ecological function; 2000 March 20-24; Billings, MT. Bozeman (MT): Montana State University, Reclamation Research Unit. p 338-345.

Kozlowski TT, Pallardy SG. 2002. Acclimation and adaptive responses of woody plants to environmental stresses. Botanical Review 68(2):270-334.

Lambrecht SC, Shattuck AK, Loik ME. 2007. Combined drought and episodic freezing effects on seedlings of low- and high-elevation subspecies of sagebrush (*Artemisia tridentata*). Physiologia Plantarum 130:207-217.

Lysne CR. 2005. Restoring Wyoming big sagebrush. In: Shaw NL, Pellant M, Monsen SB, compilers. Sage-grouse habitat restoration symposium proceedings; 2001 June 4-7; Boise, ID. Fort Collins (CO): USDA Forest Service, Rocky Mountain Research Station. Proceedings RMRS-P-38. p 93-98.

Mack RN, Thompson JN. 1982. Evolution in steppe with few large, hooved mammals. American Naturalist 119(6):757-773.

McIver J, Starr L. 2001. Restoration of degraded lands in the interior Columbia River basin: passive vs. active approaches. Forest Ecology and Management 153:15-28.

Meyer SE, Monsen SB. 1992. Big sagebrush germination patterns: subspecies and population differences. Journal of Range Management 45:87-93.

Monsen SB, McArthur ED. 1995. Implications of early intermountain range and watershed restoration practices. In: Proceedings of the wildland shrub and arid land restoration symposium; 1993 October 19-21; Las Vegas, NV. Ogden (UT): USDA Forest Service, Intermountain Research Station. General Technical Report INT-GTR-315. p 16-25.

Pierson FB, Blackburn WH, Van Vactor SS. 2007. Hydrologic impacts of mechanical seeding treatments on sagebrush rangelands. Rangeland Ecology and Management 60:666-674.

Pinto JR. 2005. Container and physiological status comparisons of *Pinus ponderosa* seedlings [MSc thesis]. Moscow (ID): University of Idaho. 32 p.

Rosentreter R. 2005. Sagebrush identification, ecology, and palatability relative to sage-grouse. In: Shaw NL, Pellant M, Monsen SB, compilers. Sage-grouse habitat restoration symposium proceedings; 2001 June 4-7; Boise, ID. Fort Collins (CO): USDA Forest Service, Rocky Mountain Research Station. Proceedings RMRS-P-38. p 3-16.

Schuman GE, Belden SE. 2002. Long-term survival of direct seeded Wyoming big sagebrush seedlings on a reclaimed mine site. Arid Land Research and Management 16:309-317.

Schuman GE, Vicklund LE, Belden SE. 2005. Establishing *Artemisia tridentata* ssp. *wyomingensis* on mined lands: science and economics. Arid Land Research and Management 19:353-362.

Welch BL. 1997. Seeded versus containerized big sagebrush plants for seed-increase gardens. Journal of Range Management 50(6):611-614.

Yoakum J. 1982. Managing vegetation for pronghorns in the Great Basin. In: Monsen SB, Shaw N, compilers. Managing intermountain rangelands—improvements of range and wildlife habitats: symposium proceedings; 1982 September 15-17; Twin Falls, ID. Ogden (UT): USDA Forest Service, Intermountain Forest and Range Experiment Station. General Technical Report INT-157.

Young JA, Evans RA, Eckert RE Jr, Kay BL. 1987. Cheatgrass. Rangelands 9(6):266-270.

Potential for Boom-Mounted Remote Sensing Applications in Seedling Quality Monitoring

Robert F. Keefe, Jan U.H. Eitel, Daniel S. Long, Anthony S. Davis, Paul Gessler, and Alistair M.S. Smith

Robert F. Keefe is a PhD candidate with the Department of Forest Resources, College of Natural Resources, University of Idaho, Moscow, ID 83843; Tel: 208.885.5165; E-mail: rkeefe@vandal.idaho.edu. **Jan U.H. Eite** is a PhD candidate with the Department of Forest Resources, College of Natural Resources, University of Idaho, Moscow, ID 83843. **Daniel S. Long** is Research Leader with the Columbia Plateau Conservation Research Center, USDA-ARS, PO Box 370, Pendleton, OR 97801. **Anthony S. Davis** is Native Plant Regeneration and Silviculture Director, Department of Forest Resources, College of Natural Resources, University of Idaho, Moscow, ID 83843. **Paul Gessler** is Associate Professor of Remote Sensing and GIS, Department of Forest Resources, College of Natural Resources, University of Idaho, Moscow, ID 83843. **Alistair M.S. Smith** is Assistant Professor of Forest Measurements, Forest and Rangeland Measurements Laboratory, Department of Forest Resources, College of Natural Resources, University of Idaho, Moscow, ID 83843.

Keefe, R.F.; Eitel, J.U.H.; Long, D.S.; Davis, A.S.; Gessler, P.; Smith, A.M.S. 2009. Potential for boom-mounted remote sensing applications in seedling quality monitoring. In: Dumroese, R.K.; Riley, L.E., tech. coords. 2009. National Proceedings: Forest and Conservation Nursery Associations—2008. Proc. RMRS-P-58. Fort Collins, CO: U.S. Department of Agriculture, Forest Service, Rocky Mountain Research Station: 48–51. Online: http://www.fs.fed.us/rm/pubs/rmrs_p058.html.

Abstract: Remotely sensed aerial and satellite sensor imagery is widely used for classification of vegetation structure and health on industrial and public lands. More intensively than at any other time in the life of a planted tree, its health and status will be maintained and monitored while under culture in a bareroot or container nursery. As a case in point, inventories to track seedling root-collar diameter, height, bud development, and merchantability at the University of Idaho Center for Forest Nursery and Seedling Research greenhouses are conducted and discussed bi-weekly. Plant moisture and nutrient status, and the presence of pests and pathogens, are monitored continuously. Many nurseries are equipped with overhead irrigation boom systems designed to deliver fertigation uniformly. Because of their slow speed and complete coverage, these systems provide an opportunistic location on which to mount lightweight, portable sensors for remote seedling quality assessment. We conducted measurements with an ASD Field SpecPro™ radiometer (Analytical Spectral Devices, Boulder, CO) in a laboratory setting to evaluate whether spectral indices used to predict biomass and nitrogen status from tractors in dryland wheat crops might also be capable of detecting differences in nitrogen effects on Scots pine (*Pinus sylvestris*). We regressed the Green Normalized Difference Vegetation Index (GNDVI) on seedling stem mass and the Canopy Chlorophyll Content Index (CCCI) on foliage chlorophyll content. GNDVI explained 77% of the variation in shoot biomass and had an average prediction error (RMSE) of 19% of the mean. CCCI predicted 61% of the variation in foliar chlorophyll content, with an average prediction error of 16%.

Keywords: seedling monitoring, container nursery

Introduction

Remote sensing technology provides a variety of measurement and monitoring tools to forest scientists and land managers. Aerial photography and satellite sensor imagery have long been used to classify vegetation types on large industrial and public lands. Recent advances in sensors, analytical methods used for spectral analysis, the ability of computers to process large amounts of geographic data, and the ready availability of public data sources over the Internet have resulted in the growth of remote sensing into an integral component of natural resource inventory and forest health monitoring (Wulder 1998). Airplane-based and satellite sensor images are commonly used to assess stand structural variables, extent of pest and pathogen outbreaks, forest successional stage, biomass and Leaf Area Index, and Net Primary Productivity (Tucker and Sellers 1986). In agriculture, hand-held spectral radiometers are also being used to automate quality monitoring in precision crop management. For example, Eitel and others (2008) monitored nitrogen status in dryland wheat crops using a portable multi-spectral radiometer.

The health and status of a bareroot or container seedling will be maintained and monitored more intensively in the nursery than at any other time in its life. While managed forests are rarely inventoried more than once in a 5-year period, nursery inventories to track seedling root-collar diameter, height development, and merchantability are conducted with greater frequency. As a typical example, inventories in the University of Idaho Center for Forest Nursery and Seedling Research (CFNSR; Moscow) greenhouses are conducted biweekly; irrigation levels, macro- and micronutrient status, and the possible presence of harmful pests and pathogens are monitored at weekly or daily intervals; and relative root and shoot biomass, bud development, tissue cold hardiness, and root growth potential are of interest throughout the growing season.

Many forestry and conservation nurseries are equipped with automated overhead irrigation boom systems. Overhead irrigation was designed to deliver fertigation to seedlings at a consistent rate and thereby minimize variability in growth characteristics within the crop (Landis and others 1989). The overhead boom is characterized by slow speed, self-propulsion, complete crop coverage, and appropriate height to allow proper water dispersal from the spray nozzles. While these characteristics exist for the purpose of delivering nutrients and moisture to seedlings, they may also make the overhead irrigation boom an opportunistic location on which to mount small, lightweight, portable sensors. In this study, we sought to evaluate whether spectral indices being used to predict biomass and nitrogen status in dryland wheat were also capable of detecting differences in nitrogen effects on Scots pine (*Pinus sylvestris*) seedlings. We regressed the Green Normalized Difference Vegetation Index (GNDVI) on seedling stem mass and the Canopy Chlorophyll Content Index (CCCI) on foliage chlorophyll content. CCCI is a metric that may be useful for detecting plant foliar chlorophyll while simultaneously accounting for differences in plant biomass. Lastly, we also described other boom-mounted remote sensing studies being conducted at the CFNSR.

Methods

Informal and formal research at the University of Idaho CFNSR is evaluating several possible boom-mounted remote sensing applications. During fall 2007, a passive multi-band spectroradiometer (MSR), the Cropscan™ (Cropscan Incorporated, Rochester, MN) was used to take readings of blue spruce (*Picea pungens*) and ponderosa pine (*Pinus ponderosa*) crops. The Cropscan™ is a passive sensor that utilizes incident ambient sunlight to measure the reflectance of particular spectral bands off of crops. While calibration procedures exist, the reliance of this MSR on incoming light provides a challenge for container seedling quality monitoring in a greenhouse environment because greenhouses are

designed to scatter light (Landis and others 1992) throughout the bays from a variety of directions. The large amount of diffuse light inside a greenhouse adds difficulty to sampling with a passive sensor.

During summer 2008, Scots pine seedlings grown by students for a University of Idaho undergraduate Forest Regeneration course were transported to the USDA Agricultural Research Service, Oregon State University laboratory (Pendleton, OR) for spectral analysis. The seedlings were grown in a 1-way factorial experiment with seven levels of fertilizer rate (2.5, 5, 7.5, 10, 12.5, 15, and 17.5 mg). The fertilizer was Osmocote® 18N:6P_2O_5:12K_2O low-start 14- to 16-month controlled release at 21 °C (70 °F) (Scotts-Sierra Horticultural Products Company, Marysville, OH). Seedlings were grown in a 50:50 mixture of vermiculite:forestry grade peat moss (v:v; Sun Gro Horticulture Distribution Incorporated, Bellevue, WA).

For each of 21 total containers, two spectral measurements were taken. The first reading targeted the individual seedling at the center position in the container, with the radiometer positioned 4.5 in (11.43 cm) above the Copperblock™ surface. The second measurement captured several seedlings, and was taken at 35.56 cm (14.0 in) above the container. Seedling root-collar diameter and stem green mass were recorded for the center seedling. Chlorophyll concentration was determined by allowing 0.2 g of foliage to soak in 80% acetone solution for 24 hours and measuring reflectance with a lab spectrometer.

Results

Effect of fertilizer treatments on shoot biomass (green weight) are shown in figure 1. Using ASD Field SpecPro™ radiometer (Analytical Spectral Devices, Boulder, CO) measurements conducted in the laboratory setting with a direct light source, it was possible to predict seedling shoot

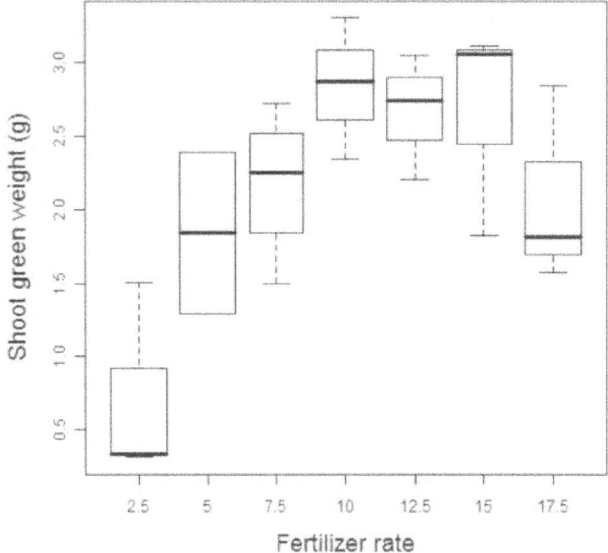

Figure 1. Relationship of fertilizer rate and shoot green weight in first year Scots pine (*Pinus sylvestris*) used in spectroradiometer study.

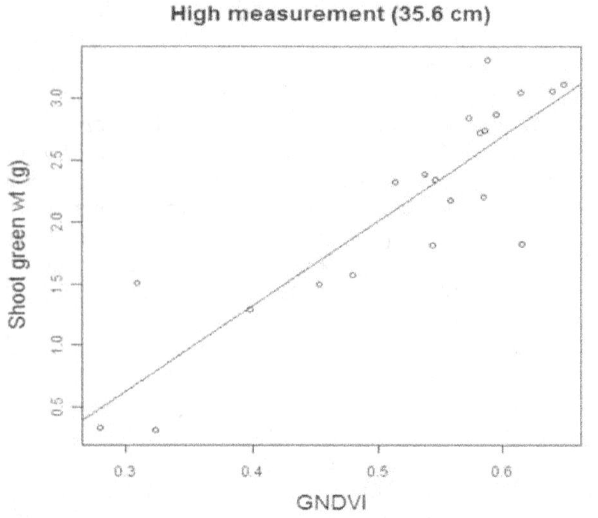

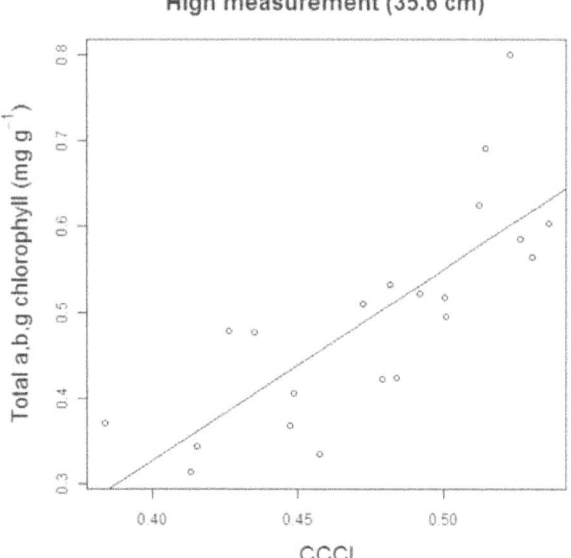

Figure 2. Relationship of GNDVI index and shoot green weight (g) (high measurement 35.6 cm [14 in]).

green weight from the spectral GNDVI index (fig. 2). The simple linear regression of shoot green mass (response) on GNDVI (predictor) had a root mean squared error (RMSE) of 0.41, indicating that the average individual prediction could be expected to vary by this amount. Expressed as a percentage of the mean, this is approximately 19% prediction error. The multiple R^2 for this model was 0.77, and residual plots satisfied linear regression model assumptions. It was also possible to predict seedling foliar chlorophyll content using from the CCCI index (fig. 3). The average prediction error (RMSE) for this model was 0.079 (16% of mean chlorophyll), and the model had a multiple R^2 of

0.61. For biomass and chlorophyll prediction, the higher spectral measurement (35.56 cm [14 in], rather than 11.43 cm [4.5 in]) provided substantially better prediction than the lower measurement.

Discussion

In this study, we have briefly explored one of many possible examples of nursery seedling quality monitoring using portable remote sensing devices. An additional preliminary experiment currently being conducted at the CFNSR is evaluating the ability of a small laser (the Acuity AccuRange™ 1000 [Schmitt Measurement Systems, Incorporated, Portland, OR]) to measure seedling heights. There are many other possibilities. An advantage of boom-mounted remote sensing applications in seedling quality monitoring is that they are more likely to detect spatial patterns in nursery crops that: (1) may not be visible to growers conducting visual assessments (due to inability to view the crop from above); and (2) may not be detected in inventories based on Simple Random Sampling, 3-P Sampling, and similar probabilistic but non-spatial sampling designs. Spatial patterning in seedling quality in a nursery crop may occur for several reasons. Variation in diffuse light characteristics, differences in temperature due to the positioning of heating and cooling units, and streaking caused by poorly performing spray nozzles may all result in patterns of seedling stress or non-uniformity. A faulty spray nozzle failing to deliver fertilizer rates correctly to a 2-cell wide swath of ponderosa pine seedlings grown in Styroblock™ 160 cell/90 mL (5.5 in³) containers at the University of Idaho Pitkin Forest Nursery would equate to 1,632 seedlings.

New, portable, active spectral sensors that should be able to function robustly in high diffuse-light environments, such as nursery greenhouses, are now available. An example of such a sensor, which will be evaluated in a similar study during the summer of 2008, is the new CropCircle™ multi-band spectral radiometer. Unlike the Cropscan™, the CropCircle™ emits its own light pattern that is detected upon return.

Although this technology is readily available, careful development of predictive equations relating appropriate spectral indices to seedling quality parameters of interest will be necessary to make seedling quality monitoring with boom-mounted sensors useful for commercial growers.

References

Eitel JUH, Long DS, Gessler PE, Hunt ER Jr. 2008. Combined spectral index to improve ground-based estimates of nitrogen status in dryland wheat. Agronomy Journal 100:1694-1702.

Eitel JUH, Long DS, Gessler PE, Smith AMS. 2007. Using in-situ measurements to evaluate the new RapidEye™ satellite series for prediction of wheat nitrogen status. International Journal of Remote Sensing 28(18):4183-4190.

El-Shikha DM, Barnes EM, Clarke TR, Hunsaker DJ, Haberland JA, Pinter PJ Jr, Waller PM, Thompson TL. 2008. Remote sensing of cotton nitrogen status using the canopy chlorophyll content index (CCCI). Transactions of the ASABE 51(1):73-82.

Landis TD, Tinus RW, McDonald SE, Barnett JP. 1989. The container tree nursery manual. Volume 4, seedling nutrition and irrigation. Washington (DC): USDA Forest Service. Agriculture Handbook 674. 119 p.

Figure 3. Relationship of total leaf chlorophyll (per gram basis) and CCCI (high measurement 35.6 cm [14 in]).

Landis TD, Tinus RW, McDonald SE, Barnett JP. 1992. The container tree nursery manual. Volume 3, atmospheric environment. Washington (DC): USDA Forest Service. Agriculture Handbook 674. 145 p.

Tucker CJ, Sellers PJ. 1986. Satellite remote sensing of primary production. International Journal of Remote Sensing 7(11):1395-1416.

Wulder M. 1998. Optical remote-sensing techniques for the assessment of forest inventory and biophysical parameters. Progress in Physical Geography 22(4):449-476.

Effects of Irrigation Frequency and Grit Color on the Germination of Lodgepole Pine Seeds

Jeremy R. Pinto, R. Kasten Dumroese, and Douglas R. Cobos

Jeremy R. Pinto is Tribal Nursery Coordinator, USDA Forest Service, Southern Research Station, 1221 S Main Street, Moscow, ID 83843; Tel: 208.883.2352; E-mail: jpinto@fs.fed.us. **R. Kasten Dumroese** is Research Plant Physiologist, USDA Forest Service, Southern Research Station, 1221 S Main Street, Moscow, ID 83843; Tel: 208.883.2324; E-mail: kdumroese@fs.fed.us. **Douglas R. Cobos** is Director of Research and Development, 2365 NE Hopkins Court, Pullman, WA 99163; Tel: 509.332.2756; E-mail: doug@decagon.com.

Pinto, J.R.; Dumroese, R.K.; Cobos, D.R. 2009. Effects of irrigation frequency and grit color on the germination of lodgepole pine seeds. In: Dumroese, R.K.; Riley, L.E., tech. coords. 2009. National Proceedings: Forest and Conservation Nursery Associations—2008. Proc. RMRS-P-00. Fort Collins, CO: U.S. Department of Agriculture, Forest Service, Rocky Mountain Research Station: 52–57. Online: http://www.fs.fed.us/rm/pubs/rmrs_p000.html.

Abstract: Nursery cultural practices during germination can be highly variable between existing production facilities. Although nursery guidebooks suggest keeping seeds moist, there are no known scientific answers indicating what sufficient moisture levels are. This study objective was to characterize differing irrigation regimes and grit color choices on different germination parameters (Germination Capacity, GC; Peak Value Germination, PV; Germination Value, GV; and Germination Rate, GR_{50}) using seedbed temperature and soil matric water potential (Ψ) measurements. No significant differences were observed between irrigation frequency and grit color for GC and GR_{50}. The indices of germination speed, PV and GV, were significant for irrigation frequency ($P < 0.05$), but not grit color. No correlations were observed between seedbed temperature and GC, PV, and GV parameters, and only weak correlations were observed between GC, GV, PV, and Ψ. Despite the lack of significance and correlations, Ψ values indicated that germinating seeds were still in contact with adequately moist soils at low irrigation frequencies. These results have implications in current nursery management and may contribute to watering reductions and potential cost savings.

Keywords: seedbed temperature, water potential, germination rate, germination capacity

Introduction

To ensure that uniform crops are grown in the nursery, considerable effort is exercised in the care of seeds before they are sown. Seed treatments, in the form of soaking, stratifying, and scarifying, are often used to break seed dormancy and increase germination capacity (Krugman and others 1974). Post sowing, the abiotic elements of light, temperature, and moisture are critical factors that also contribute to total germination (capacity) and rate of germination (Landis and others 1998). In container nurseries, seeds that have high germination capacity and fast germination rates are most desirable. Despite relative uniformity in seed treatments prior to sowing, nursery culture regimes during germination are often highly variable among existing production nurseries. Personal communication with managers of northern Idaho container tree nurseries indicate some use multiple irrigations each day to keep seeds moist (Eggleston 2006), while others use visual and tactile examination to determine irrigation (Wenny 2005). The recommendation of conifer propagation protocols advises daily misting to keep the zone around germinating seeds slightly moist to maximize germination (Wenny and Dumroese 1987, 1990, 1992).

A common feature between most forest and conservation greenhouses is that they are all heated; however, irrigation is highly variable between most facilities. Investigating the different irrigation techniques between facilities may seem trivial, but irrigation frequency during the germination period may have impacts on germination rate and the presence or absence of seedborne pathogens that cause damping-off problems during emergence (Dumroese and James 2005). While it's important for seeds to have adequate access to moisture during germination, it's also important for exposure to favorable temperatures for maximum germination.

A pilot study at the USDA Forest Service Coeur d'Alene Nursery in Idaho compared irrigation frequency on germination. Their study showed a difference in germination rates caused by irrigation frequency (Myers 2005). Unfortunately, the study was not published, and no biophysical data were collected to support the observed differences. One hypothesis is that frequent irrigation decreases seedbed temperatures, thereby contributing to lower germination rates; furthermore, by changing the color of grit (seed covering), seedbed temperatures may also be manipulated, increasing or decreasing germination. Our study objective was to analyze microsite temperature and soil matric water potential (Ψ) data at the seed level using adequate and sensitive equipment to capture differences of irrigation frequency and grit color on germination capacity and rate.

Materials and Methods

Nursery Culture

Lodgepole pine (*Pinus contorta* var. *latifolia*) seeds from Lawyers Nursery, Incorporated (Plains, MT) were cold stratified for 30 days before being sown at the USDA Forest Service Rocky Mountain Research Station greenhouse in Moscow, ID (46° 43'N, 117° 00'W). A completely randomized 3 x 3 factorial split-plot design was used on irrigation and grit color treatments with three replications. Main plots were irrigation treatments, and the split-plots were grit color. Irrigation treatments consisted of high, medium, and low frequency, where high consisted of light irrigation 3 times a day, medium was once every 2 days, and low was once every 4 days. Full irrigations (multiple passes with an irrigation boom) were carried out every 4 days to bring containers to field capacity. A per cavity breakdown of irrigation applications and rates are shown in table 1. Phosphoric acid was injected into the irrigation water to adjust the pH to 5.5. Grit treatments consisted of black, white, and neutral (natural brown). The black and white colors were made by spray painting the neutral grit color.

Seeds were sown in Styroblock™ (Beaver Plastics, Edmonton, Alberta) containers that contain 160 cavities that are each 90 ml (5.5 in³) in volume. Each container was an irrigation replication (main plot) and was split into three sections for color treatments. Containers were filled with Sphagnum peat moss:vermiculite (1:1, v:v) medium (Sun Gro Horticulture, Bellevue, WA). Each color replication contained 32 cavities sown at 3 seeds per cavity for the germination tally. A one-cell buffer row was used around each color treatment to minimize edge effects.

Germination Counts

Germination was recorded daily for 21 days after sowing and used to calculate four germination parameters: germination capacity (GC), peak value (PV), germination value (GV), and germination rate (GR_{50}). Germinated seeds were scored when hypocotyls became visible through the grit. As a measure of germination completeness, GC was calculated as the total number of germinants over the entire measured period. PV, a measure of germination speed, is the maximum value obtained using: $PV = DCG \div$ days since start of test, where DCG is the daily cumulative percent germination (Czabator 1962). GV combines germination speed and completeness, calculated by $GV = (GC \div D) \times PV$, where D is the number of days in the test. GR_{50} is equal to the number of days required for 50% of the seeds to germinate (Ching 1959). For measures of GC, PV, and GV, the higher the number, the better the germination parameter; for GR_{50}, a lower number is an indication of a better germination rate.

Instrumentation

One cell within each irrigation x grit color treatment x replication combination (n = 27) was randomly chosen for temperature collection using a copper-constantan thermocouple connected to a CR10X data logger (Campbell Scientific, Incorporated, Logon, UT). Thermocouples were placed at the soil-seed-grit interface and remained *in situ* for 21 days after sowing. Daily average temperatures for irrigation and grit treatments were calculated between the hours of 0800 and 2000. Soil water potential (matric potential) was measured in one randomly chosen cell for each irrigation x grit color treatment x replication combination (n = 27) using a T5 Tensiometer (UMS, Munich, Germany). Water potential measurements were taken in the morning prior to irrigation treatments. Greenhouse atmospheric data, including temperature and relative humidity, were also collected (Em50, Decagon Devices, Pullman, WA).

Data Analysis

Regressions and analysis of variance were done using SAS® software (SAS Institute Incorporated, Cary, NC). Assumptions for equal variances and normality were met by all data analyzed.

Results

Average daily seedbed temperature (referred to just as temperature(s) for the rest of this document) and Ψ (dependent variables) were checked for relationships to both irrigation and grit color treatments (independent variables) using 1-way analysis of variance. Grit color temperatures were significantly different ($P = 0.002$) and decreased as the color treatments moved from black to neutral to white (21.6, 21.2, and 20.9 °C [70.9, 70.2, and 69.6 °F] for black, neutral, and white, respectively; fig. 1A). Irrigation temperatures were also significantly different ($P = 0.005$), but did not show any trends (21.2, 21.6, and 20.9 °C [70.2, 70.9, and 69.6 °F] for low, medium, and high, respectively; fig. 1B). No differences were seen in Ψ and grit color ($P = 0.97$; fig.

Table 1. Average amount of water applied per cavity in each container.

Applications	Irrigation treatment		
	Low	Medium	High
	. . . . *ml*		
Single misting application	6.7	4.2	2.1
# applications every 4 days	1	2	12
Total applied every 4 days	6.7	8.4	25.4

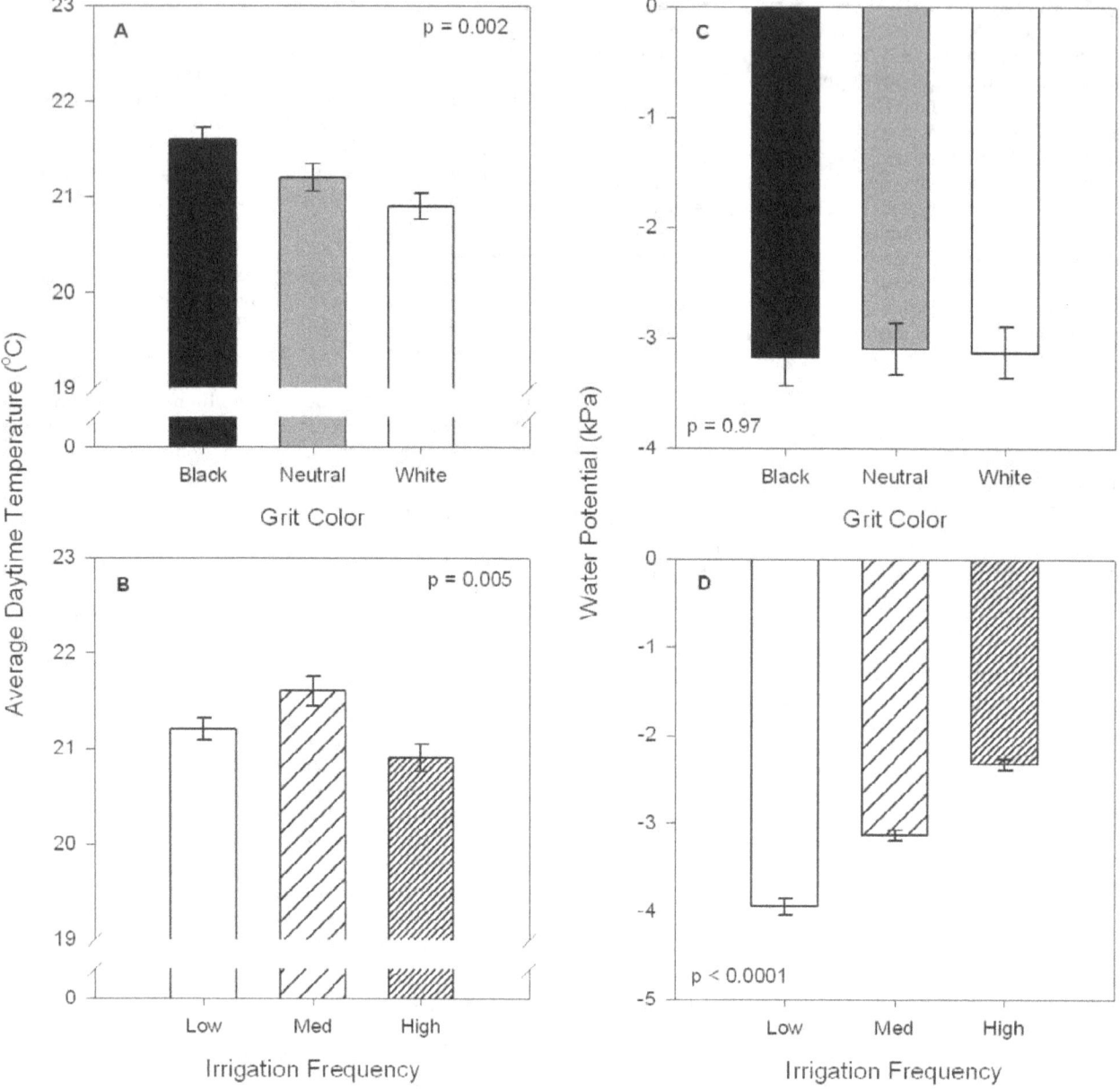

Figure 1. Irrigation frequency and grit color effects on seedbed temperature and soil matric water potential. Bars indicate standard errors of the means.

1C), but significant differences were observed in the irrigation treatments with Ψ increasing with irrigation frequency ($P < 0.0001$; fig. 1D).

Linear regression analysis was performed on germination parameters using temperature and Ψ as explanatory variables. No significant temperature relationships were detected for GC ($P = 0.45$), PV ($P = 0.69$), and GV ($P = 0.91$). Scatter plots confirm the absence of any trends (fig. 2). Conversely, significant relationships were observed with GC ($P = 0.003$; $r^2 = 0.31$), PV ($P = 0.001$, $r^2 = 0.36$) and GV ($P = 0.001$, $r^2 = 0.37$; fig. 3A, B, and C).

GC, PV, and GV all increased with increasing irrigation frequency; only PV and GV, however, yielded significant differences with irrigation frequency main effects (table 2). No significant difference in GR_{50} was observed, with the calculated day to 50% germination for all irrigation treatments occurring on day 9. Grit color showed increasing trends in PV, GV, and GR_{50}, although not significant ($P > 0.12$; table 2).

Discussion

The results of Weber and Sorensen (1990) showed that increased temperature, with 30 days of cold stratification, had a positive effect on ponderosa pine (*Pinus ponderosa*)

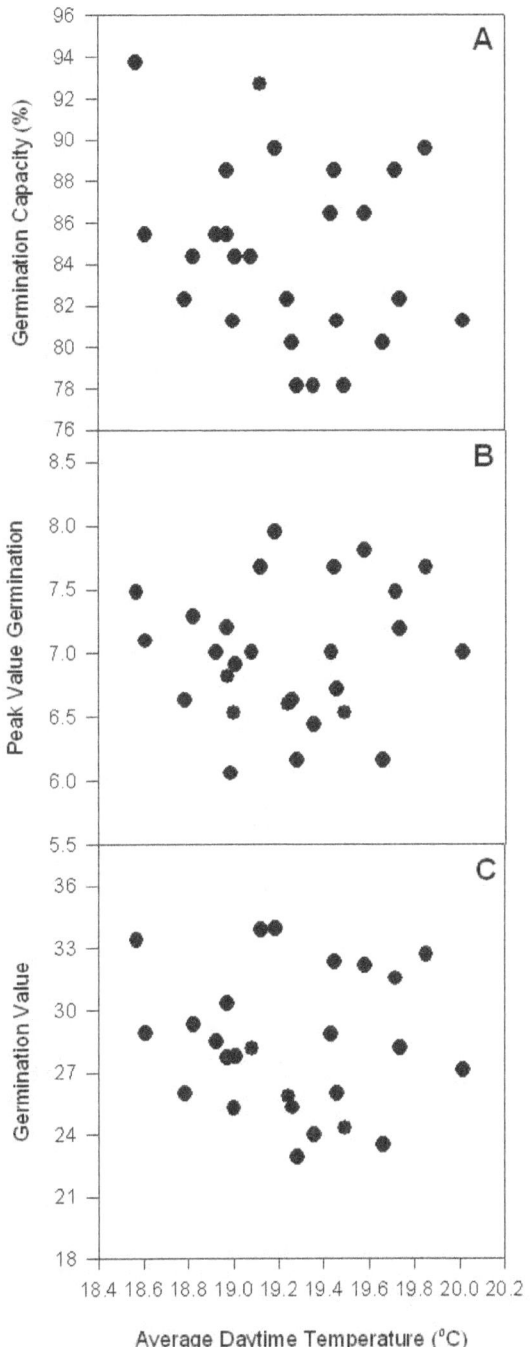

Figure 2. Average daily temperature relationship with germination capacity, peak value germination, and germination value parameters (n = 27).

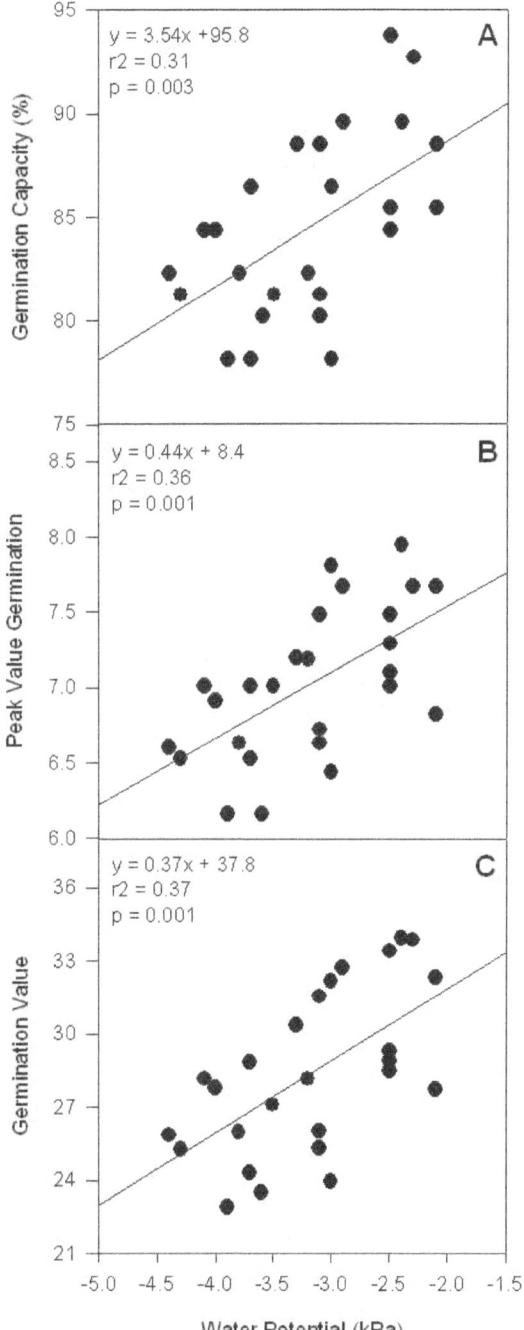

Figure 3. Seedbed soil matric water potential relationship with germination capacity, peak value germination, and germination value parameters (n = 27).

Table 2. Means (± standard errors) and *P*-values for germination parameters between three irrigation frequencies and three grit colors (α = 0.05).

Irrigation frequency	Germination capacity	Indices of germination speed		
	GC (%)	PV	GV	GR$_{50}$ (d)
Low	82.0 (0.95) a^z	6.6 (0.11) a	25.9 (0.70) a	9.6 (0.24) a
Medium	84.0 (1.42) a	7.1 (0.16) ab	28.0 (1.07) ab	9.4 (0.18) a
High	86.6 (1.94) a	7.2 (0.19) b	29.9 (1.35) b	9.7 (0.24) a
***P*-value**	0.12	0.01	0.03	0.78
Grit Color				
Black	84.6 (1.78) a	7.1 (0.20) a	28.9 (1.39) a	9.6 (0.24) a
Neutral	84.8 (1.85) a	7.1 (0.18) a	28.8 (1.28) a	9.7 (0.17) a
White	83.1 (1.09) a	6.7 (0.11) a	26.7 (0.77) a	9.4 (0.24) a
***P*-value**	0.68	0.12	0.27	0.78

^{z}Mean separation wi hin columns by Tukey (*P* < 0.05); columns with the same letter are not significant.

germination speed and uniformity. In this study, we hypothesized that frequent irrigation would have a cooling effect on lodgepole pine seeds, thus lowering germination capacity and rate. However, data obtained for this species and seedlot over the 21-day period showed little difference in average daily temperature between irrigation treatments and, consequently, little difference in germination parameters. A temperature profile plot did show a temperature decrease for high frequency irrigation treatments, but temperature recovery was relatively quick, at times less than an hour (fig. 4). Similarly, we hypothesized that grit color would also have an effect on temperature and germination parameters. Black grit was expected to yield higher temperatures

compared to neutral and white grit. Although temperature differences were statistically different, apparently it was insufficient to influence germination parameters. It is important to note the 3 weeks of the experiment were dominated mostly by cool, wet, and cloudy weather. With limited short wave radiation input, effects of grit color may be lessened.

Ψ was measured to describe free energy water potential movement from soil media to seeds. Although the technique used (soil tensiometer) only measured matric potential, and does not include osmotic potential, Vetterlein and others (1993) showed that measurement of matric potential proved adequate for describing soil water movement and availability for plants *in situ*. No relationships were seen between Ψ

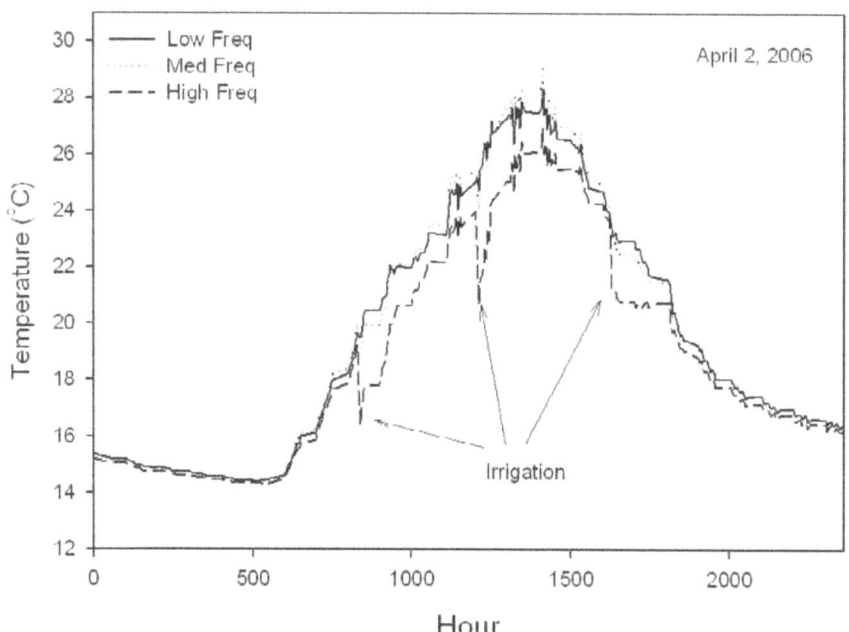

Figure 4. Average seedbed temperatures for low, medium, and high irrigation frequency treatments on 2 April 2006. Downward spikes indicate a high frequency irrigation treatment application.

and grit color and may be attributed to lack of short wave radiation input. Landis and others (1989) state that prior to germination, most soil moisture loss is due to evaporation from the top of the container. Due to decreased short wave radiation input and fixed irrigation treatments, the effects of evaporation may have been minimized, thereby creating little difference in Ψ effects with grit color.

Differences in Ψ were observed (fig. 1D) and weakly correlated with PV and GV (fig. 3B and C). A closer look at the data reveals that, despite correlations with germination parameters, the lowest irrigation frequency Ψ (−4.4 kPa [−44 bar]) was well above the field capacity value of some soils (−30 kPa [−300 bar]; Campbell and Norman 1998). Plants in soils with similar Ψ values would not be considered water stressed (Vetterlein and others 1993). Little is known about water potential of seeds in this situation. Assuming seeds germinate best at Ψ values near field capacity, the data may explain why no large significant germination differences were detected in irrigation frequencies used in this study.

Summary

Nursery managers have a plethora of cultural tools available to them when propagating seedlings in a nursery. Choosing the right tools can often be a challenge, and, in the event of wrong choices, may cost significant amounts of money. Managers turn to experts when looking for answers to specific questions about propagating seedlings, but often knowledge and/or scientific data is simply not available to guide them. This study creates a starting point in answering specific questions and addressing inconsistencies in the culturing practice of germinating seeds. Although significant differences were not seen in some germination parameters among treatments, supporting Ψ data indicated soil medium was still saturated at the lowest irrigation frequency. This elicits implications of saving person hours, water, and irrigation additives (phosphoric acid to lower soil pH) by lowering irrigation frequency. To a nursery manager, this computes to cost savings and increased nursery efficiency. Additional benefits may include reduced damping-off problems caused by over-watering germinating seeds. Further work should include other species and seedlots and hone in on specific Ψ relationships between seeds and the soil media. Additionally, further work on contributing factors, such as radiation, should also be characterized and related to improving cultural practices during germination.

References

Campbell GS, Norman JM. 1998. An introduction to environmental biophysics. 2nd ed. New York (NY): Springer. 286 p.

Ching TM. 1959. Activation of germination in Douglas-fir seed by hydrogen peroxide. Plant Physiology 34:557-563.

Czabator FJ. 1962. Germination value: an index combining speed and completeness of pine seed germination. Forest Science 8:386-396.

Dumroese RK, James RL. 2005. Root diseases in bareroot and container nurseries of the Pacific Northwest: epidemiology, management, and effects on outplanting performance. New Forests 30:185-202.

Eggleston KL. 2006. Personal communication. Coeur d'Alene (ID): USDA Forest Service, Coeur d'Alene Nursery, Horticulturist.

Krugman SL, Stein WI, Schmitt DM. 1974. Seed biology. In: Schopmeyer CS, technical coordinator. Seeds of woody plants in the United States. Washington (DC): USDA Forest Service. Agriculture Handbook 450. p 5-40.

Landis TD, Tinus RW, McDonald SE, Barnett JP. 1989. The container tree nursery manual. Volume 4, seedling nutrition and irrigation. Washington (DC): USDA Forest Service. Agriculture Handbook 674. 119 p.

Landis TD, Tinus RW, Barnett JP. 1998. The container tree nursery manual. Volume 6, seedling propagation. Washington (DC): USDA Forest Service. Agriculture Handbook 674. 167 p.

Myers JF. 2005. Personal communication. Coeur d'Alene (ID): USDA Forest Service, Coeur d'Alene Nursery, Nursery Manager.

Vetterlein D, Marschner H, Horn R. 1993. Microtensiometer technique for in situ measurement of soil matric potential and root water extraction from a sandy soil. Plant and Soil 149(2):263-273.

Weber JC, Sorensen FC. 1990. Effects of stratification and temperature on seed germination speed and uniformity in central Oregon ponderosa pine (*Pinus ponderosa* Dougl. ex Laws.). Portland (OR): USDA Forest Service, Pacific Northwest Research Station. Research Paper PNW-429. 13 p.

Wenny DL. 2005. Personal communication. Moscow (ID): University of Idaho, Center for Forest Nursery and Seedling Research, Nursery Manager/Director (retired).

Wenny DL, Dumroese RK. 1987. A growing regime for containerized ponderosa pine seedlings. Moscow (ID): University of Idaho, Forest, Wildlife and Range Experiment Station. Bulletin Number 43. 9 p.

Wenny DL, Dumroese RK. 1990. A growing regime for container-grown western redcedar seedlings. Moscow (ID): University of Idaho, Forest, Wildlife and Range Experiment Station. 8 p.

Wenny DL, Dumroese RK. 1992. A growing regime for container-grown Douglas-fir seedlings. Moscow (ID): University of Idaho, Forest, Wildlife and Range Experiment Station. 8 p.

Southern Forest and Conservation Nursery Association Biennial Meeting

Asheville, North Carolina

July 21 to 24, 2008

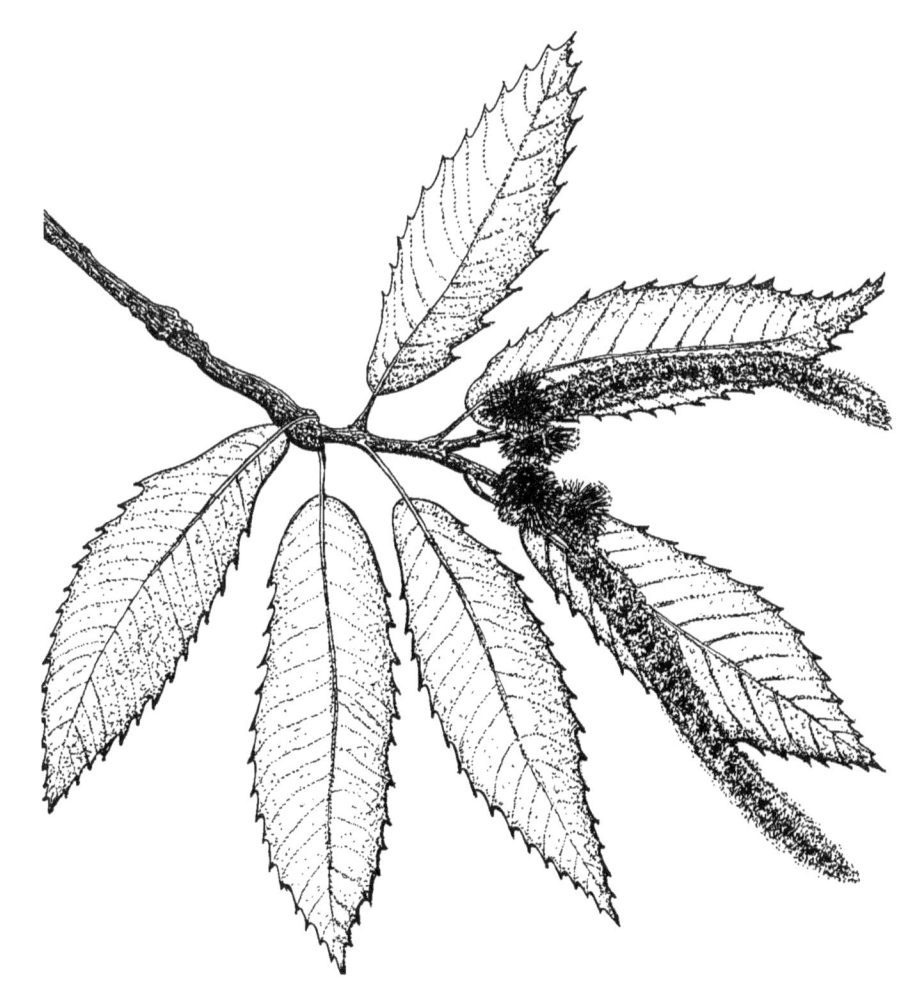

American chestnut drawing by Steven Morrison, College of Natural Resources, University of Idaho.

Outlook for Blight-Resistant American Chestnut Trees

Paul H. Sisco

Paul H. Sisco is Regional Science Coordinator, Southern Appalachian Regional Office, The American Chestnut Foundation, One Oak Plaza, Suite 308, Asheville, NC 28801; E-mail: paul@acf.org.

Sisco, P.H. 2009. Outlook for blight-resistant American chestnut trees. In: Dumroese, R.K.; Riley, L.E., tech. coords. 2009. National Proceedings: Forest and Conservation Nursery Associations—2008. Proc. RMRS-P-58. Fort Collins, CO: U.S. Department of Agriculture, Forest Service, Rocky Mountain Research Station: 61–68. Online: http://www.fs.fed.us/rm/pubs/rmrs_p058.html.

Abstract: Culminating 20 years of breeding efforts, in spring 2008, The American Chestnut Foundation (TACF) delivered its first 500 chestnuts to the USDA Forest Service for testing on National Forest lands. The expectation is that these seedlings will be more resistant to chestnut blight (*Cryphonectria parasitica*) than are pure American chestnut trees (*Castanea dentata*). Greater numbers of seeds will be distributed in coming years, as more trees start producing nuts and as these trees become larger. Meanwhile, the breeding program at TACF continues, incorporating different sources of resistance and broadening the genetic base by breeding to surviving American chestnut trees from Maine to Alabama. An additional challenge in the southern United States is the fact that American chestnut is highly susceptible to the root rot organism *Phytophthora cinnamomi*, which is found in warm, poorly-drained soils. Both Chinese (*Castanea mollissima*) and Japanese (*Castanea crenata*) chestnut trees are resistant to this soil pathogen. A volunteer member of TACF, Joseph B James of Seneca, SC, is cooperating with Clemson University scientist Steve Jeffers to breed American chestnut trees resistant to both blight and root rot. In addition, Scott Enebak of Auburn University is determining ways of keeping the root rot pathogen out of forest nurseries where chestnut seedlings are grown.

Keywords: American chestnut, *Castanea dentata*, *Cryphonectria parasitica*, *Phytophthora cinnamomi*, disease resistance, genetic diversity, ecosystem restoration

Introduction

One hundred years ago, the American chestnut (*Castanea dentata*) was a dominant canopy tree in the Appalachian Mountains, making up one quarter of the forest. Its tannin-filled, naturally rot-resistant wood was used for fences, shingles, utility poles, and industrial purposes, as well as for making furniture and decorative woodwork. The yearly nut crop, which was as abundant as it was consistent, provided a bounteous harvest for wildlife, free-range hogs and turkeys, and for humans themselves, who sold the nuts for cash income. Then, in the late 19th century, a fungal pathogen, *Cryphonectria parasitica*, was introduced on Japanese chestnut trees (*Castanea crenata*) imported to the United States in the days before there were any plant quarantine regulations. American chestnut had almost no resistance to this pathogen, which spread quickly by both airborne and sticky spores. Within 50 years of its discovery in the Bronx Zoo of New York City, chestnut blight had effectively eliminated chestnut as a freely reproducing, dominant tree species. Both the Federal government and private individuals, like Arthur Graves of Connecticut, tried to breed blight-resistant forest-type chestnut trees by crossing American chestnut with both Japanese and Chinese (*Castanea mollissima*) chestnut trees. But the hybrid F1 trees that were the product of these early breeding programs were not sufficiently resistant to the blight, and not tall enough to compete in a forest environment. The Federal program was abandoned in 1960.

Fortunately, chestnut breeding did not end with the demise of the Federal program. Charles Burnham of the University of Minnesota, a professor of corn genetics, felt that the early efforts had made a major mistake. Instead of stopping with 50/50 American/Chinese hybrids, he proposed a series of additional backcrosses to American chestnut to get more of an American-type tree, followed by at least one generation of intercrossing to bring blight resistance up to a high level. In 1983, Burnham and some fellow scientists and laymen organized The American Chestnut Foundation (TACF) as a private, non-profit corporation to pursue the backcross breeding strategy. In 1989, a farm was leased in southwest Virginia, and a scientist, Fred

---

NOTE: All Sisco figures are on pages 64 to 68.

Hebard, was hired to direct the program. Starting with the best BC1 (backcross one) progeny of the previous Federal and private programs, and taking care to promote fast growth and precocious flowering, Hebard was able to produce three more generations and complete the first stage of Burnham's program by 2005. In the spring of 2008, the first 500 BC_3F_3 seeds from selected, blight-resistant American-type trees were provided to the USDA Forest Service for testing on National Forest lands in northeast Tennessee and southwest Virginia.

TACF's breeding program has grown more ambitious and complex than Burnham originally envisioned. Additional sources of resistance from various Chinese and Japanese chestnut cultivars are being investigated, and genetic diversity is being increased by volunteer efforts in 15 state chapters from Maine to Alabama.

Unfortunately chestnut blight is not the only disease that is a threat to the survival of American chestnut. Another pathogen introduced from Asia, *Phytophthora cinnamomi*, destroyed most chestnut trees in the Piedmont South before chestnut blight arrived in North America. *Phytophthora cinnamomi* is a pathogen of many plant species, including Fraser fir (*Abies fraseri*), but it is particularly virulent on American chestnut. The disease spreads by water-borne spores in the soil. The spores are susceptible to freezing soil temperatures, so it moves slowly and doesn't survive well at high elevations. Chinese and Japanese chestnut species have resistance to the disease, so it is possible to breed for resistance to both chestnut blight and Phytophthora root rot. Joe James, a retired surgeon from Seneca, SC, has teamed up with Steve Jeffers, an expert in *Phytophthora* spp. at nearby Clemson University (Clemson, SC), to do just that.

With the dedicated efforts of professionals and volunteers, the first tests of TACF's elite hybrid trees will be planted in spring 2009. This is the beginning of a major forest restoration effort that will continue through most of the 21st century.

Materials and Methods _____

The outlines of the breeding program at TACF (fig. 1) were first presented in detail by Burnham and others (1986). A recent summary of results to date can be found in Hebard (2006). Two superior BC_1 hybrids were selected to begin TACF's breeding efforts: the 'Clapper' selection from the former USDA program (Clapper 1963), and a BC_1 tree from Arthur Graves' program in Connecticut (Anagnostakis 2007). A third source of resistance was added to the program by making a cross between the Chinese cultivar 'Nanking' and several different American chestnut trees in southwest Virginia. 'Nanking' is a selection from the old USDA program, is precocious, bears large nut crops, and, most importantly, is highly resistant to the blight (Jaynes 1979; Hebard and others 1984).

Because clearcutting was more common in the early 1980s, large numbers of flowering American chestnut trees were present in the Mount Rogers National Recreation Area of Virginia when TACF's breeding program began in 1989. The 15 state chapters of TACF have also found many flowering trees in their own areas, allowing breeding of blight-resistant chestnuts for local adaptation (fig. 2).

Selection for both blight resistance and American chestnut characteristics is practiced in each backcross generation, with only the most resistant and most American trees being advanced. Each backcross is to a different American chestnut tree to prevent inbreeding. Resistance is only partially dominant, so the selections in the backcross generations are only moderately resistant to the blight, as measured by the diameter of canker growth 5 months after inoculation (fig. 3). Backcross progeny are also selected for American characteristics, including canoe-shaped leaves, lack of leaf hairs, small stipule size, cylindrical, pointed, and hairless buds, and red stem color (fig. 4). Trees with a strong central leader are also preferred over very branchy trees, although even American chestnut will spread out when grown in the open (fig. 5).

The efforts of Joe James and Steve Jeffers to select hybrids with resistance to *Phytophthora cinnamomi* and *Cryphonectria parasitica* were outlined by Jeffers and others (2007) at an IUFRO conference at Asilomar, CA. Seeds from hybrid families, as well as pure Chinese and pure American chestnut controls, are planted in sterile soil mix in deep tubs (fig. 6). When the seedlings are 2 to 3 months old, they are inoculated with *P. cinnamomi* grown on vermiculite (fig. 7). The following December or January, the root systems of surviving seedlings are inspected and rated on a 0 to 3 scale, with "0" having no apparent lesions on the roots and "3" being dead. Surviving seedlings rated "1" or "0" are then planted on the farm of Dr. James in Seneca, SC, where *P. cinnamomi* is already present in the soil. The inoculum used on the seedlings is prepared from *P. cinnamomi* isolates from dying chestnut trees from the James farm (fig. 8). The plan is to then inoculate the trees that survived infection with *P. cinnamomi* with the chestnut blight pathogen when they reach sufficient size (> 2.5 cm [1 in] dbh).

Results and Discussion _____

In 2006, TACF's Meadowview Research Farms (Meadowview, VA) produced the first BC_3F_3 seeds from the 'Clapper' source of resistance. The first 500 seeds for testing were given to the USDA Forest Service in fall 2007. The expectation is that all of the BC_3F_3 seedlings will have higher levels of resistance than pure American chestnut, but this needs to be proven. TACF's official Testing Protocol was published in the Journal of TACF (Ad Hoc 2004). The USDA Forest Service Southern Research Station has recently devoted an entire issue of its magazine *Compass* to the American chestnut. Payne (2008) provided one of the best articles in this issue, describing the testing of chestnut seedlings by the USDA Forest Service.

Because TACF's breeding program has been ongoing for 20 years, a pent-up demand exists among TACF's members and many other landowners for the best blight-resistant seeds. Almost daily, someone in TACF gets a call from a person saying, "I have 20 acres of land I just cleared and I'd love to have some of those blight resistant chestnut seeds."

To give a reasonable and consistent answer to these callers, TACF's Science Advisory Cabinet composed the following:

> The American Chestnut Foundation (TACF) is breeding chestnut trees for ability to survive the blight disease, which killed almost all our native American chestnut. TACF's goal

is to confer on American chestnut the ability to thrive in our nation's woodlands, as it once did. Last fall, TACF began harvesting nuts that it expects will be suitable for planting back into the forest. However, these breeding lines are still in the testing phase and their value needs to be proven on many forest sites until 2015 to 2020.

A gradual increase in seed production is expected over the next few years. These will be distributed to cooperators who are assisting in a formal, rigorous testing program. In addition, seeds that are not needed for this purpose will be distributed principally to members of TACF for informal testing. At the same time, TACF is continuing its breeding program to make further gains in disease resistance and forest competitiveness.

Even with seeds of highly blight-resistant chestnut available, reforestation efforts will not be easy. Many forest creatures relish the taste of the nuts, and deer will defoliate small seedlings quickly. Seedlings need to be grown above deer browse height, transplanted, and cared for until they can survive on their own. In the past few years, drought has been a major problem. In poorly-drained sites, *P. cinnamomi* can destroy an entire planting. Other pests, such as gypsy moths (*Lymantria dispar*), Japanese beetles (*Popillia japonica*), Oriental chestnut gall wasps (*Dryocosmus kuriphilus*), and Asian ambrosia beetles (*Xylosandrus crassiusculus*) can also cause extensive damage, especially to young trees.

Nevertheless, chestnut has advantages compared to many other tree species. It can grow quickly, up to 2 m (6 ft) per year from large root systems, and, once established, can tolerate dry conditions.

Summary

The "Environmental Success Story of the 21st Century" could well be the reestablishment of American chestnut as a dominant tree species in the Appalachian forests of eastern North America. The first 500 seeds of putatively blight-resistant American chestnut trees were given to the USDA Forest Service in spring 2008, and seedlings grown from these seeds at Flint River Nursery (Montezuma, GA) will be outplanted for tests on USDA Forest Service land in the spring of 2009.

More information about the progress in breeding blight-resistant chestnuts can be found at the website of The American Chestnut Foundation (URL: http://www.acf.org).

References

[Ad Hoc] Ad Hoc Task Force on Testing. 2004. TACF adopts guidelines for testing blight-resistant American chestnuts. Journal of The American Chestnut Foundation 18(1):7-11.

Anagnostakis S. 2007. The chestnut plantation at Sleeping Giant: legacy of Arthur Harmount Graves. Journal of The American Chestnut Foundation 21:34-39.

Burnham CR, Rutter PA, French DW. 1986. Breeding blight-resistant chestnuts. Plant Breeding Reviews 4:347-397.

Clapper RB. 1963. A promising new forest-type chestnut tree. Journal of Forestry 61:921-922.

Hebard F. 2006. The backcross breeding program of The American Chestnut Foundation. In: Steiner KC, Carlson JE, editors. Restoration of American chestnut to forest lands—Proceedings of a conference and workshop; 2004 May 4-6; North Carolina Arboretum, Asheville, NC. Washington (DC): National Park Service. p 61-77.

Hebard FV, Griffin G, Elkins JR. 1984. Developmental histopathology of cankers incited by hypovirulent and virulent isolates of Endothia parasitica on susceptible and resistant chestnut trees. Phytopathology 74:140-149.

Jaynes RA. 1979. Chestnuts. In: Jaynes RA, editor. Nut tree culture in North America. Geneva (NY): The WF Humphreys Press Inc. p 111-127.

Jeffers SN, James JB, Sisco PH. 2007. Screening for resistance to Phytophthora cinnamomi in hybrid seedlings of American chestnut. In: 4th IUFRO Conference on Phytophthoras in forests and natural ecosystems; 2007 August 26-31; Asilomar, CA. URL: http://nature.berkeley.edu/IUFRO2007/phytophthora/abstracts/32_jeffers.pdf (accessed July 2008).

Payne C. 2008. Can chestnuts survive on their own? Compass (11):18-20.

THE AMERICAN CHESTNUT FOUNDATION'S BACKCROSS BREEDING PROGRAM

ADDITIONAL AMERICAN CHESTNUT CHARACTERISTICS ARE REGAINED WITH EACH BACKCROSS.

TACF expects a high level of blight resistance and American characteristics to be present in selected BC_3F_2 seed orchard parents. Their BC_3F_3 progeny will be extensively tested by TACF for blight resistance and ability to compete in the forest.

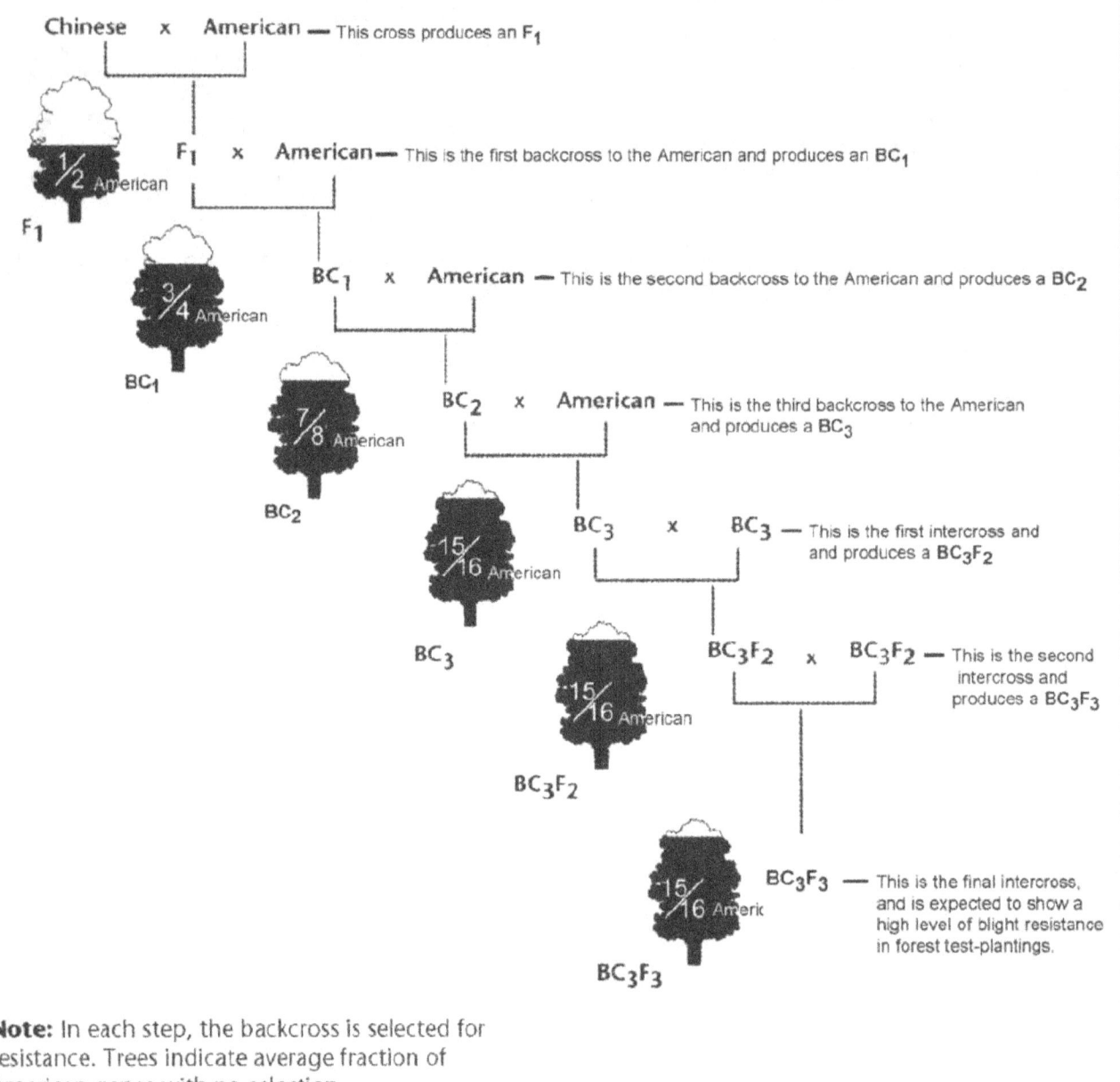

Note: In each step, the backcross is selected for resistance. Trees indicate average fraction of American genes with no selection.

Figure 1. The stages in the backcross breeding program of The American Chestnut Foundation. Each generation takes about 6 years.

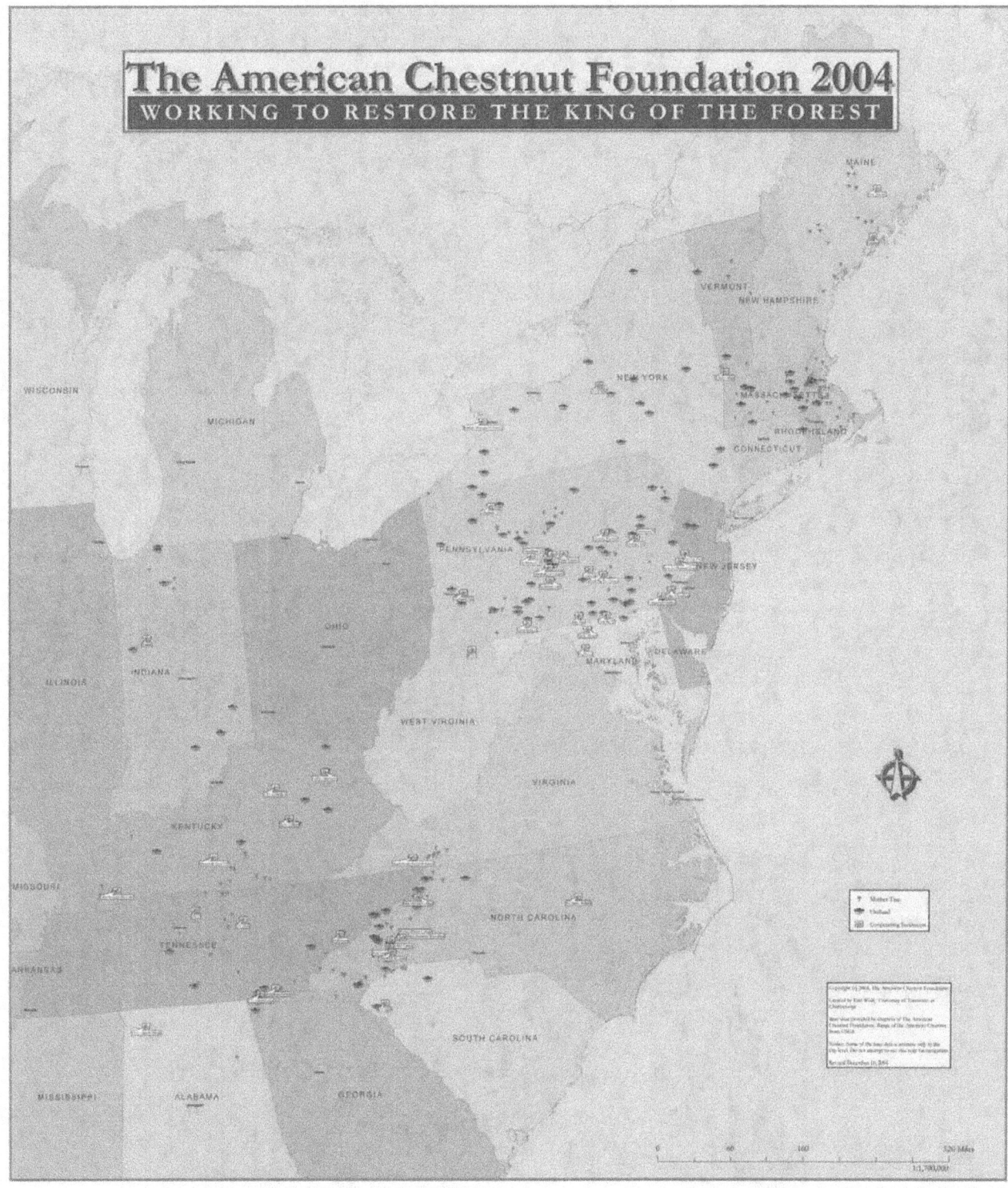

Figure 2. TACF's national effort as of 2004. Volunteers in 15 state chapters are using trees in their areas to obtain local adaptation. Each small green dot represents a surviving American chestnut tree that has been used in the breeding program. The multiple trees indicate orchards where trees are being grown.

Figure 3a. Reaction of a moderately-resistant hybrid tree after inoculation with the blight fungus. A canker walls off the growth of the fungus.

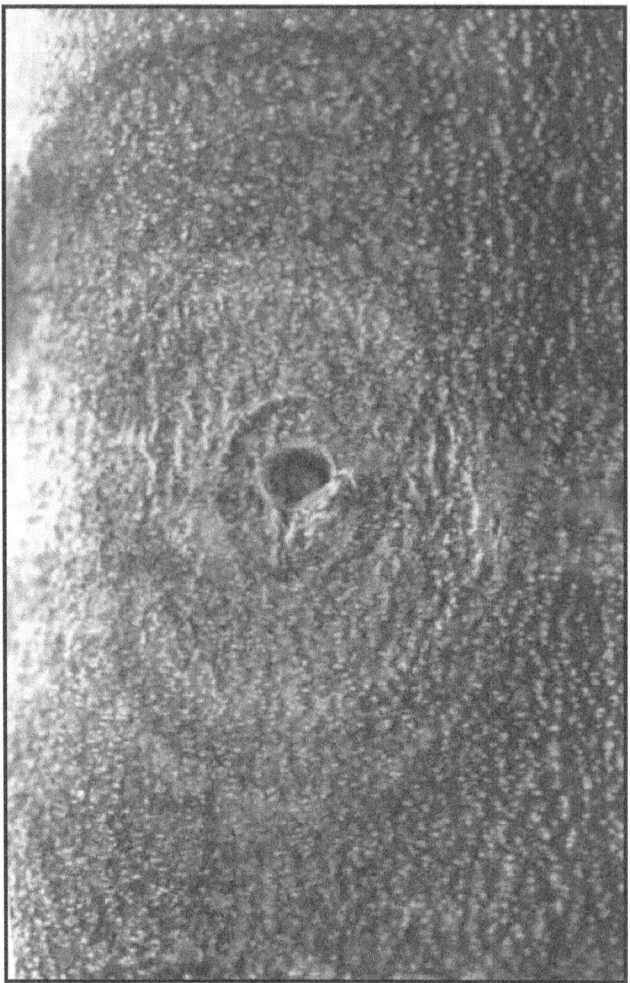

Figure 3b. Reaction of a susceptible hybrid tree after inoculation. The fungus grows in concentric circles from the inoculation point, producing a sunken canker that will soon girdle the tree.

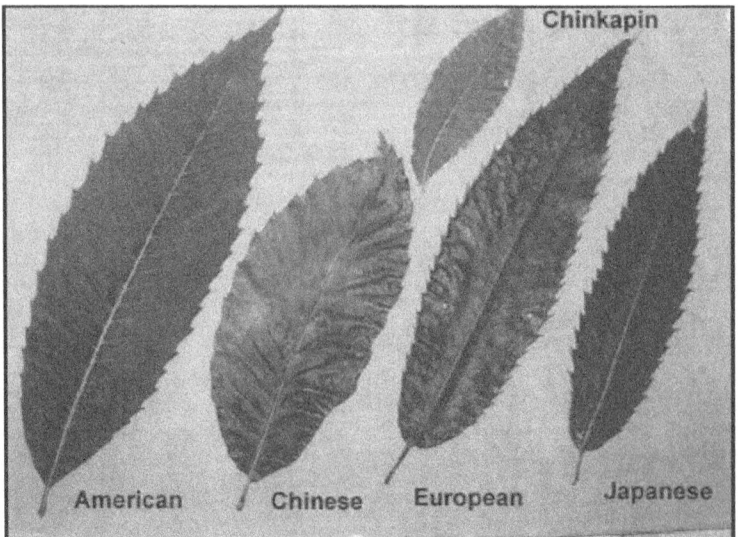

Figure 4. Leaves of the four major chestnut species, plus the leaf of the Allegheny chinkapin (*Castanea pumila*). American chestnut leaves are long in relation to their width, tapered at both ends, and their teeth are prominent and curve inward like the waves of an ocean.

Figure 5a. Surviving American chestnut tree in Dexter, ME. When grown in the open, American chestnut is a spreading, branchy tree. (Photo courtesy of Maine Chapter—TACF.)

Figure 5b. Surviving American chestnut tree in Atkinson, ME. When grown in forest competition, American chestnut easily loses its lower limbs and has a long, limbless bole. (Photo courtesy of Maine Chapter—TACF.)

Figure 6. Joe James of Seneca, SC, confers with Clemson graduate student Inga McLaughlin, while Steve Jeffers and postdoctoral research associate Jae-soon Hwang work in the background. Hybrid chestnuts from many families are planted in sterile media to test for resistance to *Phytophthora cinnamomi*. Seeds are planted close together and families are separated by colored stakes in the planting tubs.

Figure 7. Rice grains impregnated with *Phytophthora cinnamomi* are used to inoculate hybrid chestnut seedlings after about 2 months of growth in the sterile medium. More recently, vermiculite has been used in place of the rice grains to prevent contamination. (Photo courtesy of Steve Jeffers.)

Figure 8. Steve Jeffers, Professor of Plant Pathology at Clemson University, holds a dying hybrid chestnut seedling dug from the farm of Joe James in Seneca, SC. *Phytophthora cinnamomi* was isolated from such seedlings to be used in screening families of hybrid chestnut for resistance to the disease.

Nursery Profile: North Carolina Department of Forest Resources F.H. Claridge Nursery

James West

James West is Nursery Supervisor, North Carolina Forest Service F.H. Claridge Nursery, 762 Claridge Nursery Road, Goldsboro, NC 27530; Tel: 919.731.7988; E-mail: james.west@ncmail.net.

West, J. 2009. Nursery profile: North Carolina Department of Forest Resources F.H. Claridge Nursery. In: Dumroese, R.K.; Riley, L.E., tech. coords. 2009. National Proceedings: Forest and Conservation Nursery Associations—2008. Proc. RMRS-P-58. Fort Collins, CO: U.S. Department of Agriculture, Forest Service, Rocky Mountain Research Station: 69–70. Online: http://www.fs.fed.us/rm/pubs/rmrs_p058.html.

Keywords: hardwoods, *Pinus taeda*, *Pinus palustris*, bareroot, container

Who We Were

North Carolina Department of Forest Resources F.H. Claridge Nursery in Goldsboro, was founded as the Little River Nursery in 1954, and was one of five nurseries in the Forest Resources Division at the time. The early focus of the nursery was on southern yellow pine species, predominantly loblolly (*Pinus taeda*) and longleaf (*P. palustris*) pines.

In the early 1960s, the nursery was renamed in honor of F.H. Claridge, a former state forester who was a major proponent of forest nurseries.

Who We Are

Claridge Nursery has evolved into a diversified, full service nursery, offering bareroot and container pine and hardwood seedlings to a wide variety of customers. One of the nursery directives is to provide seedlings at cost to the citizens of North Carolina for a number of reasons, including reforestation, wildlife habitat, aesthetics, stream restoration, wetland mitigation.

One interesting diversification for the nursery has been the production and maintenance of the only pond pine (*P. serotina*) orchard in the world. Pond pine is a suitable species for wetland restoration and mitigation, and is very much in demand for restoration work in the Carolina bays.

Available Services

The nursery is a full service operation. "You call, we haul" anywhere, often on the same day. This service includes custom contracts and special orders, especially species for wetland and stream restoration. The nursery is a small operation, but customer care is important and keeps the nursery productive and profitable.

The nursery is self-contained, with in-house production from seeds to seedlings. Seed orchards are maintained for all softwood species grown at the nursery, as well as some hardwood species. In the Forest Resources Division, every county office is charged with its own seed collection. In addition, the nursery tailors the seed source to the deployment region. Seedlings are grown by physiographic region, for example, coastal, Piedmont, or mountain sources of poplar (*Populus* spp.).

Embracing New Technology

Loblolly Pine Performance Rating System—The nursery participates in the Loblolly Pine Performance Rating System, a simple rating system that allows customers to be informed about and compare different loblolly pine selections.

Computer System—After many years of working with an old mainframe computer system, the nursery has recently purchased a new Microsoft Windows®-based seedling order program. This new program allows the nursery staff to access customer records and order information quickly and help meet their needs.

Machinery Upgrades—Over the course of several years, the nursery has been, and is, in the process of upgrading machinery, from the field to the packing room. The field irrigation system, including pipe, risers, irrigation heads, and timers, is being replaced. Several years ago, a new pump system was installed, but the existing solid set irrigation system remained. Beginning in 2007, and continuing through 2008, all new 7.5 cm (3 in) pipe with plastic impact sprinkler heads have been installed. This new system provides very efficient water use, very few blowouts, and plenty of water with great flow rates.

Personnel

The nursery maintains a small- to moderate-sized staff to provide efficient service to its customers. This staff includes four equipment operators, a nursery technician, three field assistants, a sales coordinator/financial officer, a nursery clerk, an orchard technician, a seed plant operator, a tree improvement supervisor, and a nursery supervisor.

Inventory

Approximately 19 million seedlings comprise the 2008 inventory at Claridge Nursery. This inventory includes 13 million loblolly pine, 3.5 million container and 1 million bareroot longleaf pine, and 2.5 million hardwoods of 50 different species.

Where We Are Going

The nursery continues to expand into a variety of services and technologies. A limited amount of third-cycle loblolly pine production has occurred in 2008. In addition, the first controlled mass-pollinated seeds for loblolly pine were obtained at the nursery.

In the orchard program, testing families for the second generation longleaf pine orchards is now taking place. The nursery is one of the few sources of improved longleaf pine in the southern United States, and hopes to be the first with second generation material available.

The nursery is also greatly expanding the number of available hardwood species and other products to meet the changing demands of the citizens of North Carolina.

The content of this paper reflects the views of the authors, who are responsible for he facts and accuracy of the information presented herein.

The Christmas Tree Industry in Western North Carolina

Jill Sidebottom

Jill Sidebottom is the Area Forestry Extension Specialist with North Carolina State University for Mountain Conifer Integrated Pest Management, 455 Research Drive, Mills River, NC 28732-9244; Tel: 828.684.3562; E-mail: jill_sidebottom@ncsu.edu.

Sidebottom, J. 2009. The Christmas tree industry in western North Carolina. In: Dumroese, R.K.; Riley, L.E., tech. coords. 2009. National Proceedings: Forest and Conservation Nursery Associations—2008. Proc. RMRS-P-58. Fort Collins, CO: U.S. Department of Agriculture, Forest Service, Rocky Mountain Research Station: 71–73. Online: http://www.fs.fed.us/rm/pubs/rmrs_p058.html.

Abstract: Christmas tree production has grown in the last 50 years to one of the major farming enterprises in western North Carolina. The history, importance, and challenges to the Christmas tree industry are reviewed.

Keywords: Christmas trees, Fraser fir, western North Carolina

The North Carolina Christmas tree industry produces primarily Fraser fir (*Abies fraseri*) that is native to the highest elevations in North Carolina, eastern Tennessee, and western Virginia. Fraser fir is named for the Scottish plantsman, John Fraser (1750 to 1811). Fraser fir was probably first observed by Andre Michaux, who traveled through western North Carolina in the late 1790s. He appears to have mistaken it for balsam fir (*Abies balsamea*) (Fulcher 1998). John Fraser probably first observed Fraser fir in 1808. For a short time, Fraser and Michaux traveled together. But the two men parted company, and Fraser went to the higher elevations around Roan Mountain where he collected the tree. Frasers were growing in English gardens by 1811 (Fulcher 1998).

Despite a lack of accurate documentation, it is thought that, prior to European settlers, the spruce-fir forests occupied as much as 810,000 ha (2 million ac) of high elevation sites (McGraw 1980). These forests now exist in less than 40,500 ha (100,000 ac) in the Great Smoky Mountains, the Balsam Mountains, Roan Mountain, Mount Mitchell, and Mount Rogers.

One reason the Fraser fir Christmas industry excelled in North Carolina is because of the characteristics of the tree itself. Fraser fir possesses all the factors that make an outstanding Christmas tree that can be displayed for many weeks, including excellent needle retention, strong boughs for hanging ornaments, and a wonderful fragrance (NCCTA 2008).

Prior to World War II, most people in North Carolina used redcedar (*Juniperus virginiana*) or white pine (*Pinus strobus*) collected from the woods for Christmas trees (Beutell 2007). Trees were put up on Christmas Eve and taken down right after Christmas. After the war, as more people moved to urban areas, there was a market to purchase Christmas trees. Balsam fir trees were sold in Charlotte, Raleigh, Winston-Salem, and other larger cities. These trees were grown in the wild in Canada and Maine (Beutell 2007). As early as 1939, Fred and John Wagoners, identical twins who became founders of the industry in western North Carolina, were selling redcedar trees for US$ 2 apiece in the Greensboro area, after having paid their neighbors US$ 0.75 to collect them from fence rows (Wagoner 2007).

In western North Carolina, most farms during this time were small, producing cabbage, green beans, and tobacco, as well as small herds of beef cattle (Cartner 2007). During the war years, most farms could sell what they produced profitably. Following the war, however, prices dropped. According to Sam Cartner, a prominent Christmas tree grower who was the County Extension Agent in Avery County at the time, farmers would take their beans to market to sell, and end up dumping them on the side of the road rather than accept the low prices being offered to them (Cartner 2007).

Christmas trees would end up replacing these crops, but it would not be an easy transition for farmers used to producing annual crops with an annual income (Cartner 2007). Frasers were already being grown as nursery plants to be dug even as early as the 1920s, as well as for greenery to make wreaths (Dellinger 2007). Interest in Fraser fir as a Christmas tree was also increasing. In 1950, the first commercial cutting of Fraser fir was made on Roan Mountain (Toecane Ranger District, Pisgah National Forest) (Williams 1958). Fraser fir makes a substantially better Christmas tree than balsam fir, which was already being marketed in the area. But growing Fraser firs for Christmas trees would require several things: a source of seedlings; better understanding of production; shearing to shape trees; and growers willing to make the 7- to 10-year investment required to grow trees.

Many state and federal agencies helped get the industry started. The North Carolina Division of Forestry started growing Fraser fir seedlings at the Holmes State Nursery (Hendersonville) in 1955 and the Catawba Nursery, later to be known as the Ralph Edwards Nursery (Morganton), in 1957 (Williams 1958). In the mid 1950s, John Gilliam, a regional extension forester working for North Carolina State University (then known as State College) was asked to investigate growing Christmas trees as a profitable forestry practice for the mountains (Gilliam 2007). He made several trips to Pennsylvania, a state that already had substantial Christmas tree production brought in by German immigrants, to learn how to grow, shear, harvest, and market Christmas trees.

The first organizational meeting of what would become the North Carolina Christmas Tree Association (NCCTA) was on 8 May 1959, in Newland. Originally called the North Carolina Christmas Tree Growers Cooperative Association, this organization began in Avery County with the help of Mr. Cartner and Herman Dellinger, an agriculture high school teacher at Crossnore High School (Crossnore) (Dellinger 2007). The articles of incorporation were signed in August of that year by all Avery County growers, including Herman Dellinger, Conrad Weather, Andy Vaughn, Sammy Mortimer, and Bill Aldridge. Other important people who helped the industry grow include Fred Whitfield, Ross Douglass, and John Gray, all from NCSU; Charles Speers with the USDA Forest Service; Chuck Gardener, Ken Perry, and Waightstill Avery, all County Extension Agents; Joe Clayton, service forester in Ashe County; F.H. Claridge and B.H. Corpening with the Division of Forestry; and Jim McLauring, District Conservationist (Gilliam 2007).

In 1971, Fraser fir made national attention when Avery County grower, Kermit Johnson, took a tree to the White House. This honor is given to the winner of the national Christmas tree contest. This honor has been given to North Carolina growers more than any other state, and the tradition has continued in 2005 with Earl Deal, in 2007 with Joe Freeman, and in 2008 with Rusty Estes (NCCTA 2008).

The Christmas tree industry in North Carolina is valued at US$ 134 million, with 5 to 6 million trees harvested annually (Glenn 2008). North Carolina is second in the nation in production behind the Pacific Northwest, but is first in revenue generated. North Carolina growers supply about 15% of the nation's trees, with more than 1,500 growers on more than 12,150 ha (30,000 ac) (Glenn 2008). The majority of production is in 10 mountain counties, with the top five producers, in order, being Ashe, Avery, Alleghany, Watauga, and Mitchell counties. Ashe County is the fifth largest Christmas tree producing county in the United States based on land use (3,890 ha [9,611 ac]), fourth largest based on number of trees, and second largest based on number of Christmas tree farms (COA 2002).

Trees are sold in foot increments and are graded as premiums, #1s, #2s, or culls. Average wholesale value of trees over all sizes and grades is US$ 20 to 23, and retail values are sold for US$ 23 to 33/m (US$ 7 to 10/ft) (Glenn 2008).

In a recent survey, farm size of Christmas tree growers in western North Carolina ranged anywhere from 0.08 to 650 ha (0.2 to 1,600 ac), but 47% of growers produce 4 ha (10 ac) or less of trees. Only 29% of growers reported doing so full-time. About half of all growers produce some other crop, including nurseries, cattle, pumpkins, potatoes, or others. Most growers have been growing trees a long time, with 22% of growers having grown trees for more than 30 years (Sidebottom 2008).

Although production in western North Carolina is primarily wholesale, choose-and-cut farms are important to the industry. North Carolina has more than 400 choose-and-cut farms, selling more than 250,000 trees with a retail value of more than US$ 5 million (Glenn 2008). Value-added products, such as wreaths, roping, and centerpieces, are also important. In western North Carolina, wreath-making has been an important cottage industry since the 1930s. North Carolina has some of the largest greenery producers in the country (Glenn 2008).

The value of the Christmas tree industry is more than just the wholesale value of the trees themselves. It is estimated that every dollar earned by growers cycles as much as 2.5 times in local communities as the wages are spent and profits reinvested in buildings, equipment, and vehicles. Christmas trees have provided an economic incentive to landowners to keep their land from being developed (NCCTA 2008).

Impacts of Christmas trees to western North Carolina are more than economic. For each tree grown, there is 2.3 m^2 (25 ft^2) of green space for wildlife. As an "early successional forest," a Christmas tree farm provides habitat for grouse and quail when ground covers are managed properly. Macroinvertebrate surveys in streams below tree farms have demonstrated little negative impacts of tree production on water quality (Sidebottom 2003). In a recent survey of pesticide use, Christmas tree growers have also greatly reduced the use of pesticides in recent years. Using Integrated Pest Management techniques, growers have reduced insecticide and herbicide use by 40% based on active ingredient per acre. In 2006, growers used only an average of 3.9 kg ai/ha (3.5 lb ai/ac) of herbicides and insecticides, averaged over all ages of trees. Fungicides are not used to produce Christmas trees in western North Carolina (Sidebottom 2008).

Although Christmas tree production continues to be strong in western North Carolina, the industry faces many challenges. Phytophthora root rot continues to reduce areas where Fraser fir can be grown. Land prices continue to increase, making development more attractive to growers. And although production costs continue to rise due to increase costs of fuel, fertilizer, and labor, the price of trees is starting to decline because of a nationwide oversupply of trees (Glenn 2008). This is caused by the increased useage of artificial Christmas trees. In 2000, there were an estimated 129 million households in the United States. According to figures generated by the National Christmas Tree Association, 27% of households bought a real tree in 2007, using approximately 35 million trees. However, 58% of households displayed an artificial tree, and 15% of households didn't have a Christmas tree at all (CTCS 2008).

Summary _____

In 2009, the NCCTA will celebrate its fiftieth anniversary. Christmas tree growers in western North Carolina have built a nationally renowned industry using their native fir. Although faced with challenges for future growth, the industry continues to provide mountain families with a reliable income supported by the efforts of state and federal agencies.

References _____

Beutell TC. 2007. Personal communication. Tuckasegee (NC): Wolf Creek Tree Farm, Christmas tree grower.

Cartner S. 2007. Personal communication. Asheville (NC): Former Avery County Cooperative Extension Director and Christmas tree grower, Cartner Christmas Tree Farm.

[COA] Census of Agriculture. 2002. Table 35. Woodland Crops: 2002 and 1997. URL: http://www.nass.usda.gov/census/census02/volume1/nc/st37_2_035_035.pdf (accessed July 2008).

[CTCS] Christmas Tree Checkoff Study. 2008. URL: http://www.checkoffstudy.com/ (accessed July 2008).

Dellinger H. 2007. Personal communication. Crossnore (NC): Christmas tree grower.

Fulcher B. 1998. Muir, Michaux, and Gray on the Roan. The Tennessee Conservationist. URL: http://cleanairtn.org/environment/tn_consv/archive/roan.htm (accessed July 2008).

Glenn B. 2008. Personal communication. Raleigh (NC): North Carolina Department of Agriculture and Consumer Services, Area Marketing Specialist.

Gilliam J. 2007. Personal communication. Raleigh (NC): North Carolina State University, Former Forestry Extension Specialist, and Christmas tree grower.

McGraw JR. 1980. Past and present importance of the red spruce-Fraser fir forest resource of the southern Appalachians. Limbs & Needles 8(3):13-16.

[NCCTA] North Carolina Christmas Tree Association. URL: http://www.NCChristmastrees.com/ (accessed July 2008).

Sidebottom JR. 2003. Evaluation of the Christmas tree industry in western North Carolina on surface water quality. URL: http://www.ces.ncsu.edu/Christmastrees/environment/water_summary.html (accessed July 2008).

Sidebottom JR. 2008. Crop profile for Christmas trees in North Carolina (mountains). URL: http://www.ipmcenters.org/CropProfiles/docs/NCchritmastrees.pdf (accessed July 2008).

Wagoner F. 2007. Personal communication. Laurel Springs (NC): Christmas tree grower.

Williams WK. 1958. Fraser fir as a Christmas tree. Washington (DC): USDA Forest Service in cooperation with the Extension Service. 9 p.

Successes and Failures in Controlling Weeds in Hardwood Seedbeds at the Arkansas Forestry Commission Baucum Forest Nursery

Allan Murray

Allan Murray is Nursery Manager for the Arkansas Forestry Commission Baucum Forest Nursery, 1402 Highway 391 North, North Little Rock, AR 72117; Tel: 501.907.2485; E-mail: baucumnursery@arkansas.gov.

Murray, A. 2009. Successes and failures in controlling weeds in hardwood seedbeds at the Arkansas Forestry Commission Baucum Forest Nursery. In: Dumroese, R.K.; Riley, L.E., tech. coords. 2009. National Proceedings: Forest and Conservation Nursery Associations—2008. Proc. RMRS-P-58. Fort Collins, CO: U.S. Department of Agriculture, Forest Service, Rocky Mountain Research Station: 74–75. Online: http://www.fs.fed.us/rm/pubs/rmrs_p058.html.

Keywords: fumigation, methyl bromide, herbicides, hand weeding, oak

Fumigation with methyl bromide is essential in the production of hardwood seedlings in nurseries in the southern United States. However, the proposed rules under the 2008 U.S. Environmental Protection Agency (EPA) Risk Mitigation will further restrict the use of methyl bromide for nursery use.

The Arkansas Forestry Commission Baucum Forest Nursery in North Little Rock fumigates nursery seedbeds in the first year for hardwood crops. In 2008, hardwood species were grown on 12 ha (30 ac), of which 11 ha (28 ac) were treated with methyl bromide. The difference in weed growth between the treated and nontreated areas was significant.

Weed Control

Pre-Emergent

If fumigation with methyl bromide is not available, or becomes more restricted, use of pre-emergent herbicides becomes extremely important. At Baucum Nursery, Goal® 2XL is used for almost all hardwood crops, with the exception of some small-seeded species (for example, mulberry [*Morus* spp.]). Once germination begins, however, we have a 5- to 6-week window when no applications can occur because any treatment will stunt or kill germinating seedlings. During this time, it is necessary to use a "health squad," or hand crews, to remove weeds as quickly as possible.

Post-Emergent

The number of herbicides that can be applied to broadleaf crop species is limited. The nursery has used GoalTender® over the top of a few species, including Nuttall oak (*Quercus nuttallii*), with very little damage. Use of this herbicide on other species of oaks, for example, Shumard oak (*Q. shumardii*), has resulted in significant damage to new top growth. Therefore, the decision must be made as to whether to use chemicals at a younger age or wait until the trees are larger.

When hardwood species begin to grow and achieve canopy closure on the seedbeds, weeds become less of a problem. At that point, weeds can be managed with a hand crew. Every day, the nursery runs a hand crew of seven to nine people with a supervisor. Because the nursery grows up to 12 ha (30 ac) of hardwoods annually, or 6 to 6.5 million seedlings comprised of 25 different species, weed control is extremely important.

Problems and Solutions

Nut grass (*Cyperus* spp.) is a problem weed at Baucum Nursery. The nursery has had success using hand mops with Roundup®. If the seedlings are small enough and the nut grass is tall, a wiper rig can be used over the top of the seedbeds.

Broadleaf weed species, however, are the biggest challenge in the hardwood seedbeds. These species can be removed by costly hand weeding. The nursery has made several attempts at using shielded sprayers, and each sprayer has been a failure. The sprayers are successful for two to three beds, but usually break down at that point. In addition, the seedlings must be large enough to apply the herbicide under the crop foliage. If seedlings have attained this size, it is usually unnecessary to apply herbicides because the foliage has covered the beds.

Nursery culturing has changed in an effort to lower herbicide use. Hardwood beds are now sown with five drills instead of the traditional four drills. The result is faster foliage cover on the beds, resulting in faster shading, less weeds, and less herbicide treatments. Although hand control is still done on a daily basis, the hardwood beds at the nursery remain fairly clean.

The content of this paper reflects the views of the authors, who are responsible for the facts and accuracy of the information presented herein.

Hardwood Weed Control: Iowa Department of Natural Resources Forestry, Iowa State Nursery

Roger Jacob

Roger Jacob is Nursery Manager for Iowa Department of Natural Resources Forestry, Iowa State Nursery, 2404 South Duff Avenue, Ames, IA 50010-8037; Tel: 800.865.2477; E-mail: roger.jacob@dnr.iowa.gov.

Jacob, R. 2009. Hardwood weed control: Iowa Department of Natural Resources Forestry, Iowa State Nursery. In: Dumroese, R.K.; Riley, L.E., tech. coords. 2009. National Proceedings: Forest and Conservation Nursery Associations—2008. Proc. RMRS-P-58. Fort Collins, CO: U.S. Department of Agriculture, Forest Service, Rocky Mountain Research Station: 76–78. Online: http://www.fs.fed.us/rm/pubs/rmrs_p058.html.

Keywords: fumigation, methyl bromide, herbicides

Background

The Iowa Department of Natural Resources Forestry, Iowa State Nursery in Ames grows approximately 4 to 8 million seedlings, consisting of about 50 species. Most of our production is hardwoods. We have not been fumigating very much, if at all, for about 20 years and, with the proposed rules under the 2008 U.S. Environmental Protection Agency (EPA) Risk Mitigation, many other nurseries may be joining us.

Weed Control

We determined that most fumigation was being done for weed control, and that it was not doing a very good job in our rich loam prairie soil. We were using Vorlex at the time. The nursery did some trials using methyl bromide, chloropicrin, and Vorlex, and compared them to different herbicide treatments. After establishing which herbicide treatments were most effective, we then tested their safety on the crops we were growing. As we add new species, the herbicides will again have to be tested. The result is that we have developed an effective herbicide program for our nursery.

Pre-Emergent Treatments

We have a pre-emergent herbicide that we apply on each species after sowing and before germination. These, of course, vary by species groups, and the timing can be altered for weather and other factors.

Post-Emergent Treatments

Post-emergent treatments may be used during the growing season according to weather and weed growth. We will normally apply an application of Pendulum® 3.3EC (4.7 L /ha [2 qt/ac]) around the first of July. This is usually done during irrigation to avoid spotting of the leaves and consequential stunting of plants. We may also apply a treatment of Vantage® or Fusilade® DX if we have enough grass pressure to warrant this application. Spot treatments of Lontrel® or Stinger® may be applied, mainly for thistle. Spot treatments of Classic® may also be used for yellow nutsedge (*Cyperus esculentus*). In areas of known yellow nutsedge pressure, we will use Pennant® as a pre-emergent wherever it is safe on the crop.

We have also developed shielded sprayers for spraying between rows, between beds, and along pipeline areas. These sprayers are mainly used with Roundup® Original, although pre-emergent herbicides are often added to try to discourage regrowth.

Precautions

Before using any herbicide applications in your nursery, make sure that you test the chemicals to make sure they are safe. Make sure you get the proper labeling in your state, as Iowa has some 24C state labeling. Some products that are soil-active, such as Princep® 4L or Simazine, may have to be changed for various soil types. The Ames program and the Montrose program (tables 1 and 2) differ for this reason. Montrose has very sandy soils, whereas Ames has very loamy soils.

Table 1. Iowa State Forest Nursery, Ames 2008 Herbicide Program.

Herbicide used	Application rate	Nursery crop	Stocktype (seedling/ cutting)
Surflan®	4.7 L/ha (2 qt/ac)	Serviceberry (*Amelanchier* spp.)	S
		Ninebark (*Physocarpus* spp.)	S
		Elderberry (*Sambucus* spp.)	S
Pendulum® 3.3EC	4.7 L/ha (2 qt/ac)	Buttonbush (*Cephalanthus occidentalis*)	S
		Arrowwood (*Viburnum recognitum*)	S
		Nannyberry (*Viburnum lentago*)	S
		Cranberry (*Viburnum opulus*)	S
		Basswood (*Tilia americana*)	S
		Hard maple (*Acer* spp.)	S
		Hackberry (*Celtis occidentalis*)	S
		Chokeberry (*Aronia* spp.)	S
Pendulum® 3.3EC	2.4 L/ha (1 qt/ac)	Sycamore (*Platanus occidentalis*)	S
		River birch (*Betula nigra*)	S
Princep® 4L	2.4 L/ha (1 qt/ac)	Gray dogwood (*Cornus racemosa*)	S
Pendulum® 3.3EC	4.7 L/ha (2 qt/ac)	Red-osier dogwood (*Cornus stolonifera*)	S
		Silky dogwood (*Cornus amomum*)	S
		Wild plum (*Prunus* spp.)	S
		Chokecherry (*Prunus virginiana*)	S
		Nanking cherry (*Prunus tomentosa*)	S
		Black cherry (*Prunus serotina*)	S
		Kentucky coffeetree (*Gymnocladus dioicus*)	S
Goal® 2XL	4.7 L/ha (2 qt/ac)	White pine (*Pinus strobus*)	S
Pendulum® 3.3EC	2.4 L/ha (1 qt/ac)	Red pine (*Pinus resinosa*)	S
		Scotch pine (*Pinus sylvestris*)	S
		Jack pine (*Pinus banksiana*)	S
		Redcedar (*Juniperus virginiana*)	S
		Norway spruce (*Picea abies*)	S
		White spruce (*Picea glauca*)	S – No Pendulum
		White ash (*Fraxinus americana*)	S
Goal® 2XL	9.4 L/ha (4 qt/ac)	Green ash (*Fraxinus pennsylvanica*)	S
		Poplar (*Populus* spp.)	C
		Cottonwood (*Populus* spp.)	C
		Willow (*Salix* spp.)	C
Goal® 2XL	2.4 L/ha (1 qt/ac)	All carryover conifers	1-3 yr.
Princep® 4L	2.4 L/ha (1 qt/ac)		
Pendulum® 3.3EC	4.7 L/ha (2 qt/ac)		
Princep® 4L	4.7 L/ha (2 qt/ac)	Silver maple (*Acer saccharum*)	S
Pendulum® 3.3EC	4.7 L/ha (2 qt/ac)		
Princep® 4L	7.1 L/ha (3 qt/ac)	All oaks (*Quercus* spp.)	S
Goal® 2XL	2.4 L/ha (1 qt/ac)	Walnut (*Juglans* spp.)	S
Pendulum® 3.3EC	4.7 L/ha (2 qt/ac)	Pecan (*Carya illinoensis*)	S
Roundup® Original	4.7 L/ha (2 qt/ac)	Hickory (*Carya* spp.)	S
		All carryover hardwoods	1-3 yr.
Princep® 4L	4.7 L/ha (2 qt/ac)	Hazelnut (*Corylus americana*)	S
Pendulum® 3.3EC	4.7 L/ha (2 qt/ac)	All carryover shrubs	1-2 yr.

Goal® 2XL can be used as a post-emergent at 5 weeks after germination at 1.2 to 2.4 L/ha (1 pt to 1 qt/ac) on conifers.
Goal® 2XL can be used as a post-emergent before and after candling at 1.2 to 2.4 L/ha (1 pt to 1 qt/ac) on conifers.
Vantage® or Fusilade® can be used as a post-emergent to kill grasses over all species, except during the first 3 weeks after germination.
A second application of Pendulum® 3.3EC may be applied, if needed, after plants reach approximately 5 cm (2 in) in height. This usually occurs in mid-June to July. When applying, wet the plants first and water immediately after, or apply while watering.
Stinger® or Lontrel® can be applied over the crop for some broadleaf control, particularly thistle.
Scepter® can be applied over the crop to control some broadleaf species, particularly in poplar and oak species.
Classic® can be applied over the crop to control nusedge, particularly in oak species.

Table 2. Iowa State Forest Nursery, Montrose 2008 Herbicide Program.

Herbicide used	Application rate	Nursery crop	Stocktype (seedling/ cutting)
Surflan®	4.7 L/ha (2 qt/ac)	Serviceberry (*Amelanchier* spp.)	S
Pendulum® 3.3EC	4.7 L/ha (2 qt/ac)	Buttonbush (*Cephalanthus occidentalis*)	S
		Basswood (*Tilia americana*)	S
		Hard maple (*Acer* spp.)	S
		Hackberry (*Celtis occidentalis*)	S
		Chokeberry (*Aronia* spp.)	S
Pendulum® 3.3EC	2.4 L/ha (1 qt/ac)	Sycamore (*Platanus occidentalis*)	S
		River birch (*Betula nigra*)	S
Goal® 2XL	4.7 L/ha (2 qt/ac)	White pine (*Pinus strobus*)	S
Pennant®	3.6 L/ha (1.5 qt/ac)	Red pine (*Pinus resinosa*)	S
		Scotch pine (*Pinus sylvestris*)	S
		Jack pine (*Pinus banksiana*)	S
		Redcedar (*Juniperus virginiana*)	S
		Norway spruce (*Picea abies*)	S
		White spruce (*Picea glauca*)	S – No Pennant
		White ash (*Fraxinus americana*)	S
		Green ash (*Fraxinus pennsylvanica*)	S- Goal @ 3 qt/ac
Goal® 2XL	2.4 L/ha (1 qt/ac)	All carryover conifers	1-3 yr.
Princep® 4L	2.4 L/ha (1 qt/ac)		
Pennant®	3.6 L/ha (1.5 qt/ac)		
Princep® 4L	4.7 L/ha (2 qt/ac)	Silver maple (*Acer saccharum*)	S
Pendulum® 3.3EC	4.7 L/ha (2 qt/ac)		
Princep® 4L	4.7 L/ha (2 qt/ac)	All oaks (*Quercus* spp.)	S
Goal® 2XL	2.4 L/ha (1 qt/ac)	Walnut (*Juglans* spp.)	S
Pennant®	3.6 L/ha (1.5 qt/ac)	Pecan (*Carya illinoensis*)	S
Roundup® Original	4.7 L/ha (2 qt/ac)	Hickory (*Carya* spp.)	S
		All carryover hardwoods	1-3 yr.
Princep® 4L	4.7 L/ha (2 qt/ac)	Hazelnut (*Corylus americana*)	S
Pennant®	3.6 L/ha (1.5 qt/ac)	All carryover shrubs	1-2 yr.

Goal® 2XL can be used as a post-emergent at 5 weeks after germination at 1.2 to 2.4 L/ha (1 pt to 1 qt/ac) on conifers.

Goal® 2XL can be used as a post-emergent before and after candling at 1.2 to 2.4 L/ha (1 pt to 1 qt/ac) on conifers.

Vantage® can be used as a post-emergent to kill grasses over all species, except during the first 3 weeks after germination.

A second application of Pendulum® 3.3EC may be applied, if needed, after plants reach approximately 5 cm (2 in) in height. This usually occurs in mid-June to July. When applying, wet the plants first and water immediately after, or apply while watering.

Weed Management at ArborGen, South Carolina SuperTree Nursery

Mike Arnette

Mike Arnette is with ArboGen, South Carolina SuperTree Nursery, 5594 Highway 38 South, Blenheim, SC 29516; Tel: 843.528.3203; E-mail: dmarnet@arborgen.com.

Arnette, M. 2009. Weed management at ArborGen, South Carolina SuperTree Nursery. In: Dumroese, R.K.; Riley, L.E., tech. coords. 2009. National Proceedings: Forest and Conservation Nursery Associations—2008. Proc. RMRS-P-58. Fort Collins, CO: U.S. Department of Agriculture, Forest Service, Rocky Mountain Research Station: 79. Online: http://www.fs.fed.us/rm/pubs/rmrs_p058.html.

Keywords: bareroot nursery, hardwoods, weed control

Weed management is vital to producing healthy hardwood seedlings. Several methods are available to each nursery, and it is common knowledge that what works for one situation may not work for another. The weed control methods used in nursery beds of hardwood species at the South Carolina SuperTree Nursery (Blenheim) are listed below.

Weed Control

Pre-Emergent Treatments

Nursery beds are fumigated with methyl bromide at a rate of 450 kg/ha (400 lb/ac). No pre-emergent herbicides are applied to certain spring sown species or to any fall sown species. In spring, Goal® 2XL is applied at a rate of 1.6 L/ha (22 oz/ac) over oaks (*Quercus* spp.).

Post-Emergent Treatments

In our hardwood seedbeds, contract hand-weeding crews control weeds until Pendulum® 3.3 EC and Endurance® can be applied at the label rate. Our general rotation is Endurance® (1.1 kg/ha [1 lb/ac]), Pendulum® 3.3 EC (4.7 L/ha [2 qt/ac]), and Endurance® at the previous rate. These treatments are usually sufficient to control weeds for the rest of the growing season.

Summary

Each nursery uses different weed control methods. Varying conditions and species dictate which methods work best. Weed control is necessary to produce a healthy crop.

The content of this paper reflects the views of the authors, who are responsible for the facts and accuracy of the information presented herein.

A Century of Progress in Weed Control in Hardwood Seedbeds

David B. South

David B. South is Professor, School of Forestry and Wildlife Sciences, Auburn University, 602 Duncan Drive, Auburn, AL 36849; Tel: 334.844.1022; E-mail: southdb@auburn.edu.

South, D.B. 2009. A century of progress in weed control in hardwood seedbeds. In: Dumroese, R.K.; Riley, L.E., tech. coords. 2009. National Proceedings: Forest and Conservation Nursery Associations—2008. Proc. RMRS-P-58. Fort Collins, CO: U.S. Department of Agriculture, Forest Service, Rocky Mountain Research Station: 80–84. Online: http://www.fs.fed.us/rm/pubs/rmrs_p058.html.

Abstract: Weeds have existed in nurseries since before the time Bartram grew hardwoods during the 18th century. Hand weeding was the primary method of weed control during the first part of the 20th century. From 1931 to 1970, advances in chemistry increased the use of herbicides, and advances in engineering increased the reliance on machines for cultivation. Many managers now rely on chemical treatments, including methyl bromide, chloropicrin, and various selective herbicides. The last 3 decades of the 20th century saw an increase in regulation of chemicals due to health and environmental concerns. If soil fumigation becomes impractical due to governmental regulation, hand-weeding times in hardwood seedbeds will likely increase unless managers adapt to the change. Some managers will increase their use of sanitation practices and herbicides. Although a few herbicides are registered for use on hardwoods, many herbicides that may be used on food crops cannot be legally applied to hardwood seedbeds. In general, grasses can be effectively controlled with properly timed, selective herbicides. The germination of many small-seeded broadleaf weeds can be suppressed with pre-emergence herbicides. Several perennial weeds and various broadleaf weeds, however, are difficult to control with pre-emergence herbicides. For some difficult-to-control weeds, a few nursery managers use shielded herbicide sprayers to apply non-selective herbicides between drills.

Keywords: herbicides, fumigation, integrated pest management

Introduction

In 1908, Dr. Carl Schenck hosted a 3-day forestry meeting (26-28 November 1908) at Asheville, NC. The Battery Park Hotel was the headquarters for the meeting, and those in attendance included state foresters from New York and Massachusetts, a U.S. senator, and more than 80 other individuals. On 26 November, the tour included several pine and hardwood plantations. That evening, dinner was at the hotel. The next day, the group visited the Biltmore Nursery and greenhouses, the Biltmore Dairy, and an afforestation site on Coxehill. In the evening, there was a possum hunt with a barbecue and much rejoicing (Anonymous1908). At one point during the meeting, Schenck said that "no tree do I hold more dear than the yellow poplar" (*Liriodendron tulipifera*).

A century later, history is repeated. Greg Pate and the North Carolina Division of Forest Resources hosted a 3-day meeting at the Crown Plaza Resort in Asheville on 22-26 July 2008. On 22 July, those in attendance visited a nursery and greenhouse at Crossnore, with an enjoyable barbecue lunch and a talk by the State Forester of North Carolina. The next day, the attendees visited the Biltmore estate and were given a forest history tour by Bill Alexander, Landscape and Forest Historian. The group visited what was once the old Biltmore Dairy, now America's most visited winery, and most likely saw some of the same trees that were planted by Schenck and his students. Although there was no opportunity to hunt possums, participants were given a bottle of "possum water" as a gift.

Another common factor between now and 1908 involves managers growing hardwoods and controlling weeds. In fact, weeds have been a problem in hardwood nurseries for more than 200 years. In 1784, John Bartram was growing various species, including oaks (*Quercus* spp.), sweetgum (*Liquidambar styraciflua*), and yellow poplar. Today, nursery managers are fighting some of the same weed species that Bartram had in his nursery. Although hand weeding is still used, the number of tools available to combat weed competition has increased. This paper reviews some of the common practices that have been used to suppress weeds in hardwood seedbeds.

1891 to 1930

The Biltmore Nursery (Asheville) was established in 1889. By 1893, it contained more than 1.8 million tree seedlings. The nursery (which contained seedbeds, transplant beds, shadehouses, and greenhouses) was managed by Chauncy Beadle. He helped propagate more varieties of plants than Kew Gardens in London. Oak and white ash (*Fraxinus americana*) seedlings, and cottonwood (*Populus deltoides*) were sold to the public for US$ 0.20 each, and plants were shipped in either boxes or bales (Alexander 2007). Unfortunately, it was situated adjacent to the Swannona River, and a flood destroyed the nursery and greenhouses in 1916.

Dr. Carl Schenck started the first forestry school in North America. To keep seedling costs low, his students established several "shifting" nurseries. A "shifting" nursery produces a few crops and is then abandoned. Dr. Schenck's students used knives, forks, hoes, and special weeding wheels to weed seedbeds (fig. 1). Because the "shifting" nurseries were typically established on forest soil, they did not suffer from an excess of weeds that developed at stationary nurseries

Figure 1. A photo taken by Dr. Carl Schenck on 1 September 1909. (Photo courtesy of the Forest History Society, Durham, NC.) The two weeders are forestry students at the Biltmore Forestry School. The "stationary" nursery at the Biltmore Estate (managed by Chauncey Beadles) operated until it was destroyed by a flood in 1916. As part of their instruction, students at the Biltmore Forestry School operated several "shifting" nurseries. At least two of these temporary nurseries were already abandoned by 1908, one being an oak nursery. In his lecture on "remedies against fungi in nurseries," Schenck (1909) mentioned "sterilized soil in nursery beds" and spraying with a fungicide including copper and lime.

like the Biltmore Nursery (Schenck 1907). Therefore, one method of weed control involved abandoning the nursery and shifting to a new, less weedy location. One "shifting" oak nursery established by Schenck was abandoned in 1905 (Anonymous 1908).

Seeds with good germination were sown in drills 12.5 to 25 cm (5 to 10 in) apart, and the rows made weeding easier (Schenck 1907). Mulch (moss, sawdust, straw, twigs, and so on) was placed between drills to keep weeds down. In contrast, when seeds were broadcast, Schenck employed high seedbed densities as a weed-control method. He said, "Weeding can be dispensed with in dense, broadcast seedbeds. In thinly stocked beds planted broadcast, it is most necessary and most difficult." Seed broadcast was used for seeds of low germination, including birch (*Betula alba*), elm (*Ulmus americana*), beech (*Fagus grandifolia*), alder (*Alnus glutinosa*) and yellow poplar. Of course, weeds should be removed before they produce seeds (Meier 1897).

Horses were used to cultivate transplants, but soon machines were developed to assist in weeding seedbeds. At the Clearfield Nursery in Pennsylvania, a gasoline motor cultivator was developed for use in drill-sown beds (Dague 1925). This was a cheaper method than using hand weeders in broadcast beds. Schenck (1909) listed soil sterilization as a method to control soil fungi in nurseries, and Dague (1925) suggested weeds might be suppressed by steam sterilization of seedbeds.

At this time, some nurseries sold hardwood seedlings for US$ 0.002 to 0.01 each (Tillotson 1916).

1931 to 1970

Before 1930, only a few forest nurseries were in operation, but the number increased after the establishment of the Civilian Conservation Corps in 1933. During that time, cheap labor was plentiful and mechanical weed control was discouraged (Augenstein 1949). However, when the availability of tractors increased and labor costs increased, many managers adopted mechanical weed control (McComb and Steavenson 1936). One nursery developed a gas-powered cultivator specifically for hardwoods that could be moved by either two workers or one tractor (Mony 1954).

During this 4-decade period, managers began to experiment with chemical weed control. In some places, nurseries applied ally alcohol to seedbeds to kill weed seeds before sowing. Mineral spirits were applied to guayule (*Parthenium argentatum*) and, due to its success with this plant, this herbicide was tested on both conifer and hardwood seedlings. Most hardwoods were injured by the treatment, but some managers found that sweetgum seedlings had some tolerance (Vande Linde 1973).

Soil fumigation with methyl bromide showed promising results, and the weed control reductions were great. Kopitke and Langford (1952) remarked, "Cottonwood, commonly acknowledged as a difficult crop to grow because the seedbeds must be kept moist during the germination period with a resultant high population of weeds, has been grown on methyl bromide treated soil with no hand weeding whatever." Because mineral spirits were not used in most hardwood seedbeds, many managers quickly adopted the use of soil fumigation.

1971 to 2010 _____

The next 4 decades saw an increase in chemical regulations. In 1972, Congress passed the Federal Insecticide, Fungicide, and Rodenticide Act (FIFRA) to regulate the use and labeling of pesticides. As a result, most herbicides that were permitted for use on food were no longer permitted for use in hardwood seedbeds (if the label did not list ornamental, non-cropland, or nurseries). As a result, at some nurseries, managers had to rely on fumigation and hand weeding, because they could no longer legally apply the herbicides they had used on hardwoods in 1970. For example, simazine could be used on oaks in 1970, but not in 1973. It was only recently labeled for use on oak seedbeds using a state label (Wichman 2005). In general, EPA is not sympathetic to the plight of minor-use, non-food crops (Fennimore and Doohan 2008).

In 1983, several environmental groups sued the USDA Forest Service over the use of herbicides in the forest. As a result, a U.S. District Court Order temporarily banned the use of herbicides on National Forest lands in Washington and Oregon. The consequence of ceasing the use of herbicides in a nursery weed management program was documented by observing the effect on weed management costs at the USDA Forest Service J. Herbert Stone Nursery (Central Point, OR). Even with soil fumigation (that is, methyl bromide with 33% chloropicrin) and mechanical cultivation, hand-weeding costs in 1-year seedbeds after the ban were up to 5 times greater than the total weed management costs in 1983 (when herbicides were used). In addition, seed efficiency at the USDA Forest Service Wind River Nursery (Carson, WA) was reduced to the point where 25% more seeds were required to produce the same number of plantable seedlings. The herbicide ban was lifted in 1989, but "only when other methods are ineffective or will increase project costs unreasonably."

In 1993, the Forest Stewardship Council (FSC) was established to promote responsible forest and plantation management. To earn FSC certification, plantation owners should not obtain hardwood seedlings from nurseries that use certain herbicides. Nursery chemicals not permitted in FSC certified nurseries include: ally alcohol, methyl bromide, metam sodium, atrazine, diquat dibromide, fluziflop-butyl, hexazinone, isoxaben, MSMA, oryzalin, oxyfluorfen, simazine, pendimethalin, and trifluralin. In addition, managers of FSC plantations "shall make every effort to move away from chemical pesticides and fertilizers, including their use in nurseries." As someone who supports the use of pesticides and urea in forest nurseries, I assume "every effort" really means "every effort."

Current Weed Management Practices

At the request of USDA Forest Service specialists with the Regeneration, Nurseries, and Genetics Resources (RNGR) group, Douglass Jacobs and Amy Ross-Davis (Purdue University, West Lafayette, IN) developed a hardwood nursery questionnaire. In 2006, 91 questionnaires were sent to nurseries in the eastern United States. From a return of 26 surveys, it was learned that 21 nurseries use soil fumigation, 20 nurseries use herbicides, 19 nurseries sow oak seeds in the fall, 25 use hand weeders, and 6 use mechanical cultivation.

One question that was asked: "What are the three (3) most troublesome pests (including weeds) with regard to hardwood seedling production?" Half (13) indicated that weeds were the number one pest. Of the remaining half (13), five said weeds were the second most troublesome pest, and four said weeds were their third most troublesome pest. Four managers did not list weeds among the top three pests (although one of these indicated his nursery required about 250 hours of hand weeding/ha [100 hours/ac]). Several managers listed specific weeds as troublesome (table 1).

Questions were also asked about the amount of time required to mechanically weed or hand weed seedbeds. Some managers did not keep good records and could not answer this question, or answered "as needed." Twenty managers included a number. The maximum amount of hand weeding time was 309 hours/ha [125 hours/ac], and one nursery

Table 1. Weeds mentioned by hardwood nursery managers in 2006.

Common name	Species	State
Barnyardgrass	*Echinochloa crus-galli*	Michigan
Hairy crabgrass	*Digitaria sanguinalis*	Wisconsin
Goosegrass	*Eleusine indica*	Arkansas
Sourgrass	*Digitaria insularis*	Alabama
Witchgrass	*Panicum capillare*	New Hampshire
Yellow nutsedge	*Cyperus rotundus*	Alabama, Iowa
Carpetweed	*Mollugo verticillata*	New Hampshire
Creeping charlie	*Glechoma hederacea*	Iowa
Chickweed	*Stellaria media*	Michigan
White clover	*Trifolium repens*	Minnesota, West Virginia
Dayflower	*Commelina communis*	Iowa
Eclipta	*Eclipta alba*	Oklahoma
Horseweed	*Conyza canadensis*	Michigan, Wisconsin
Redroot pigweed	*Amaranthus retroflexus*	Louisiana, New Hampshire
Common purslane	*Portulaca oleracea*	New Hampshire, Wisconsin
Spurge	*Chamaesyce maculata*	Alabama, New Hampshire, Wisconsin

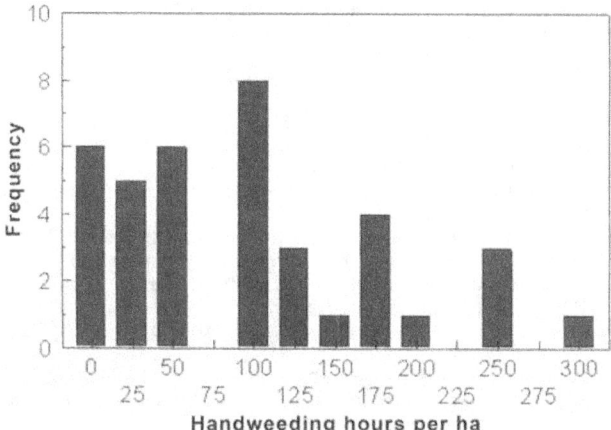

Figure 2. Annual hand weeding required in hardwood seedbeds (data from a 2006 survey of hardwood nurseries). One nursery with no hand weeding employed sanitation practices, soil fumigation, and multiple applications of herbicides.

required no hand weeding (fig. 2). On average, hardwood seedbeds required 92 hours of hand weeding/ha (37 hours/ac). One nursery, that did not report any use of herbicides, employed 100 seasonal employees, while 6 nurseries employed less than 11 seasonal employees. There was no relationship between nursery production and number of seasonal employees. In fact, one nursery that produced 2.4 million hardwood seedlings and over 50 million pine seedlings employed only two seasonal workers.

The reliance on seasonal labor varies with nursery and with the cost of labor. In some cases, prison labor is used, and the cost of hand weeding may be relatively low. At some nurseries, the cost of contract labor is US$ 20/hour, and the cost of 100 hours of hand weeding might exceed US$ 2000/ha (US$ 810/ac). Therefore, the use of herbicides depends, in part, on the cost of hand weeding. At some nurseries, herbicides are used and no hand weeding is required, while other managers rely on hand weeding and, except for soil fumigants, do not apply herbicides to hardwood seedbeds. Currently, hardwood nursery managers use a number of herbicides, including DCPA, fluziflop-butyl, glyphosate, isoxaben, napropamide, oryzalin, oxyfluorfen, paraquat, sethoxydim, simazine, pendimethalin, trifluralin. Although several granular herbicides are registered for use on hardwoods (South and Carey 2005), most managers of bareroot nurseries avoid their use due to the additional cost associated with granular herbicides.

When asked "Do you fumigate your soil?" five managers said, "No." Of the 21 who fumigate, three used dazomet (300 to 350 kg ai/ha [270 to 310 lb ai/ac]) and two used sodium methyldithiocarbamate (267 to 307 kg ai/ha [238 to 274 lb ai/ac]). The remaining treated either with methyl bromide+33% chloropicrin (392 kg ai/ha [350 lb ai/ac]) or with methyl bromide + 2% chloropicrin (336 kg ai/ha [300 lb ai/ac]). Dazomet was applied in September and sodium methyldithiocarbamate was applied in August. Fumigation with methyl bromide and chloropicrin occurred either in the summer (6), fall (9), or spring (6). One advantage of methyl bromide and chloropicrin is that they can be used relatively close to fields containing seedlings. In some situations,

injury to adjacent crops has occurred when dazomet (or sodium methyldithiocarbamate) was applied without a tarp (Scholtes 1989; Buzzo 2003). In addition, dazomet is not as effective as methyl bromide in controlling nutsedge (*Cyperus* spp.) (Carey 1995; Carey and South 1999; Fraedrich and Dwinell 2003).

Because hardwood seedbeds often contain either four or five drills, sometimes mechanical cultivation is used to control weeds once seedlings are tall enough to withstand some mechanical disturbance. Of the 21 managers, 6 indicated they used some "mechanical weeding." The time required for this practice averaged 15 hours/ha/year (6 hours/ac/year), but one nursery required 37 hours/ha/year (15 hours/ac/year).

Efficient weed management systems for hardwoods involve a combination of methods that may include: sanitation (Wichman 1982, 2005), living mulch (Ensminger 2002; Hawkins 2005), soil fumigation, herbicides (South 1984; Rentz 1999; South and Carey 2005), and mechanical cultivation (Barham 1980; South 1988). Less efficient systems usually rely on just one or two methods of weed management and do not incorporate a "24/7" weed management program.

Future Practices

No one is certain what the future will hold, but I will "go out on a limb" and predict that weeds will continue to exist in hardwood seedbeds (as long as bareroot nurseries exist). What might not last is the ability to effectively control weeds with chemicals. Perhaps advances in robotic technology will produce robots that will weed seedbeds mechanically (Fennimore and Doohan 2008). This would result in a loss of jobs, but would virtually eliminate problems associated with nursery workers waiting 3 days before reentering herbicide- or insecticide-treated fields.

A harder prediction involves how governmental regulations will affect the cost of hardwood weed control. Will governmental regulators ban the use of chemicals, or will they impose restrictions that make their use impractical? For example, recently imposed regulations by EPA will likely increase costs associated with use of both herbicides and fumigants. Buffer restrictions will reduce the potential fumigated area and will increase the cost of hardwood seedlings. In some cases, regulations and urban sprawl might result in the closing of some bareroot nurseries. Some may decide to convert to 100% container production, while others might be relocated to remote locations. In some cases, these changes will double seedling cost so a hardwood seedling might have a retail cost of US$ 0.70 or more.

Acknowledgments

The author wishes to thank Ron Overton (Area Regeneration Specialist with the USDA Forest Service) and George Hernandez (Southern Region Nursery Specialist with the USDA Forest Service) for their assistance with nursery selection, survey development, and follow-up contact with non-respondent nurseries. Douglass Jacobs and Amy Ross-Davis (Associate Professor and Post-Doctoral Research Scientist in the Department of Forestry and Natural Resources, Purdue University) for designing and conducting the survey. Thanks also goes to Edward Loewenstein (Assistant Professor in the

School of Forestry and Wildlife Sciences, Auburn University),
Ken McNabb (Professor and Interim Special Assistant to the
Provost, Auburn University), and Tom Landis (Consultant
and Research Nursery Specialist) for assistance with survey
development. Elizabeth Bowersock (Outreach Assistant with
the Southern Forest Nursery Management Cooperative)
assisted with obtaining nursery contact information and
follow-up contact with non-respondent nursery managers.
I especially thank the 26 hardwood nursery managers who
were willing to take the time to answer the questionnaire.

References

Alexander B. 2007. The Biltmore Nursery—a botanical legacy.
Charleston (SC): Natural History Press. 288 p.

Anonymous. 1908. Three days' forest festival on the Biltmore Estate.
American Lumberman. December 19. p 43-45.

Augenstein JW. 1949. Weed control. In: Meeting of Forest Tree
Nurserymen; 17 January 1949; Seattle, Washington. Seattle
(WA): University of Washington. p 11-18.

Barham RO. 1980. Handweeding times reduced in hardwood
seedbeds by a modified rolling cultivator. Tree Planters' Notes
31(4): 30-32.

Buzzo RJ. 2003. Phytotoxicity with metam sodium. In: Riley LE,
Dumroese RK, Landis TD, technical coordinators. National pro-
ceedings: forest and conservation nursery associations—2002. Fort
Collins (CO): USDA Forest Service, Rocky Mountain Research
Station. Proceedings RMRS-P-28. p 79-83.

Carey WA. 1995. Chemical alternatives to methyl bromide. In: Landis
TD, Dumroese RK, technical coordinators. National proceedings,
forest and conservation nursery associations—1994. Fort Collins
(CO): USDA Forest Service, Rocky Mountain Forest and Range
Experiment Station. Gen. Tech. Rep. RM-257. p 4-11.

Carey WA, South DB. 1999. Effect of chloropicrin, Vapam and
herbicides for the control of purple nutsedge in southern pine
seedbeds. In: Landis TD, Barnett JP, technical coordinators.
National proceedings, forest and conservation nursery associations. Asheville (NC): USDA Forest Service, Southern Research
Station. Gen. Tech. Rep. SRS-25. p 39-40.

Dague WF. 1925. Manual labor saving devices in nursery practice.
Journal of Forestry 22:790-792.

Ensminger P. 2002. Nursery practices in Tennessee. In: Dumrose RK,
Riley LE, Landis TD, technical coordinators. National Proceedings:
Forest and Conservation Nursery Associations—1999, 2000, and
2001. Fort Collins (CO): USDA Forest Service, Rocky Mountain
Research Station. Proceedings RMRS-P-24. p 281-283.

Fennimore SA, Doohan DJ. 2008. The challenges of specialty crop
weed control, future directions. Weed Technology 22:364-372.

Fraedrich SW, Dwinell LD. 2003. Effect of dazomet, metam sodium and oxamyl on Longidorus populations and loblolly pine
seedling production. Southern Journal of Applied Forestry
29(3):117-122.

Hawkins R. 2005. Panel discussion: cover crops used at Vallonia
Nursery, Indiana Division of Forestry . In: Dumroese RK, Riley
LE, Landis TD, technical coordinators. National Proceedings:
Forest and Conservation Nursery Associations—2004. Fort Collins
(CO): USDA Forest Service, Rocky Mountain Research Station.
Proceedings RMRS-P-35. p 31-32.

Kopitke JC, Langford JKR. 1952. Weed control with methyl bromide.
Journal of Forestry 50(3):208-211.

McComb AL, Steavenson HA. 1936. Some new nursery equipment.
Journal of Forestry 7:698-701.

Meier FR. 1897. How to start a forest nursery. Chapter 11. In: TJ
Rothrock, Commissioner of Forestry. Third Annual Report of the
Pennsylvania Department of Agriculture, Part 2. Harrisburg
(PA): William Stanley Ray State Printer. p 234-251.

Mony CC. 1954. Vallonia rotary tooth cultivator. Tree Planters'
Notes 16:17-20.

Rentz R. 1999. Hardwood seedling production. In: Landis TD, Bar-
nett JR, technical coordinators. National Proceedings: Forest and
Conservation Nursery Associations—1996. Asheville (NC): U.S.
Department of Agriculture, Forest Service, Southern Research
Station. Gen. Tech. Rep. SRS-25. p 22-24.

Schenck CA. 1907. Biltmore lectures on silviculture. Albany (NY):
Brandow Printing Company.

Schenck CA. 1909. Forest protection. Asheville (NC): The Inland
Press.

Scholtes JR. 1989. Soil fumigation at J Herbert Stone Nursery. In:
Landis TD, Cregg B, technical coordinators. National Proceedings,
Forest and Conservation Nursery Associations. Portland (OR):
USDA Forest Service, Pacific Northwest Research Station. Gen.
Tech. Rep. PNW-GTR-365. p 80-83.

South DB. 1984. Chemical weed control in southern hardwood
nurseries. Southern Journal of Applied Forestry 8:16-22.

South DB. 1988. Mechanical weed control for the forest nursery.
Atlanta (GA): Georgia Forestry Commission. Research Report
No 1. 10 p.

South DB, Carey WA. 2005. Weed control in bareroot hardwood
nurseries. In: Dumroese RK, Riley LE, Landis TD, technical
coordinators. National proceedings, forest and conservation
nursery associations—2004. Fort Collins (CO): USDA Forest
Service, Rocky Mountain Research Station. Proceedings RMRS-
P-35. p 34-38.

Tillotson CR. 1916. The care and improvement of the woodlot.
Washington (DC): USDA Farmers Bulletin 711. 21 p.

Vande Linde F. 1973. Hardwood nursery practices. In: Hardwood
short course. Raleigh (NC): North Carolina State University,
School of Forest Resources, Industry Cooperative Program. p
44-52.

Wichman JR. 1982. Weed sanitation program at the Vallonia Nursery. Tree Planters' Notes 33(4):35-36.

Wichman JR. 2005. Weed control practices in seedbeds of deciduous
trees and shrubs in the Indiana Department of Natural Resources
Nursery program. In: Dumroese RK, Riley LE, Landis TD, technical coordinators. National proceedings, forest and conservation
nursery associations—2004. Fort Collins (CO): USDA Forest
Service, Rocky Mountain Research Station. Proceedings RMRS-
P-35. p 41-42.

Root-Collar Diameter and Third-Year Survival of Three Bottomland Hardwoods Planted on Former Agricultural Fields in the Lower Mississippi Alluvial Valley

Emile S. Gardiner, Douglass F. Jacobs,
Ronald P. Overton, and George Hernandez

Emile S. Gardiner is Research Forester, USDA Forest Service, Southern Research Station, Center for Bottomland Hardwoods Research, PO Box 227, Stoneville, MS 38776; Tel: 765.496.6686; E-mail: egardiner@fs.fed.us. Douglass F. Jacobs is Associate Professor, Hardwood Tree Improvement and Regeneration Center, Department of Forestry and Natural Resources, Purdue University, West Lafayette, IN 47907; E-mail: djacobs@purdue.edu. Ronald P. Overton is Area Regeneration Specialist, Northeastern Area State and Private Forestry, USDA Forest Service, West Lafayette, IN 47907; E-mail: roverton@fs.fed.us. George Hernandez is Regeneration Specialist, Region 8, USDA Forest Service, Atlanta, GA 30367; E-mail: ghernandez@fs.fed.us.

Gardiner, E.S.; Jacobs, D.F.; Overton, R.P.; Hernandez, G. 2009. Root-collar diameter and third-year survival of three bottomland hardwoods planted on former agricultural fields in the lower Mississippi Alluvial Valley. In: Dumroese, R.K.; Riley, L.E., tech. coords. 2009. National Proceedings: Forest and Conservation Nursery Associations—2008. Proc. RMRS-P-58. Fort Collins, CO: U.S. Department of Agriculture, Forest Service, Rocky Mountain Research Station: 85–89. Online: http://www.fs.fed.us/rm/pubs/rmrs_p058.html.

Abstract: Athough the Lower Mississippi Alluvial Valley (LMAV) has experienced substantial afforestation of former agricultural fields during the past 2 decades, seedling standards that support satisfactory outplanting performance of bottomland hardwood tree species are not available. A series of experimental plantations, established on three afforestation sites in the LMAV, provided an opportunity to examine relationships between initial root-collar diameter and the probability of third-year survival for Nuttall oak (*Quercus nuttallii*), sweet pecan (*Carya illinoensis*), and green ash (*Fraxinus pennsylvanica*). Three years after planting, the probability of survival for Nuttall oak and sweet pecan seedlings improved with increasing initial root-collar diameter. The probability of survival for Nuttall oak and sweet pecan seedlings increased 26% and 33%, respectively, over the range of initial root-collar diameters (2 to 18 mm [0.08 to 0.71 in]). Intensive vegetation control during the first growing season also increased the probability of survival for both species. In contrast, green ash seedlings maintained a third-year survival of 95% across the three study sites, and the probability of survival was not influenced by initial root-collar diameter or first-year vegetation control. These results suggest that morphological variables, such as root-collar diameter, can provide practical, species-specific indices of potential survival for bottomland hardwood seedlings outplanted on former agricultural fields in the LMAV.

Keywords: afforestation, seedling survival, *Quercus nuttallii*, *Carya illinoensis*, *Fraxinus pennsylvanica*

Introduction

For over 2 decades, government programs, including the Wetland Reserve Program (WRP) and Conservation Reserve Program (CRP), have promoted restoration of forest cover on previously farmed acreage in the Lower Mississippi Alluvial Valley (LMAV) (Kennedy 1990). Participation in these incentive programs has been enthusiastic as landowners target replacement of economically marginal farmland with forest cover capable of enhancing wildlife habitat, establishing timber production, improving water quality, and promoting other environmental objectives (Schoenholtz and others 2001). For a multitude of reasons, natural regeneration is often not a reliable practice for establishing forest cover on former agricultural land in the LMAV (Allen 1997; Stanturf and others 2001). Managers, therefore, typically practice afforestation to establish native tree species on enrolled acreage (Stanturf and others 1998). Accordingly, the extensive afforestation employed to establish forest cover in the LMAV has spiked the demand for bottomland hardwood tree seedlings.

Although state and private nurseries have increased production to meet demand, hardwood seedlings raised by various growers can differ substantially in morphological and physiological attributes that may influence seedling field performance (Jacobs and others 2005a; Gardiner and others 2007). Indeed, field observations in the LMAV indicate a wide range of outplanting performance for hardwood seedlings, and some of these differences may be attributed to cultural practices that affect morphological or physiological condition of lifted stock (Jacobs and others 2005a; Wilson and Jacobs 2006; Gardiner and others 2007). Although it is established that seedling morphology and physiology can determine outplanting performance, scientifically based standards for the production and grading of bottomland hardwood seedlings are currently unavailable. Furthermore, afforestation programs implemented throughout the LMAV often maintain seedling specification policies that differ from state to state. Clearly, there is a need to acquire additional knowledge on the factors that determine outplanting success of bottomland hardwood seedlings so that nursery growers can target specific seedling characteristics, and landowners can purchase quality planting stock. This study is part of a larger research effort designed to examine linkages between nursery practices, seedling morphology, and outplanting performance of several bottomland hardwood species commonly planted on afforestation sites in the LMAV. Knowledge gained from this effort could eventually be used to develop hardwood seedling standard recommendations for afforestation in the LMAV. The objective of this manuscript is to present preliminary analyses of the relationships between initial root-collar diameter and third-year survival of outplanted Nuttall oak (*Quercus nuttallii*), sweet pecan (*Carya illinoensis*), and green ash (*Fraxinus pennsylvanica*) seedlings.

Methods

Overview

In February 2003, a series of experimental plantations were established on former agricultural sites in the LMAV to examine bottomland hardwood seedling quality, as affected by nursery source and competition control, on outplanting performance. The chosen sites in Louisiana, Mississippi, and Arkansas were privately owned and enrolled in either the WRP or CRP, and site conditions were representative of other acreage recently enrolled in these conservation programs. Jacobs and others (2005a) and Gardiner and others (2007) provide comprehensive details on the design, establishment, and measurement of this bottomland hardwood seedling quality research. Methods presented in this manuscript are a subset from that larger research effort, and are restricted to those most relevant to our examination of the relationships between initial root-collar diameter and third-year survival of Nuttall oak, sweet pecan, and green ash seedlings.

Seedling Material and Laboratory Procedures

Nuttall oak, sweet pecan, and green ash seedlings were obtained from the Louisiana Department of Agriculture and Forestry Monroe Nursery in Monroe, the Mississippi Forestry Commission Winona Nursery in Winona, and the Arkansas Forestry Commission Baucum Nursery in North Little Rock. The 1+0 bareroot seedlings were lifted on 30-31 January 2003, then stored at 4 °C (39 °F) in refrigerated lockers located at the Center for Bottomland Hardwoods Research, Stoneville, MS, and the Theodore Roosevelt National Wildlife Refuge Complex, Hollandale, MS. Prior to outplanting, each seedling was tagged with a unique number referencing its nursery of origin and measured values for several morphological variables. Root-collar diameter, measured with calipers to the nearest 0.1 mm, was among the variables measured on each seedling in the laboratory.

Field Sites and Design

Three locations in the LMAV, scheduled to receive afforestation, were selected as experimental sites for this study. The sites were former agricultural fields in Madison Parish, LA (32° 26' N, 91° 25' W), Bolivar County, MS (33° 53' N, 91° 00' W), and Chicot County, AR (33° 03' N, 91° 22' W). On each site, a factorial arrangement of nursery (three levels—Louisiana, Mississippi, Arkansas) and weed control (two levels—no weed control, complete weed control) treatments were assigned within three blocks of six experimental plots established for each species. Treatment plots consisted of a 5 by 10 grid of planting spots spaced 1.8 m (6 ft) apart. Thus, a total of 900 seedlings for each species, 300 from each nursery, were planted on each of the three experimental sites (2,700 total seedlings for each species).

On each site, experimental plantations were delineated on soils suited for each species such that Nuttall oak and green ash were assigned to Sharkey clay (very-fine, smectitic, thermic Chromic Epiaquerts) at the Madison Parish and Bolivar County sites, and Perry clay (very-fine, smectitic, thermic Chromic Epiaquerts) at the Chicot County site. Sweet pecan was assigned to the better drained Dundee loam (fine-silty, mixed, active, thermic Typic Endoaqualfs) at the Madison Parish site, Commerce silt loam (fine-silty, mixed, superactive, nonacid, thermic Fluvaquentic Endoaquepts) at the Bolivar County site, and Robinsonville loam (coarse-loamy, mixed, superactive, nonacidic, thermic Typic Udifluvents) at the Chicot County site.

Planting and Tending Practices

All three study sites were planted in February 2003. A professional planting crew was contracted to plant the Madison Parish and Chicot County sites, while the authors and forestry technicians planted the Bolivar County site. The experimental seedlings on all sites were hand-planted using hardwood planting shovels that had a 16.5 cm (6.5 in) wide x 25 cm (10 in) long blade. Vegetation control practices were initiated on designated plots immediately after planting to remove all competing vegetation through the first growing season (Corbin and others 2004). Herbicide applications included a pre-emergent broadcast application of Goal® 2XL (oxyfluorfen) applied at a rate of 4.7 L/ha (2 qt/ac) in early March 2003, broadcast applications of Select® 2EC (clethodim) applied as needed throughout the growing season at a rate of 0.6 or 0.9 L/ha (0.5 or 0.75 pt/ac), and directed applications of Derringer (glufosinate-ammonium) applied at a rate of 118 ml/L (4 oz/gal) of water as needed throughout the growing season. Additionally, mechanical weed control by mowing and hand-hoeing was employed as needed to aid in competition control.

Data Analysis

The experimental design as described above is structured for an "ANOVA-type" analysis of experimental factors. This design, however, also allows for exploration of relationships between seedling morphological characteristics and variables of outplanting performance. To meet the objectives of this manuscript, logistic regression was used to estimate the probability of seedling survival at year 3 from initial measurements of root-collar diameter. Third-year survival and initial root-collar diameter data from all three study sites were pooled, and the probability of seedling survival over the range of measured root-collar diameters was modeled as:

$$P = 1 / 1 + e^{-(a + b \cdot \text{initial root-collar diameter})}$$

In this model, e is the base of the natural logarithm (2.718), while a and b are estimated model parameters. The probability of survival (P) is unitless and can range between 0 and 1 such that probabilities near 0 indicate little chance of occurrence and probabilities near 1 indicate a high chance of occurrence. For each species, separate models were developed for seedlings receiving weed control and seedlings that did not receive weed control. Model significance was determined at $P = 0.05$.

Results and Discussion

Knowledgeable and conscientious afforestation foresters and planting crews operating on former agricultural fields in the LMAV have demonstrated success in establishing bottomland hardwood plantations that maintain relatively high survival rates. Plantation failures, however, are still frequent, particularly if adequate care is not taken to assure suitable species selections, site preparation, procurement of quality planting stock, and proper seedling storage, handling, and planting (Gardiner and others 2002). In this study, third-year survival of bareroot seedlings planted on former agricultural fields in the LMAV ranged from 95% for green ash to 67% for sweet pecan across all three study sites. Nuttall oak was intermediate with 85% survival across all sites. These percentages, particularly for Nuttall oak and green ash, are as good as, or higher than, other reported survival rates from the LMAV (Krinard and Kennedy 1987; Ozalp and others 1997; Michalek and others 2002; Patterson and Adams 2003). As in this study, green ash survival rates on afforestation sites are generally higher than other bottomland species, and it is not uncommon to observe less than 5% mortality of this species 3 years after outplanting in the LMAV (Krinard and Kennedy 1987; Groninger and Babassana 2002). This may be due, in part, to the ability of green ash to readily develop adventitious roots (Kennedy 1972). Less is known about the artificial establishment of sweet pecan on afforestation sites, but Krinard and Kennedy (1987) reported fourth-year survival of this species averaged 57% on a cleared forest site in the LMAV.

With recent advances in herbicide labeling and application technologies, practitioners in the LMAV are beginning to employ vegetation control practices during plantation establishment. Operational vegetation control practices are generally known to benefit bottomland hardwood seedling growth (Gardiner and others 2002; Groninger and others 2004), but improving seedling survival through vegetation control practices has not been consistently observed. Greatest gains in survival following vegetation control have perhaps been observed in establishment years of low rainfall (Ezell and Catchot 1997; Ezell and Hodges 2002). In this study, complete weed control during the first growing season reduced seedling mortality for Nuttall oak and sweet pecan. Ninety percent of the planted Nuttall oak seedlings survived 3 years when established in plots receiving weed control, whereas 80% survived the same period without weed control. Third-year survival for sweet pecan averaged 75% in plots that received first-year weed control as compared to 58% in plots that did not receive weed control. Removing unwanted vegetation did not benefit green ash survival, averaging 95% across all three study sites regardless of weed control treatment. The complete weed control practiced for the purpose of this experiment is not operationally feasible for large-scale plantations. Our results, however, do illustrate potential detriments of competing vegetation on survival of the three species examined.

While the plantation survival results described above contribute to our general knowledge of bottomland hardwood establishment on afforestation sites in the LMAV, exploring potential morphological indices of seedling survival is more important to the objective of this manuscript. Other authors working with various broadleaved species have identified variables such as root-collar diameter, root volume, and the number of first-order lateral roots as promising indices of some measures of hardwood seedling field performance (Dey and Parker 1997; Spetich and others 2002; Davis and Jacobs 2005; Jacobs and others 2005b). Our examination of the relationships between initial root-collar diameter and third-year seedling survival is revealing. Nuttall oak seedlings outplanted without receiving weed control showed third-year survival probabilities that ranged from 0.67 to 0.93 (fig. 1). The probabilities of survival were, in part, determined by initial root-collar diameter (P > Chi Square < 0.001), as the lowest probabilities were associated with the smallest root-collar diameters and the greatest probabilities for survival were projected for seedlings with the largest root-collar diameters (fig. 1). Removing competing vegetation had a positive impact on the probabilities of survival for Nuttall oak, with the response curve shifting upwards to probabilities that ranged from 0.80 to 0.98 (fig. 1).

Plotting the response curve for probability of survival over initial root-collar diameter can be useful for identifying a target seedling size that corresponds to a threshold survival level. For example, to achieve an arbitrary 0.85 probability of survival 3 years after planting, a Nuttall oak seedling planted without receiving weed control would need a minimum root-collar diameter of about 11 mm (0.43 in) (fig. 1). Understandably, because competing vegetation reduced the probability of survival for Nuttall oak, the threshold root-collar diameter needed to achieve an 0.85 probability of survival is reduced to about 4 mm (0.15 in) if

Gardiner, Jacobs, Overton, and Hernandez

Root-Collar Diameter and Third-Year Survival of Three Bottomland Hardwoods . . .

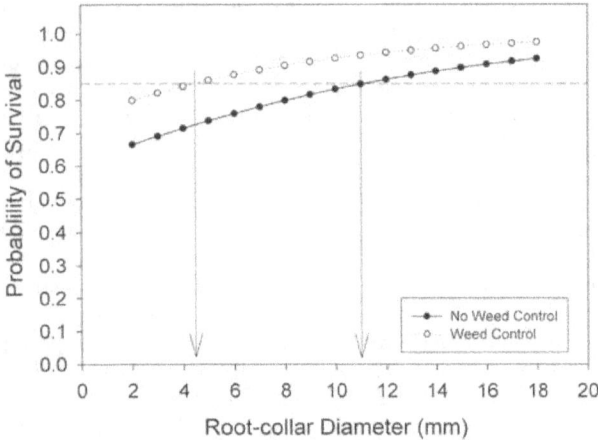

Figure 1. Third-year probability of survival for bareroot Nuttall oak seedlings established on three former agricultural fields in the LMAV. The dashed, horizontal line represents an arbitrary 0.85 probability of survival. Arrows indicate the minimum initial root-collar diameter that provides a 0.85 probability of survival.

complete weed control is practiced during the first growing season (fig. 1).

Third-year probabilities of survival for sweet pecan seedlings could be partially ascribed to initial root-collar diameter ($P >$ Chi Square < 0.001). Survival probabilities ranged between 0.47 for seedlings with initial root-collar diameters of 2 mm (0.08 in) and 0.80 for seedlings with initial root-collar diameters of 18 mm (0.71 in) (fig. 2). The probabilities of survival for this species also responded to first-year weed control, that is, the response curve shifted upwards to a range of third-year survival probabilities from 0.66 to 0.90 (fig. 2). For sweet pecan, achieving an arbitrary 0.85 probability of survival appears unlikely without intensive control of competing vegetation (fig. 2). An initial

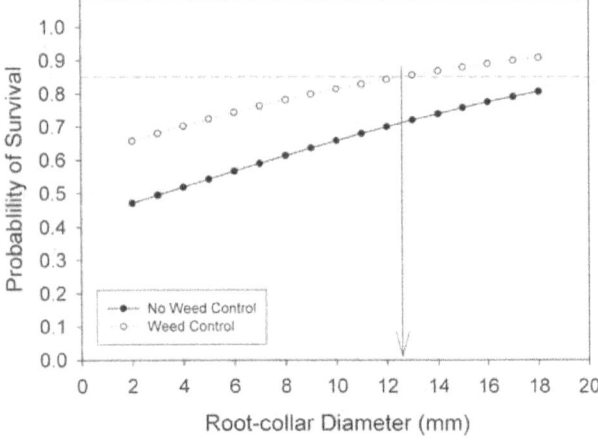

Figure 2. Third-year probability of survival for bareroot sweet pecan seedlings established on three former agricultural fields in the LMAV. The dashed, horizontal line represents an arbitrary 0.85 probability of survival. The arrow indicates the minimum initial root-collar diameter that provides a 0.85 probability of survival with competition control.

root-collar diameter of 13 mm (0.51 in), along with first-year weed control, would be needed to attain this probability of survival (fig. 2).

In contrast to the other species, the probabilities of survival for green ash seedlings could not be referenced to initial root-collar diameter ($P >$ Chi Square $= 0.77670$). Third-year survival probabilities for this species were high across the entire range of initial root-collar diameters, indicating a large capacity for survival within a broad range of seedling morphology (fig. 3). Additionally, probabilities of survival for this species were not improved with first-year competition control (fig. 3).

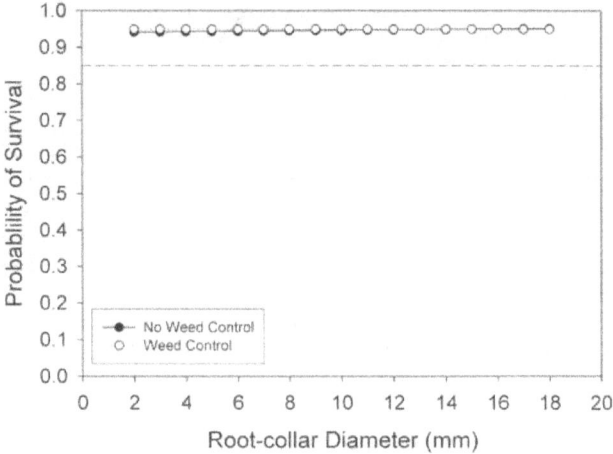

Figure 3. Third-year probability of survival for bareroot green ash seedlings established on three former agricultural fields in the LMAV. The dashed, horizontal line represents an arbitrary 0.85 probability of survival.

Conclusions

Bottomland hardwood tree seedlings have traditionally been raised, processed, planted, and tended with little regard for species-specific requirements. Lack of knowledge of bottomland hardwood seedling quality as it relates to outplanting success limits the implementation of species-specific standards. In this study, Nuttall oak, sweet pecan, and green ash exhibited differing abilities to survive outplanting on former agricultural fields in the LMAV. Three years after planting, the range in initial root-collar diameter was associated with differing probabilities of survival for Nuttall oak and sweet pecan seedlings. Survival probabilities for seedlings planted without weed control improved 26% for Nuttall oak and 33% for sweet pecan as initial root-collar diameter increased from 2 to 18 mm (0.08 to 0.71 in). The probability of survival for these species also responded to vegetation control, showing marked increases when seedlings were established in plots free of competing weeds. In contrast, the probability of survival for green ash seedlings showed little variation throughout the range of initial root-collar diameter. This species maintained a consistently high capacity for survival, even when planted with competing vegetation. These results suggest that seedling survival on afforestation sites in the LMAV could be improved through implementation of species-specific quality standards for planting stock. Morphological variables, such as root-collar diameter, can provide practical indices of potential survival for some bottomland hardwood species. Additionally, consideration of how the plantation will be managed, such as accounting for future vegetation control practices, during plantation establishment could lead to more informed decisions regarding seedling quality. The assessment of this seedling quality research will continue into the future, with more in-depth analyses of the relationships between seedling morphology and outplanting performance to support development of practical indices of bottomland hardwood seedling quality for afforestation sites on former agricultural fields in the LMAV.

References

Allen JA. 1997. Reforestation of bottomland hardwoods and the issue of woody species diversity. Restoration Ecology 5:125-134.

Corbin ME, Gardiner ES, Jacobs DF. 2004. Initial effects of complete weed control on survival and growth of two bottomland hardwood species established on former agricultural fields. Proceedings of the Southern Weed Science Society 57:192-197.

Davis AS, Jacobs DF. 2005. Quantifying root system quality of nursery seedlings and relationship to outplanting performance. New Forests 30:295-311.

Dey DC, Parker WC. 1997. Morphological indicators of stock quality and field performance of red oak (Quercus rubra L.) seedlings underplanted in a central Ontario shelterwood. New Forests 14:145-156.

Ezell AW, Catchot AL Jr. 1997. Competition control for hardwood plantation establishment. In: Waldrop TA, editor. Proceedings of the ninth biennial southern silvicultural research conference. Asheville (NC): USDA Forest Service, Southern Research Station. General Technical Report SRS-20. p 42-43.

Ezell AW, Hodges JD. 2002. The importance of competition control for restoration of oaks in the southern United States. In: Frochot H, Collet C, Ballandier P, compilers. Popular summaries from the fourth international conference on forest vegetation management. Champenoux (France): Institut National de la Recherche Agronomique.

Gardiner ES, Russell DR, Oliver M, Dorris LC Jr. 2002. Bottomland hardwood afforestation: state of the art. In: Holland MM, Warren ML, Stanturf JA, editors. Proceedings of a conference on sustainability of wetlands and water resources: how well can riverine wetlands continue to support society into the 21st century? Asheville (NC): USDA Forest Service, Southern Research Station. General Technical Report SRS-50. p 75-86.

Gardiner ES, Salifu KF, Jacobs DF, Hernandez G, Overton RP. 2007. Field performance of Nuttall oak on former agricultural fields: initial effects of nursery source and competition control. In: Riley LE, Dumroese RK, Landis TD, technical coordinators. National proceedings, forest and conservation nursery associations—2006. Ogden (UT): USDA Forest Service, Rocky Mountain Forest and Range Experiment Station. Proceedings RMRS-P-50. p 120-125.

Groninger JW, Babassana DA. 2002. Accelerating planted green ash establishment on an abandoned soybean field. In: Outcalt KW, editor. Proceedings of the eleventh biennial southern silvicultural research conference. Asheville (NC): USDA Forest Service, Southern Research Station. General Technical Report SRS-48. p 270-272.

Groninger JW, Baer SG, Babassana DA, Allen DH. 2004. Planted green ash (Fraxinus pennsylvanica Marsh.) and herbaceous vegetation responses to initial competition control during the first 3 years of afforestation. Forest Ecology and Management 189:161-170.

Jacobs DF, Gardiner ES, Salifu KF, Overton RP, Hernandez G, Corbin ME, Wightman KE, Selig MF. 2005a. Seedling quality standards for bottomland hardwood afforestation in the Lower Mississippi River Alluvial Valley: preliminary results. In: Dumroese RK, Riley LE, Landis TD, technical coordinators. National proceedings, forest and conservation nursery associations—2004. Ogden (UT): USDA Forest Service, Rocky Mountain Forest and Range Experiment Station. Proceedings RMRS-P-35. p 9-16.

Jacobs DF, Salifu KF, Seifert JR. 2005b. Relative contribution of initial root and shoot morphology in predicting field performance of hardwood seedlings. New Forests 30:235-251.

Kennedy HE Jr. 1972. Horizontal planting of green ash cuttings looks promising. New Orleans (LA): USDA Forest Service, Southern Forest Experiment Station. Research Note SO-147. 4 p.

Kennedy HE Jr. 1990. Hardwood reforestation in the South: landowners can benefit from Conservation Reserve Program incentives. New Orleans (LA): USDA Forest Service, Southern Forest Experiment Station. Research Note SO-364. 6 p.

Krinard RM, Kennedy HE Jr. 1987. Planted hardwood development on clay soil without weed control through 16 years. New Orleans (LA): USDA Forest Service, Southern Forest Experiment Station. Research Note SO-343. 4 p.

Michalek AJ, Lockhart BR, Dean TJ, Keeland BD, McCoy JW. 2002. Hand planting versus machine planting of bottomland red oaks on former agricultural fields in Louisiana's Mississippi Alluvial Plain: sixth-year results. In: Outcalt KW, editor. Proceedings of the eleventh biennial southern silvicultural research conference. Asheville (NC): USDA Forest Service, Southern Research Station. General Technical Report SRS-48. p 352-357.

Ozalp M, Schoenholtz SH, Hodges JD, Miwa M. 1997. Influence of soil series and planting methods on fifth-year survival and growth of bottomland oak re-establishment in a farmed wetland. In: Waldrop TA, editor. Proceedings of the ninth biennial southern silvicultural research conference. Asheville (NC): USDA Forest Service, Southern Research Station. General Technical Report SRS-20. p 277-280.

Patterson WB, Adams JC. 2003. Soil, hydroperiod and bedding effects on restoring bottomland hardwoods on flood-prone agricultural lands in North Louisiana, USA. Forestry 76:181-188.

Schoenholtz SH, James JP, Kaminski RM, Leopold BD, Ezell AW. 2001. Afforestation of bottomland hardwoods in the Lower Mississippi Alluvial Valley: status and trends. Wetlands 21:602-613.

Spetich MA, Dey DC, Johnson PS, Graney DL. 2002. Competitive capacity of Quercus rubra L. planted in Arkansas' Boston Mountains. Forest Science 48:504-517.

Stanturf JA, Schweitzer CJ, Gardiner ES. 1998. Afforestation of marginal agricultural land in the Lower Mississippi River Alluvial Valley, U.S A. Silva Fennica 32:281-297.

Stanturf JA, Schoenholtz SH, Schweitzer CJ, Shepard JP. 2001. Achieving restoration success: myths in bottomland hardwood forests. Restoration Ecology 9:189-200.

Wilson BC, Jacobs DF. 2006. Quality assessment of temperate zone deciduous hardwood seedlings. New Forests 31:417-433.

From Lifting to Planting: Root Dip Treatments Affect Survival of Loblolly Pine (*Pinus taeda*)

Tom E. Starkey and David B. South

Tom E. Starkey is Research Fellow, Southern Forest Nursery Cooperative, School of Forestry and Wildlife Sciences, Auburn University, 602 Duncan Drive, Auburn, AL 36849; Tel: 334.844.8069; E-mail: starkte@auburn.edu. **David B. South** is Professor, School of Forestry and Wildlife Sciences, Auburn University, 602 Duncan Drive, Auburn, AL 36849; E-mail: southdb@auburn.edu.

Starkey, T.E.; South, D.B. 2009. From lifting to planting: Root dip treatments affect survival of loblolly pine (*Pinus taeda*). In: Dumroese, R.K.; Riley, L.E., tech. coords. 2009. National Proceedings: Forest and Conservation Nursery Associations—2008. Proc. RMRS-P-00. Fort Collins, CO: U.S. Department of Agriculture, Forest Service, Rocky Mountain Research Station: 90–94. Online: http://www.fs.fed.us/rm/pubs/rmrs_p000.html.

Abstract: Hydrogels and clay slurries are the materials most commonly applied to roots of pines in the southern United States. Most nursery managers believe such applications offer a form of "insurance" against excessive exposure during planting. The objective of this study was to examine the ability of root dip treatments to: (1) support fungal growth; and (2) protect roots from injury during exposure for 1, 2, or 4 hours. Four treatments were tested: kaolin clay, two grades of polyacrylamide hydrogels, and a cornstarch-based hydrogel. In laboratory tests, kaolin clay was the only treatment that inhibited the growth of three soilborne fungi (*Pythium* spp., *Fusarium* spp., *Rhizoctonia* spp.). When applied to roots, however, the clay slurry did not effectively prevent permanent root damage during exposure of more than 1 hour. Gel treatment provided some protection when roots were exposed to air for 2 or 4 hours. Current use of root gels is still good "insurance" against poor handling of the seedlings after they leave the nursery.

Keywords: hydrogel, clay, polyacrylamide, cornstarch, seedlings, dessication

Introduction

During the 19th century, roots were often kept moist at the nursery during counting and sorting to improve the chance of seedling survival (Hodges 1883). The practice of "puddling" has been used for more than a century; this involved dipping roots into a mixture of clay and water (the consistency of paint) either at the nursery (Goff 1897) or at the planting site (Hodges 1883; Pinchot 1907).

Several materials have been added to roots before packing seedlings. Sphagnum moss was preferred during the 19th and first half of the 20th century; as moss became harder to acquire, alternative treatments were investigated (Davey 1964; Fisher 1974). Slocum and Maki (1956, 1959) reported benefits of treating roots with clay when seedlings were exposed to an hour or two of drying. In 1960, Weyerhaeuser asked that their seedlings be treated with clay at the nursery (Bland 1964), and this practice was quickly adopted by the North Carolina Forest Service Nursery (Goldsboro). Soon after, other researchers began to report on tests using clay slurries (Dierauf and Marler 1967, 1971), and the practice spread.

During the 1980s, nursery managers began operational use of polyacrylamide gels. In some cases, use of gels increased survival compared with roots treated with a clay dip (Venator and Brissette 1983). Polyacrylamide gels are likely preferred over clay because they usually cost less, require less storage space, and are less messy (Bland 1964). A nursery that produces 25 million seedlings may only need a pallet of product, while clay might require the delivery of 23 tonnes (25 tons) (Pryor 1988). Most managers agree with Alm and Stanton (1993), who believe that polymer gels "offer a form of insurance against survival loss resulting from seedlings being exposed to drying during the planting process."

Despite this "insurance" aspect, no economic studies support the use of either gels or clays in the production of loblolly pine (*Pinus taeda* L.). Therefore, these trials were initiated to examine the effects of three root dip treatments on their ability to: (1) support fungal growth; and (2) protect roots from injury during exposure.

From Lifting to Planting: Root Dip Treatments Affect Survival of Loblolly Pine . . .

Starkey and South

Materials and Methods _____

Study I: Fungal Growth

This study was designed to address concerns that root treatments may support the growth of soil-borne fungi. In some cases this might be detrimental to seedling survival. Treatments included: kaolin clay; two grades of polyacrylamide hydrogels (PAM gels "A" and "B"[Soil Moist®, JRM Chemicals, Cleveland, OH]); and a cornstarch-based hydrogel, CSB gel (Zeba®, Absorbent Technologies, Beaverton, OR). Samples of the kaolin clay and PAM gels were obtained from the nursery, while the CSB gel was provided by the manufacturer. A comparison of particle size for the root dip treatments is provided in figure 1. The rate of material used for each treatment is provided in table 1 and is comparable to nursery use. Companies offer different gel formulations based on particle size (Venator and Brissette 1983). Particle size can affect physical properties such as water-holding capacity and ability to go into suspension. The fungi used were pathogenic isolates of *Pythium* spp., *Fusarium* spp., and *Rhizoctonia* spp.

Water agar is a basic medium made with distilled water that supports minimal fungal growth. A 3-mm (0.12-in) plug of the fungus was placed on the center of a water-agar Petri plate (85 mm diameter [3.3-in]) that had been augmented with either clay, PAM gel "A" or "B," or CSB gel as provided in table 1. Control plates were water agar without any gel or clay amendments. Each treatment was replicated 12 times. The radial growth of each fungus was recorded daily. Differences in fungal growth on the various amended media demonstrate the ability of the gel or clay to support fungal growth relative to that of non-amended media.

Study II: Seedling Survival Following Exposure

Each treatment was mixed in a separate bucket with 7.5 L (2 gal) of tap water at the rates indicated in table 1. The clay had to be stirred continuously during treatment because it doesn't dissolve. Both PAM gels went into suspension with less than 1 minute of stirring; gel "A" went into suspension faster than gel "B." The CSB gel, however, was very difficult to mix. When it was placed in the water, it immediately clumped and required considerable stirring and agitation to break up the clumps. Once this was done, it was similar in appearance to the PAM gels.

The amount of gel sprayed operationally on roots of machine-lifted loblolly pine seedlings is approximately 3.6 g (0.13 oz) per seedling. Dipping roots of 20 seedlings 5 times removed about 72 g (2.5 oz) of gel solution, or about 3.6 g (0.13 oz) of gel per seedling. All root gel or clay treatments were hand-dipped five times before exposure.

Seedlings were treated with one of four root treatments (table 1), while the roots of control seedlings were dipped into water. The seedlings (20 per experimental unit) were laid on an expanded metal bench in the greenhouse for 0, 1, 2, or 4

Table 1. Rate of material used expressed as total mass of material per liter (L) of water (1L = 0.26 gal).

	Clay	PAM gel "A"	PAM gel "B"	CSB gel
Mass (g)	300	2.2	3.3	1.8
Mass (oz)	10.582	0.077	0.116	0.063

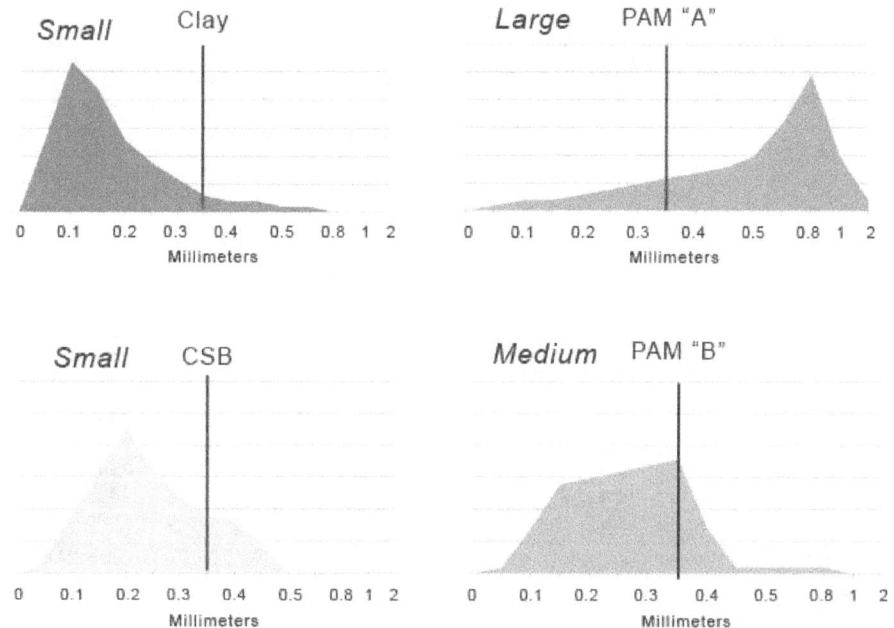

Figure 1. Comparison of particle size of root dip treatments. The Y-axis in each graph is a measure of relative proportion. The vertical black line at 0.35 mm is for comparative purposes.

Starkey and South

From Lifting to Planting: Root Dip Treatments Affect Survival of Loblolly Pine . . .

hours. Greenhouse temperatures during exposure ranged from 28 to 37 °C (82 to 99 °F); relative humidity ranged from 16% to 38%. The average solar radiation measured within the greenhouse was 22,700 lumen/m² (2,100 lux).

After exposure, seedlings were planted in the Southern Forest Nursery Cooperative's seedling testing facility. This facility consists of six pits (23 m [75 ft] by 23 m [75 ft] by 1 m [3 ft]) containing 100% sand. Twenty treatments (5 root by 4 exposure treatments) were replicated 12 times in a randomized complete block design with five seedlings per experimental unit. The sand in the pits was irrigated for 4 hours before planting. In order to obtain a separation among treatments, irrigation was withheld after transplanting. Rainfall for the test period from 7 February to 7 May 2007 totaled 15.9 cm (6.3 in): 5.0 (2 in), 7.1 (2.8 in), 3.8 (1.5 in), and 0.0 cm (0 in) for February, March, April, and May, respectively. At the end of the study period (7 May 2007), seedling survival was recorded.

Study III: Root Growth Potential

Root growth potential (RGP) is a measure of the ability of the seedling to initiate and elongate roots when placed in an environment favorable for root growth. The gel and clay treatments for this study were the same as above (table 1). After root treatments had been applied, the seedlings were exposed for 1, 2, or 4 hours. Greenhouse environmental conditions were similar to those in the previous study.

The trial used two seedlings per experimental unit, with 18 replications (a total of 36 seedlings per treatment-exposure); 15 experimental units were contained in one aquarium (5 treatments by 3 exposure times). Seedling roots were suspended in aerated water, and the water level in each aquarium was adjusted daily. After 4 weeks, the numbers of new white root tips greater than 0.5 cm (0.2 in) on each seedling were counted.

Data from each study were analyzed by analysis of variance (ANOVA) for a randomized complete block design. When the F-test for treatment was significant ($\alpha = 0.05$), treatment means were separated using Duncan's New Multiple Range Test. SPSS® software (SPSS Incorporated, Chicago, IL) was used for all data analysis.

Results

Study I: Fungal Growth

Particle size varied considerably among the gel treatments. PAM gel "A" had a greater percentage of large particles; the CSB gel had a greater percentage of fine material (fig. 1). The water-agar control was the baseline for each fungus tested. Therefore, any growth less than that observed in control plates indicated an inhibitory effect on the fungus (table 2), whereas more growth than in the controls indicated that the fungus was able to use the amendment as a food source. *Rhizoctonia* spp. grew the fastest, with one or more treatments reaching the edge of the petri plate before day 6.

In all cases, clay inhibited fungal growth. All of the gel treatments inhibited growth of *Pythium* spp., but the clay treatment had the greatest effect. More plate-to-plate variation occurred with the *Pythium* spp. than the other fungi. The growth of *Fusarium* spp. on the CSB gel was greater than for the control plates; clay was the only inhibitory treatment. Growth of *Rhizotonia* spp. was increased by all gels.

Study II: Seedling Survival Following Exposure

Treatments significantly affected seedling survival, but no differences were detected among treatments with 0 or 1 hour of exposure (table 3). The root gels increased survival after 2 or 4 hours of exposure. Clay or water dips, however, did not protect the roots exposed to these longer times of desiccation. This is very evident at 4 hours of exposure, where the gel treatments increased survival by 40% or more.

Study III: Root Growth Potential

The RGP study showed similar trends as the survival study. In the water-only treatment, 1 hour of exposure reduced RGP by half, compared with the clay or CSB gel. In both the 2- and 4-hour desiccation treatments, RGP was reduced to fewer than four roots in both the clay and water treatments (table 4). Even when placed in water, the desiccated roots were not able to recover and produce new root

Table 2. Fungal growth (mm) on amended or unamended water agar medium.

Amendment	Pythium (day 6)	Fusarium (day 6)	Rhizoctonia (day 4)
Clay	10d[1]	51c	58c
PAM gel "A"	26c	60b	75a
PAM gel "B"	31c	60b	74a
CSB gel	42b	63a	76a
Control	69a	61b	70b
lsd$_{(0.05)}$	6.5	1.6	2.8

[1]Means in columns followed by he same letter are not significantly different ($\alpha = 0.05$; Duncan's New Multiple Range Test).

Table 3. Loblolly pine survival (percentage) after 3 months, as affected by root dip treatment and length of exposure.

Dip treatment	Length of exposure (hours)			
	0	1	2	4
PAM gel "B"	94.5a[1]	86.8a	87.0b	60.0b
PAM gel "A"	82.6a	88.9a	93.5b	56.1b
CSB gel	79.2a	76.2a	85.9b	52.8b
Clay	91.2a	87.9a	52.9a	12.1a
Water	97.8a	85.7a	77.2ab	12.1a
lsd$_{(0.05)}$	23.8	13.5	30.3	15.0

[1]Means in columns followed by the same letter are not significan ly different (α = 0.05; Duncan's New Mul iple Range Test).

Table 4. Average number of white root tips at 4 weeks in RGP testing, as affected by root dip treatment and length of exposure.

Treatment	Length of exposure (hours)		
	1	2	4
PAM gel "B"	32.1ab[1]	29.3b	19.9a
PAM gel "A"	41.3a	16.8c	22.6a
CBS gel	45.3a	39.3a	14.9a
Clay	43.1a	1.2d	0.0b
Water	22.0b	3.4d	0.0b
lsd$_{(0.05)}$	12.4	8.3	7.9

[1]Means in columns followed by the same letter are not significan ly different (α = 0.05; Duncan's New Mul iple Range Test).

tips. The gels provided some protection during the extended desiccation periods.

Discussion

When seedlings are handled carefully, not exposed to drying conditions, and not stored, outplanting survival can be greater than 80% (Venator and Brissette 1983). Under ideal conditions, roots would never be exposed for 2 to 4 hours of desiccation and would always be planted in moist soil. However, nursery managers typically have no control of seedling care after stock is shipped from the nursery. Every nursery manager has a file full of examples of seedlings transported incorrectly, stored in the sun at the planting site, and handled incorrectly by the planting crew.

Many studies have exposed roots after treatment with clay or gels (Slocum and Maki 1956; Williston 1967; Miller and Reines 1974; Dierauf and Gardner 1975; Alm and Stanton 1993). In this study, we decided to subject treated seedlings to various times of desiccation and then transplant them into moist sand to allow seedlings to become established.

Results from the survival and RGP studies agreed, but the RGP test detected treatment differences after just 1 hour of desiccation. Ritchie (1985) proposes that root growth potential is a good indicator of the ability of seedlings to become establish when outplanted, assuming adequate moisture and nutrients. Our data agree with those of others who found that gels provided an increase in survival (Echols and others 1990; Alm and Stanton 1993). Although clay was not effective in preventing permanent root damage to the seedlings in our study, clay did improve seedling survival in a previous study (Slocum and Maki 1959).

A concern during the 1980s was that fermentation of wood fiber mulches or starch gels would result in deterioration of seedlings stored in the shade (Barnard and others 1981). People thought that the wood fibers (or starch) were providing a substrate for pathogenic microbes. Therefore, some nursery managers have expressed a concern that root gels, especially the starch-based gels, could support the growth of soil-borne fungi. In order for disease to develop, three factors must occur. First, the environment must be conducive to disease development (generally optimal moisture and temperature). Second, the host must be susceptible. In some cases, the host may be too old to be susceptible. Third, you must have a virulent pathogen.

Of the four root dips tested, kaolin clay was the only treatment that did not support, and in fact inhibited, the growth of the three soil-borne fungi tested. The other root dips tested stimulated fungal growth, especially of *Fusarium* spp. and *Rhizoctonia* spp. Because these are common nursery fungi, they could utilize the polyacrylamide hydrogels or the cornstarch-based hydrogel as a food source. Thus, the gels might have negative ramifications during seedling storage, especially the CSB gel in the presence of *Fusarium* spp.

Management Implications and Conclusions

When freshly lifted seedlings were exposed for 1 hour, some protection (as measured by RGP) was provided by the kaolin clay and the PAM gel root dip treatments. When seedlings were exposed for 2 hours or more, only the gel root dip treatments increased seedling survival and RGP. Thus, continued use of gel root dip treatments by nursery managers as "insurance" against poor handling after seedlings leave the nursery is worth the cost of the materials. Kaolin clay inhibited all three soil-borne fungi, whereas gel-based root dips increased growth of *Rhizoctonia* spp. In all cases, treating loblolly pine roots with root gels kept short roots alive so they could elongate when placed into a favorable environment. The current view by nursery managers that root gels provide "insurance" against poor handling after leaving the nursery is valid.

Results from these studies are applicable only when seedlings are transplanted within a few days of treatment. Additional research is required to determine if gels affect fungal growth during long-term, cool storage (for example, 1 to 2 °C [34 to 36 °F]) of seedlings.

Acknowledgments

This research was funded by the USDA Forest Service State and Private Forestry under terms of the Forest and Rangeland Renewable Resources Research Act of 1978.

References

Alm A, Stanton J. 1993. Polymer root dip increases survival of stressed bareroot seedlings. Northern Journal of Applied Forestry 10(2):90-92.

Barnard EL, Rowan SJ, Lantz CW. 1981. Wood fiber mulch and gelatinized starch should be carefully evaluated as seedling packing media. In: Lantz CW, technical coordinator. Southern pine

Starkey and South

From Lifting to Planting: Root Dip Treatments Affect Survival of Loblolly Pine . . .

nursery handbook. Atlanta (GA): USDA Forest Service, State and Private Forestry. p 10.13-10.17.

Bland WA. 1964. New packaging method for forest tree planting stock—North Carolina's "mudding." In: Hitt RG, technical coordinator. Proceedings, Region 8 Forest Nurserymen's Conference; 1964 August 19-20; Morganton, NC. Atlanta (GA): USDA Forest Service, State and Private Forestry. p 50-52.

Davey CB. 1964. Current studies on clay slurry root dips. In: Hitt RG, technical coordinator. Proceedings, Region 8 Forest Nurserymen's Conference; 1964 August 19-20; Morganton, NC. Atlanta (GA): USDA Forest Service, State and Private Forestry. p 53-59.

Dierauf TA, Garner JW. 1975. A test of Agricol as a root dip. Charlottesville (VA): Virginia Division of Forestry. Occasional Report 47. 5 p.

Dierauf TA, Marler RL. 1967. Clay dipped vs. bare rooted seedling survival. Charlottesville (VA): Virginia Division of Forestry. Occasional Report 27. 5 p.

Dierauf TA, Marler RL. 1971. Effect of exposure, clay treatment, and storage on survival and growth of loblolly pine seedlings. Charlottesville (VA): Virginia Division of Forestry. Occasional Report 34. 10 p.

Echols RJ, Meier CE, Ezell AW, McKinley CR. 1990. Dry site survival of bareroot and container seedlings of southern pines from different genetic sources given root dip and ectomycorrhizal treatments. Tree Planters' Notes 41(2):13-32.

Fisher D. 1974. Packing material for seedlings—are there suitable alternatives to moss? In: McConnell JL, technical coordinator. Southeastern nurserymen's conference; 1964 August 6-8; Gainesville, FL. Atlanta (GA): USDA Forest Service, State and Private Forestry. p 135-137.

Goff ES. 1897. Principles of plant culture. Madison (WI): Published by author. 276 p.

Hodges LB. 1883. The forest tree planters' manual. 3rd ed. St Paul (MN): HM Smyth Printing Co. 116 p.

Miller AE, Reines M. 1974. Survival and water relations in loblolly pine seedlings after root immersion in alginate solution. Forest Science 20(2):192-194.

Pinchot G. 1907. How to pack and ship young forest trees. Washington (DC): USDA Forest Service. Circular 55. 2 p.

Pryor WL. 1988. Kaolin clay dipping at Union Camp's Bellville Forest Tree Nursery. In: Hagwood R, chairman. Southern Forest Nursery Association; 1988 July 25-28; Charleston, SC. Atlanta (GA): USDA Forest Service, State and Private Forestry. p 19-24.

Ritchie GA. 1985. Root growth potential: principles, procedures and predictive ability. In: Duryea ML, editor. Proceedings, evaluating seedling quality: principles, procedures, and predictive ability of major tests; 1984 October 16-18; Corvallis, OR. Corvallis (OR): Oregon State University, Forest Research Laboratory. p 93-106.

Slocum GK, Maki TE. 1956. Exposure of loblolly pine planting stock. Journal of Forestry 54(5):313-315.

Slocum GK, Maki TE. 1959. Exposure of longleaf pine planting stock. Journal of Forestry 57(11):825-827.

Venator CR, Brissette JC. 1983. The effectiveness of superabsorbent materials for maintaining southern pine seedlings during cold storage. In: Brissette J, Lantz C, compilers. Proceedings, southern nursery conferences; 1982 July 12-15; Savannah, GA. Atlanta (GA): USDA Forest Service, State and Private Forestry. Technical Publication R8-TP4. p 240-245.

Williston HL. 1967. Clay slurry root dip impairs survival of loblolly pine seedlings in Mississippi. Tree Planters' Notes 18(4):28-30.

Stunt Nematode (*Tylenchorhynchus claytoni*) Impact on Southern Pine Seedlings and Response to a Field Test of Cover Crops

Michelle M. Cram and Stephen W. Fraedrich

Michelle M. Cram is a Plant Pathologist, Forest Health Protection, USDA Forest Service, 320 Green Street, Athens, GA 30602-2044; Tel: 706.559.4233; E-mail: mcram@fs.fed.us. **Stephen W. Fraedrich** is a Research Plant Pathologist, Southern Research Station, USDA Forest Service, Athens, GA 30602-2044; E-mail: sfraedrich@fs.fed.us.

Cram, M.M.; Fraedrich, S.W. 2009. Stunt nematode (*Tylenchorhynchus claytoni*) impact on southern pine seedlings and response to a field test of cover crops. In: Dumroese, R.K.; Riley, L.E., tech. coords. 2009. National Proceedings: Forest and Conservation Nursery Associations—2008. Proc. RMRS-P-58. Fort Collins, CO: U.S. Department of Agriculture, Forest Service, Rocky Mountain Research Station: 95–100. Online: http://www.fs.fed.us/rm/pubs/rmrs_p058.html.

Abstract: The stunt nematode, *Tylenchorhynchus claytoni*, was found to cause a reduction in root volume (cm^3) of loblolly pine at population densities equivalent of 125 nematodes/100 cm^3 (6 in^3) soil and greater. The results of a host range test conducted in containers under controlled conditions determined that buckwheat cultivar (*Fagopryum esculentum* 'Mancan'), velvetbean (*Mucuna pruriens*), Kobe lespedeza (*Lespedeza striata* 'Kobe'), bicolor lespedeza (*Lespedeza bicolor*), and purple nutsedge (*Cyperus rotundus*) are suitable hosts for the stunt nematode. Previous container studies concluded that pearl millet (*Pennisetum glaucum*) hybrid 'ET-300' was a nonhost for the stunt nematode. A 2-year field test of sorghum-sudangrass hybrid 'Sugar Graze,' pearl millet hybrid 'Tifleaf 3,' and fallow found that the use of pearl millet as a cover crop greatly restricts population development of the stunt nematode in infested fields, and its use would be a good alternative to fallow.

Keywords: nematode, stunt, stubby-root, *Tylenchorhynchus claytoni*, *Paratrichodorus minor*, *Pinus taeda*, pine, cover crops, sorghum-sudangrass, pearl millet, fallow, *Fagopyrum esculentum*, *Mucuna pruriens*, *Lespedeza striata*, *Lespedeza bicolor*, *Cyperus rotundus*

Introduction

Loblolly (*Pinus taeda*) and slash pine (*P. elliottii*) are known hosts for the stunt nematode, *Tylenchorhynchus claytoni* (Ruehle 1966), and stunting of loblolly pine seedlings has been associated with high population densities of this nematode (Hopper 1958; Ruehle 1969). However, the only southern pine species that has been shown to be stunted by this nematode is longleaf pine (*P. palustris*) (Ruehle 1973). The population densities at which *T. claytoni* can damage loblolly and slash pine seedlings remains a basic gap in our understanding of this nematode and the impact it has on pine seedling production.

Cover crops are alternated with tree seedlings in southern forest tree nurseries for maintaining organic matter and soil stabilization, as well as other benefits (Boyer and South 1984). In the southern United States, sorghum-sudangrass, corn, rye, and oats have been common cover crops in forest nurseries (Boyer and South 1984). Unfortunately, these cover crops are hosts for the stunt nematode *T. claytoni* (Cram and Fraedrich 2007). Based on host range tests conducted under controlled conditions, hybrid pearl millet (*Pennisetum glaucum*) 'ET-300' cultivar from the East Texas Seed Company (Tyler, TX) appeared to be a nonhost for *T. claytoni* (Cram and Fraedrich 2007). The search for other nonhosts and the testing of common cover crops used by southern nursery managers, as well as a noxious weed (purple nutsedge [*Cyperus rotundus*]), is continued in this paper. The growth chamber tests provide a practical way of screening species for host status, but field testing is necessary to determine crop performance and nematode population changes over time under field conditions.

Materials and Methods

Pathogenicity

The effect of *T. claytoni* population density on loblolly and slash pine seedlings was evaluated in a growth chamber experiment. Containers were filled with approximately 400 cm^3 (24 in^3) of a loamy sand soil that was microwaved in 2,000-g

(70.5-oz) batches for 8 minutes. Containers were planted with five germinating loblolly pine seeds. Nematodes were reared on roots of loblolly pine seedlings and subsequently extracted with Baermann funnels (Shurtleff and Averre 2000). Nematodes were added to containers at rates of 0, 500, 1,000, 2,000, and 4,000 individuals/container, and there were four replications of each nematode dose. Containers were placed in growth chambers at 25 °C (77 °F) with a 14-hour photoperiod and watered every 1 to 3 days, as needed. After 10 weeks, plants were removed from the containers and placed in tap water for 15 to 30 minutes to remove soil and nematodes from plant roots. These nematodes were washed back into the soil sample using a 325-mesh screen, and soil samples were mixed thoroughly. Roots were placed in plastic bags and stored at 6 °C (43 °F). Root volume (cm^3) was calculated by WinRHIZO Version 2003b scanning system (Regent Instruments, Quebec, Canada). Nematodes were extracted from 100 cm^3 (6 in^3) of soil using the centrifugal-flotation method (Shurtleff and Averre 2000). The relationship between the initial *T. claytoni* dose and root volumes were determined by regression analysis using a nonlinear, negative exponential model. The analysis was conducted using the regression analysis package of SigmaPlot®, Version 8.0 (SYSTAT, San Jose, CA). The criteria for fit of the model were based on the mean square error (MSE), r-square values, and the significance of the overall regression.

Host Suitability

Host suitability was evaluated for loblolly pine, buckwheat (*Fagopryum esculentum* 'Mancan'), velvetbean (*Mucuna pruriens*), Kobe lespedeza (*Lespedeza striata* 'Kobe'), bicolor lespedeza (*Lespedeza bicolor*), and purple nutsedge (*Cyperus rotundus*). A fallow treatment was also included. Soil was treated as previously described and each container held about 1,600 cm^3 (98 in^3) of the loamy sand soil. In each experiment, four containers for each plant species were sown. Stunt nematodes were produced as previously described, extracted with Baermann funnels, and 500 nematodes were added to each container. Containers were placed in a growth chamber at 25 °C (77 °F) with a 14-hour photoperiod for 12 weeks. Plants were removed from the containers and placed in water for 15 to 30 minutes to separate the soil and nematodes from the roots. Nematodes were extracted from the water using a 325-mesh screen, washed back into the soil sample, and soil samples were thoroughly mixed. Nematodes were extracted from 100 cm^3 (6 in^3) of soil using the centrifugal-flotation method (Shurtleff and Averre 2000). Statistical comparisons were conducted among treatments on the final population densities of nematodes by an ANOVA and Tukey's HSD test. Data were transformed with the log10$^{(x+1)}$ transformations prior to analysis, but only non-transformed values are presented in tables.

Field Cover Crop Trial

The site selected for a field trial was surveyed in 2005 and found to be infested with the stunt nematode *T. claytoni* (Cram and Fraedrich 2007). The soil type of the field was a sandy loam soil in the Wagram Sand soil series. The field had been fumigated in the fall of 2004 with methyl bromide (67%) and chloropicrin (33%), then sown with loblolly pine seeds in 2005. In spring 2006, a test was established of sorghum-sudangrass hybrid 'Sugar Graze,' pearl millet hybrid 'Tifleaf 3,' and fallow treatments. Each treatment had five blocks. 'Tifleaf 3' was selected because this cultivar was readily available to the nursery, and the nursery was switching from sorghum-sudangrass to the pearl millet and was using this cultivar operationally. A previous test found this cultivar was not a host of the stubby-root nematode *Paratrichodorus minor*, and we hypothesized that 'Tifleaf 3' would also prove to be a nonhost for the stunt nematode *T. claytoni*.

The checkerboard pattern of plots was created by dividing the field into three 3-m (10-ft) widths by ten 15.3-m (50-ft) lengths and leaving sections between the treatment plots as fallow buffers (fig. 1). Sorghum-sudangrass and pearl millet were sown on 25 April 2006 and again on 4 May 2007. The sowing rate was 33.6 kg/ha (30 lb/ac) for sorghum-sudangrass and 16.8 kg/ha (15 lb/ac) for pearl millet. The study area was watered with approximately 2.5 cm (1 in) of water per week for 12 weeks. One application of granular ammonium nitrate at a rate of 57.2 kg/ha (51 lb/ac) of N was applied after 6 weeks. Fomesafen sodium (Reflex®) and lactofen (Cobra®) were each applied at 2.3 L/ha (1 qt/ac) in fallow areas at sowing. Glyphosate (Gly-4 Plus) was added as a 5% solution as needed during the growing season.

Soil samples were obtained in April (prior to sowing), May, June, September, and November each year. The soil was systematically sampled from the center of each treatment

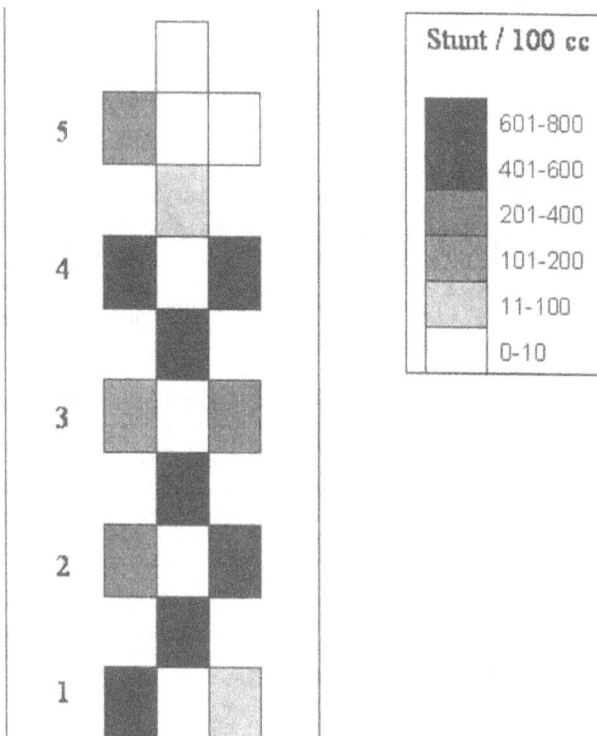

Figure 1. Field diagram of stunt nematode populations by plot in April 2006.

plot and consisted of six cores taken to a 15 cm (6 in) depth. Soil samples from each plot were composited and nematodes were extracted from a 100 cm³ (6 in³) subsample using the centrifugal-flotation method (Shurtleff and Averre 2000). The percentage of organic matter for soil samples collected in April 2007 and 2008 was determined using the Dumas combustion elemental analysis at the University of Georgia Institute of Ecology, Soil Biology Laboratory (Athens, GA).

Statistical comparisons were conducted on the nematode population densities between cover crop treatments by an ANOVA using the PROC GLM procedure of SAS® software (SAS Institute Incorporated, Cary, NC), and mean separation was performed by Tukey's HSD test. Prior to analysis, block 5 was removed due to low initial nematode population. Data were transformed with the square root (x + ½) transformations prior to analysis, but only nontransformed values are presented in graphs.

Results

Loblolly and slash pine root volume decreased with respect to the initial populations of the stunt nematode *T. claytoni* (fig. 2). The relative fit of the negative exponential model, based on the R^2 values and MSEs, was slightly better for loblolly pine (MSE = 0.0027; R^2 = 0.92) than slash pine (MSE = 0.0073; R^2 = 0.82). Initial population densities as low as 500 nematodes per 400 cm³ (25 in³) soil (125/100 cm³ [6 in³]) reduced the root volume of both pine species. The level of damage was similar for all doses of the stunt nematode.

Host Range Tests

All crops and purple nutsedge were hosts for the stunt nematode *T. claytoni* (table 1). Only the fallow treatment had a lower population of stunt nematodes than the original inoculum of 500 nematodes. In all crop and weed treatments,

Table 1. Population densities of stunt nematodes in containers with various crop and weed species 12 weeks after infestation with 500 stunt nematodes/container (1600 cm³ [98 in³] soil).

Plant species	Stunt nematodes per 100 cm³ (6 in³) soil[a]		Stunt nematodes per container[+]	
Buckwheat 'Mancan'	798	a	12760	a
Velvetbean	615	a	9840	a
Loblolly pine	318	a	5080	a
Kobe lespedeza	243	a	3880	a
Bicolor lespedeza	159	a	2540	a
Purple nutsedge	135	a	2160	a
Fallow	5	b	80	b

[a]Non-tranformed means followed by the same letter do not differ significantly (α = 0.05) according to Tukey's HSD test. Logarithmic transformation of nematode counts performed before analysis.

the number of nematodes increased. No significant differences in stunt nematode population densities were observed among hosts.

Field Test

The stunt nematode *T. claytoni* was the predominant nematode species isolated from treatment plots in the field study. Some plots also had stubby-root nematodes, *Paratrichodorus minor*, at less than 10 individuals/100 cm³ (6 in³), and predacious nematodes (*Mylonchulus* spp., *Mononchus* spp.) at less than 15 individuals/100 cm³ (6 in³) soil. One other plant parasitic nematode, *Paratrichodorus porosus*, was found during the second year of the field test in the sorghum-sudangrass treatments only. Population densities of *P. porosus* were usually less than 50 nematodes/100 cm³ (6 in³) soil.

The population densities of the stunt nematode within plots at the time of sowing in April 2006 ranged from 0 to 788 individuals/100 cm³ (6 in³) soil. The stunt nematodes were not uniformly distributed among plots, and few to no nematodes were found in some treatment plots of block 5 (fig. 1).

Over a 2-year period, the average population densities of the stunt nematode decreased significantly in the fallow and pearl millet cover crop treatments (fig. 3). The population of stunt nematodes in the fallow treatment fell below 100 individuals/100 cm³ (6 in³) soil by the end of the first year. The number of stunt nematodes within the pearl millet treatment did not fall below 100 individuals/100 cm³ (6 in³) soil until the second year. An examination of the average population densities of the stunt nematode in the sorghum-sudangrass over the 2-year study indicated nematode densities decreased during August and September sampling dates and increased greatly in the winter and spring.

The population densities of the stubby-root nematode *P. minor* were greater in the sorghum-sudangrass and pearl millet plots than in the fallow, although the densities remained under 100 nematodes/100 cm³ (6 in³) soil during the 2 years (fig. 4). Population densities of predacious nematodes remained low (0.5 to 17.5 predators/100 cm³ [6 in³]) throughout the 2-year study and did not appear to be affected by season.

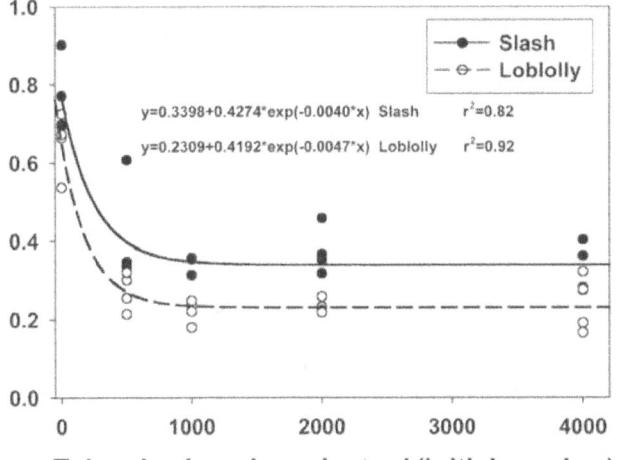

Figure 2. Relationship between initial population of stunt nematode (*T. claytoni*) and root volume (cm³) of seedlings after 10 weeks.

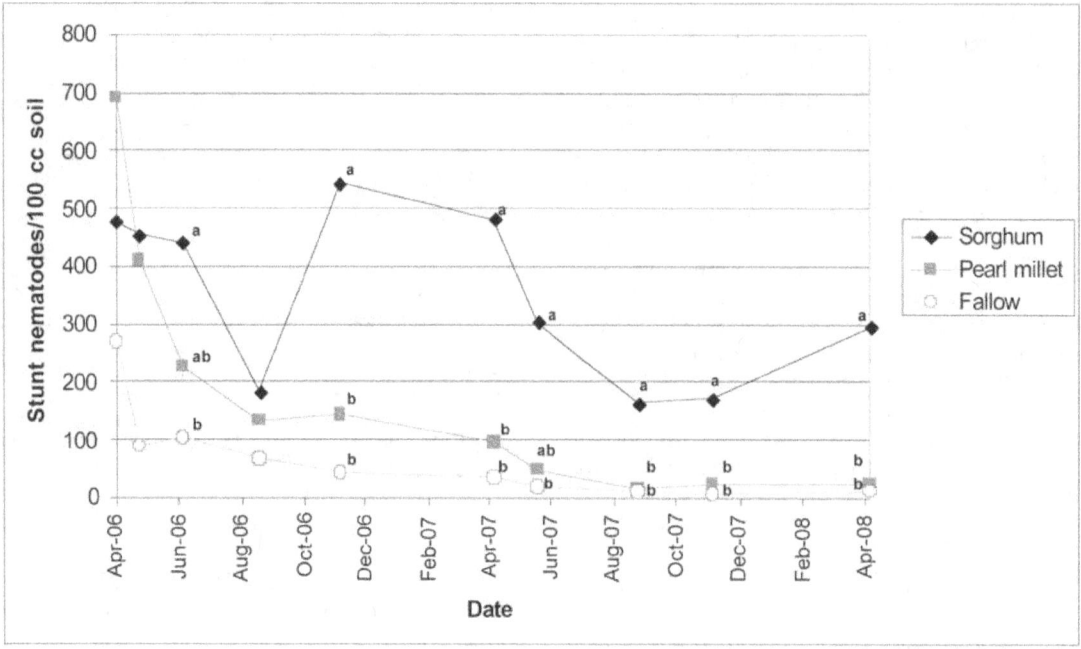

Figure 3. Relationship between stunt nematode (*T. claytoni*) population densities and cover crop treatment over 2 years. Data was transformed by square root of (x + ½); treatments in block 5 were removed from analysis due to low initial nematode population. Data points followed by different letters by date are significantly different using Tukey's HSD test (α = 0.05).

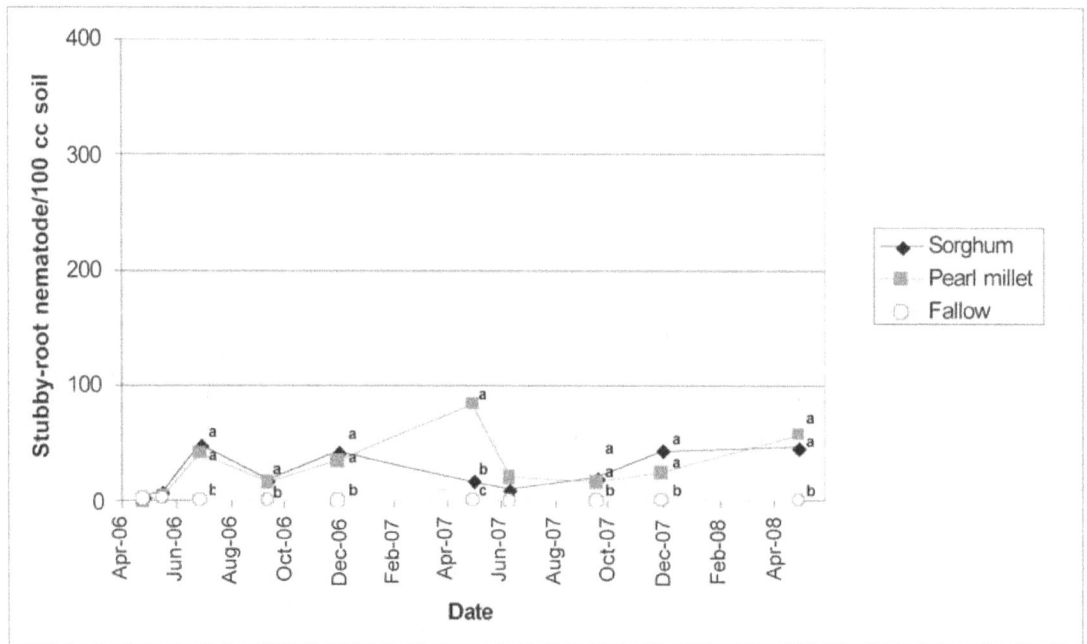

Figure 4. Relationship between stubby-root nematode (*M. minor*) population densities and covercrop treatment over 2 years. Data transformed by square root of (x + ½); treatments in block 5 were removed from analysis due to low initial nematode population. Data points followed by different letters by date are significantly different using Tukey's HSD test (α = 0.05).

Table 2. Percentage of carbon as a measure of organic matter in soil by cover crop after the first and second year of treatment.

Cover crops	April 2007 carbon (%)[a]		April 2008 carbon (%)[a]	
Sorghum-sudangrass	0.79	ab	0.89	a
Pearl millet 'Tifleaf 3'	0.89	a	0.86	a
Fallow	0.57	b	0.51	b

[a]Means within columns followed by the same letter to not differ significantly (α = 0.05) according to Tukey's HSD test.

Soil organic matter was similar for the sorghum-sudangrass and the pearl millet treatments by April of both years (table 2). Pearl millet significantly improved the percentage of organic matter in the soil as compared to the fallow treatment.

Discussion

The results of the dosage response trials indicate that the stunt nematode, *T. claytoni*, can directly cause stunting of loblolly and slash pine root systems when the nematode is present during seed germination and growth of young seedlings. The impact of the stunt nematode on loblolly and slash pine seedlings during the first 10 weeks in this study is similar to what occurs on these pine species in nursery beds (Hopper 1958; Ruehle 1973). The results of our pathogenicity test also suggest that the high densities of the stunt nematodes present in the field study on 25 April 2006 would probably have led to areas of seedling damage and losses had the nursery produced pine seedlings in the field.

Our host range test failed to identify a new nonhost of the stunt nematode, although some of the crops may be less favorable hosts than others. The buckwheat cultivar 'Mancan,' Kobe lespedeza, and bicolor lespedeza have been grown in some southern forest tree nurseries, and are now confirmed hosts for the stunt nematode. Our finding that purple nutsedge is a host for the stunt nematode adds to the list of common weeds that are hosts of *T. claytoni*. Other host weeds include: crabgrass (*Digitaria ischaemum* and *D. sanguinalis*), redwort pigweed (*Amaranthus retroflexus*), witchgrass (*Panicum capillare*), stinkgrass (*Eragrostis cilianensis*), carpet weed (*Molugo verticillata*), and dandelion (*Taraxacum officinale*) (Miller and Ahrens 1969).

The velvetbean species, *M. pruriens*, had shown some promise as a less favored host than sorghum-sudangrass for the stunt nematode in Florida (Crow and others 2001). Extracts from velvetbean stems and roots have also been shown to have nematicidal effects on a root-knot nematode when tested under laboratory conditions (Zasada and others 2006). Our results indicate that this species of velvetbean is a good host for the stunt nematode *T. claytoni*; however, we did not test the potential toxic effects of this species on nematode populations after plant parts are incorporated into the soil. Perhaps more research on velvetbean is warranted before it is entirely ruled out as a control option for fields infested with the stunt nematode.

The hybrid pearl millet, 'Tifleaf 3,' is not a host for the stunt nematode *T. claytoni* and appears to be a good alternative to fallow as a means to decrease nematode populations in fields. These field results mirror the container study with pearl millet 'ET-300' and fallow treatment (Cram and Fraedrich 2007). Other pearl millet cultivars have also been found to be resistant to plant-parasitic nematodes, including *P. minor*, *Meloidogyne* spp., *Belonolaimus longicaudatus*, and *Pratylenchus brachyurus* (Timper and others 2002; Timper and Hanna 2005).

The host test conducted under controlled conditions in a previous paper found that pearl millet 'ET-300' and 'Tiff' (abbreviated for 'Tifleaf 3') were nonhosts for the stubby-root nematode *P. minor*, and that sorghum-sudangrass was a preferred host (Cram and Fraedrich 2007). Our field test results for the stubby-root nematode in this study did not mirror the results of previous container studies. The low levels of stubby-root nematodes in the sorghum-sudangrass plots could be the result of many factors including less favorable environmental conditions and competition by stunt nematodes. In general, the densities of stubby-root nematodes in the field were too low to have expected substantial damage on loblolly or slash pine seedlings (Ruehle 1969).

The predacious nematodes (*Mylonchulus* spp., *Mononchus* spp.) appeared to have no impact on the stunt nematode population, as their densities did not change over time. The low population of predators and lack of effect on other nematodes has been noted in other studies that have monitored these nematodes (Ferris and others 1996; MacGuidwin and Layne 1995). Predacious nematodes are only one component of the organisms that control plant parasitic nematodes, and it is possible that they are neither effective, nor even suited, as predators of the stunt nematode.

The threshold population density of stunt nematodes that young loblolly and slash pine seedlings can tolerate without stunting remains unknown, but seedling size can be significantly reduced at 125 stunt nematodes/100 cm^3 (6 in^3), as indicated by the pathogenicity test. Although population levels of nematodes are lowered significantly by pearl millet in 1 year, it may take 2 years to get population densities sufficiently low that they will not damage pine seedlings. Nurseries that use a 2:1 rotation of seedling production to cover crops may be better off using fallow (or a combination of organic matter treatments and fallow). Unfortunately, stunt nematode populations in the fallow treatments were not reduced to zero in all plots over the 2 years of this study. Managers need to be aware that populations of the stunt nematode *T. claytoni* can explode quickly because its lifecycle is relatively short (31 to 38 days) (Wang 1971), and each female can produce 1 to 15 eggs (Krusberg 1959).

Fields that have stunt nematodes may not be able to have successive pine crops without the use of a fumigant before each crop. Other options depend on nursery land base and access to organic amendments. Managers may consider alternative cropping strategies, such as a 1:1 rotation of pine with fallow (including organic amendments if needed). Crop rotations with hardwoods, pine, and cover crops may also be possible. Associations between the stunt nematode and stunting of hardwood tree seedlings have not been well documented (Ruehle 1968). The only known nonhost hardwood species identified to date is sweetgum (*Liquidambar styraciflua*), while yellow poplar (*Liriodendron tulipifera*) is a very poor host (Ruehle 1971). Hardwoods tolerant to stunt nematodes could be used in a rotation with a pine crop (for example, a pine crop followed by summer fallow with weed control and fall planting of hardwoods). Further investigation into nematode population response to hardwood crops over time may be required before implementing a hardwood/pine/cover crop rotation.

Acknowledgments

We wish to thank the nursery manager who cooperated with us to establish and care for the field study. A special thanks also goes to Susan Best for her assistance in sample processing and data collection, and to Dr. Zafar Handoo for identifying nematodes to species.

References

Boyer JN, South DB. 1984. Forest nursery practices in the South. Southern Journal of Applied Forestry 8(2):67-73.

Cram MM, Fraedrich SW. 2007. Detection and management of stunt and stubby-root nematodes in a southern forest nurseries. In: Riley LE, Dumroese RK, Landis TD, technical coordinators. National Proceedings: forest and conservation nursery associations—2006. Fort Collins (CO): USDA Forest Service, Rocky Mountain Research Station. Proceedings RMRS-P-50. p 91-96.

Crow WT, Weingartner DP, Dickson DW, McSorley R. 2001. Effect of sorghum-sudangrass and velvetbean cover crops on plant-parasitic nematodes associated with potato production in Florida. Journal of Nematology 33(4S):285-288.

Ferris H, Venette RC, Lau SS. 1996. Dynamics of nematode communities in tomatoes grown in conventional and organic farming systems, and their impact on soil fertility. Applied Soil Ecology 18:13-29.

Hopper BE. 1958. Plant-parasitic nematodes in the soils of southern forest nurseries. Plant Disease Reporter 42:308-314.

Krusberg LR. 1959. Investigation on the life cycle, reproduction, feeding habits and host range of *Tylenchorhynchus claytoni* Steiner. Nematologica 4:187-197.

MacGuidwin AE, Layne TL. 1995. Response of nematode communities to sudangrass and sorghum-sudangrass hybrids grown as green manure crops. Journal of Nematology 27(4S):609-616.

Miller PM, Ahrens JF. 1969. Influence of growing marigolds, weeds, two cover crops and fumigation of subsequent populations of parasitic nematodes and plant growth. Plant Disease Report 53:642-646.

Ruehle JL. 1966. Nematodes parasitic on forest trees I. Reproduction of ectoparasites on pine. Nematologica 12:443-447.

Ruehle JL. 1968. Plant-parasitic nematodes associated with southern hardwoods and coniferous forest trees. Plant Disease Reporter 52:837-839.

Ruehle JL. 1969. Influence of stubby-root nematode on growth of southern pine seedlings. Forest Science 15:130-134.

Ruehle JL. 1971. Nematodes parasitic on forest trees. III. Reproduction on selected hardwoods. Journal of Nematology 3:170-173.

Ruehle JL. 1973. Nematodes and the forest trees—types of damage to tree roots. Annual Review of Phytopathology 11:99-118.

Shurtleff MC, Averre CW III. 2000. Diagnosing plant diseases caused by nematodes. St Paul (MN): The American Phytopathological Society.

Timper P, Hanna WW. 2005. Reproduction of *Belonolaimus longicaudatus, Meloidogyne javanica, Paratrichodorus minor*, and *Pratylenchus brachyurus* on pearl millet (*Pennisetum glaucum*). Journal of Nematology 37:214-219.

Timper P, Wilson JP, Johnson AW, Hanna WW. 2002. Evaluation of pearl millet grain hybrids for resistance to meloidoghne spp. and leaf blight caused by *Pyricularia grisea*. Plant Disease 86:909-914.

Wang LP. 1971. Embryology and life cycle of *Tylenchorhynchus claytoni* Steiner. Journal of Nematology 3:101-107.

Zasada IA, Klassen W, Meyer SLF, Codallo M, Abdul-Baki AA. 2006. Velvetbean (*Mucuna pruriens*) extracts: impact on *Meloidogyne incognita* survival and on *Lycopersicon esculentum* and *Lactuca sativa* germination and growth. Pest Management Science 62:1122-1127.

2008 Interim Guidelines for Growing Longleaf Pine Seedlings in Container Nurseries

R. Kasten Dumroese, James P. Barnett, D. Paul Jackson, and Mark J. Hainds

R. Kasten Dumroese is a Research Plant Physiologist, USDA Forest Service, formerly Southern Research Station, currently Rocky Mountain Research Station, 1221 South Main Street, Moscow, ID 83843; Tel: 208. 883.2324; E-mail: kdumroese@fs.fed.us. **James P. Barnett** is an Emeritus Scientist, USDA Forest Service, Southern Research Station, Pineville, LA, 71360; E-mail: jpbarnett@fs.fed.us. **D. Paul Jackson** was a Biological Science Technician, USDA Forest Service, Southern Research Station, but is currently a graduate student at Auburn University, AL 36849. **Mark J. Hainds** is Research Coordinator, The Longleaf Alliance, Solon Dixon Forestry Education Center, Andalusia, AL 36420.

Dumroese, R.K.; Barnett, J.P.; Jackson, D.P.; Hainds, M.J. 2009. 2008 Interim guidelines for growing longleaf pine seedlings in container nurseries. In: Dumroese, R.K.; Riley, L.E., tech. coords. 2009. National Proceedings: Forest and Conservation Nursery Associations—2008. Proc. RMRS-P-58. Fort Collins, CO: U.S. Department of Agriculture, Forest Service, Rocky Mountain Research Station: 101–107. Online: http://www.fs.fed.us/rm/pubs/rmrs_p058.html.

Abstract: Production of container longleaf pine (*Pinus palustris*) seedlings for reforestation and restoration plantings exceeds that of bareroot production, but information on container production techniques has been slow to develop. Because success of those outplantings requires quality seedlings, interim guidelines were proposed in 2002 to assist nursery managers and tree planters in developing and using the best stock possible. The guidelines were intended to be updated as new information was generated. During the past 6 years, additional studies have confirmed most provisions of the interim guidelines, except that presence of buds (number and color) as originally described in the guidelines does not appear to be a useful metric. In addition, some new parameters have been added. This report synthesizes that new information and revised guidelines are presented.

Keywords: root-collar diameter, clipping, root development

Introduction

Longleaf pine (*Pinus palustris*) forests once were a dominant ecosystem across the southeastern United States, but intense harvesting during the past century reduced this forest type from nearly 36 million ha (90 million ac) to about 800,000 ha (2 million ac) (Noss and others 1995; Outcalt 2000; Barnett 2002; Shibu and others 2006). Restoration of this forest type has been encouraged by federal incentive programs (Hainds 2002) and because survival and growth of container longleaf pine is often better after outplanting (Boyer 1989; Barnett and McGilvray 1997; South and others 2005), use of this stocktype has increased dramatically. In 2008, about 64 million container seedlings were produced compared to about 12 million bareroot seedlings (Longleaf Alliance data).

Despite demand for container longleaf pine, very little detailed research exists concerning the production of this relatively new stocktype. This information gap led to a major problem, that is, an absence of container seedling standards and subsequent variation in stock quality (Hainds 2004). Although stock quality can be described in the nursery, what really matters is how well it performs on the outplanting site (Landis and Dumroese 2006). Plants characterized as "poor" in the nursery may perform well in the field if site factors are favorable (for example, proper site preparation, planting techniques, weed control, and/or ample precipitation). On the other hand, "high" quality plants may do poorly if those same factors are poorly done or precipitation is below normal. Even with the existing information gaps, Barnett and others (2002a,b) published interim guidelines to help growers "zero-in" on container types and seedling quality attributes for growing longleaf pine seedlings in containers. These guidelines were generated based on the limited research results, experience of growers, and the expertise of regional specialists with the intention that they would be revised as new information became available.

Since 2002, some additional studies have been completed or are in the final stages of completion. Although most of these projects have not yet been vetted by the scientific community through refereed journal publications, we feel that some of the information gleaned from them can be used to update the interim guidelines. Some preliminary results of this work include Dumroese and others (2005), Hainds and Barnett (2006), Jackson (2006), Jackson and others (2007), and Jackson and others (forthcoming).

2002 Interim Guidelines _____

The 2002 interim guidelines focused on needles, roots, root-collar diameter (RCD), buds, container size, and other important attributes, such as presence of "sondereggers" (Barnett and others 2002a,b). For each parameter, we summarize the "2002 interim guideline" as published in Barnett and others (2002a), describe the "rationale" behind each original guideline, and provide a "2008 update" that synthesizes new information that collaborates or refines the 2002 guidelines.

Needles

2002 Interim Guideline—If clipped, needles should be 15 to 25 cm (6 to 10 in) long, but not less than 10 cm (4 in). If not clipped, needles should be 20 to 30 cm (8 to 12 in) long. The appearance of many fascicles is preferred, and needles should have a pale to dark green color.

Rationale—Barnett (1984) showed that repeated clipping of longleaf needles to maintain a length of 5 cm (2 in) reduced RCD, shoot weight, and root weight during nursery production, but seedlings given single or multiple clippings to maintain a needle length of 25 cm (10 in) were similar to their non-clipped cohorts. In addition, survival of seedlings clipped to maintain the 5-cm (2-in) length was poorer under higher levels of moisture stress than seedlings with longer needles. Barnett (1984) also reported that seedlings clipped once to 25 cm (10 in) immediately before outplanting under severe moisture stress conditions survived better than control seedlings and seedlings clipped too frequently. These results are similar to the conclusions of South (1998) who noted that clipping needles of bareroot seedlings improved survival, presumably because of reduced transpiration on sites where seedlings are under significant moisture stress. Clipping needles in the nursery can prevent their lodging and reduce subsequent susceptibility to disease by improving air circulation, reducing humidity levels, and allowing more uniform irrigation. Poor irrigation uniformity leads to overwatering and can increase root disease (Enebak and Carey 2002). Barnett (1989) found that seedlings grown in shade during nursery production were much smaller and suggested that clipping could allow more uniform light exposure (Barnett 1984). Seedlings with fascicles are preferred; Wakeley (1954) and Barnett (1980) reported that seedlings with fascicles perform better after outplanting. A healthy "green" color is indicative of proper nutrient status, rather than the "yellow" (chlorotic) foliage resulting from nutrient deficiencies.

2008 Update—To our knowledge, no new work has been published on clipping. However, we found that needle length of container seedlings is a function of nitrogen fertilizer rate (Jackson 2006; Jackson and others 2007). We also determined that a rate of 2 to 3 mg nitrogen/seedling/week

for 20 weeks produced seedlings in Ropak® Multipot #3-96® containers (depth = 12 cm [4.8 in]; volume = 98 cm^3 [6 in^3]; density = 441 per m^2 [41 per ft^2]) with needles within the original interim guidelines without the need for clipping. After outplanting, these seedlings survived and grew well (Jackson 2006; Jackson and others 2007). Seedlings given 4 mg nitrogen/week for 20 weeks had needles that would have required clipping under operational conditions to prevent lodging (we did not clip them, however, in the experiment); no additional benefit in terms of seedling survival or growth was noted for this stocktype. It should be noted that many other fertilizer regimes appear to produce longleaf seedlings without the need for clipping (Dumroese and others 2005). It may be, however, that nutrient loading longleaf pine seedlings in the nursery (Hinesley and Maki 1980; Dumroese 2003) in concert with clipping may improve outplanting performance, particularly because of unpublished work conducted at Auburn University. Researchers there found that clipping longleaf pine seedlings to 20 cm (8 in) reduced water loss in a greenhouse during the first 4 days after clipping (South 2008). This short-term affect may be beneficial to outplanting performance.

Roots

2002 Interim Guideline—RCD, measured at the base of the needles, should be 6.35 mm (0.25 in) or more, and no less than 4.75 mm (0.19 in). Roots should be light brown in color with white root tips, free of disease symptoms, and without circling. Presence of mycorrhizae is encouraged.

Rationale—Because longleaf pine seedlings generally exit the grass stage when their RCDs are about 25 mm (1 in) (Wahlenberg 1946), obtaining large RCDs in the nursery could shorten the grass stage after outplanting. In addition, larger RCDs are associated with better survival of bareroot stock (White 1981). The minimum value was based on observations that seedlings with less than 4.75 mm (0.19 in) diameter grown in Ropak® Multipot #6-45® containers (described below) were "floppy" and had reduced survival. ("Floppy" seedlings, when held horizontally by the terminal bud, "flopped" over because of insufficient development of roots within the root plug [Hainds and Barnett 2004, 2006]). Light brown roots with white root tips indicate a healthy root system and show potential for new root development. Black roots require close scrutiny, particularly if a large portion of the root system is black, because they are likely diseased. Presence of mycorrhizae indicates a healthy root system, but applying inoculant is usually unnecessary because windborne spores typically inoculate seedlings naturally (Barnett and Brissette 1986).

2008 Update—In general, the recommendation for RCDs greater than 4.75 mm (0.19 in) for typical 100 cm^3 (6 in^3) containers seems acceptable. In this stocktype, we note that most fertilizer regimes produce seedlings above this threshold (Jackson 2006; Jackson and others 2007). Seedlings below this threshold have reduced survival (Hainds and Barnett 2004, 2006), and it appears that seedlings with increasing RCDs have increasingly better performance in terms of reduced time in the grass stage (Jackson and others 2007, forthcoming). South and others (2005) report a critical threshold of 5.5 mm (0.22 in); seedlings with lower RCDs had poorer survival across a variety of sites than those with greater RCDs. Recent work shows, however, that RCD cannot be increased indefinitely without a decline in survival and growth—when the ratio of RCD to the diameter of the growing container (the Root Bound Index [RBI]) was greater than 27%, seedling survival was compromised (fig. 1) (South and others 2005; South and Mitchell 2006). Our observation is that this critical threshold may be difficult to achieve in a 20- to 30-week growing cycle for seedlings in Ropak® Multipot #3-96® containers, but, as Salonius and others (2002) point out, could be easily achieved when seedlings are grown too long in the containers, or "held over" in the nursery in anticipation of being sold the following year.

Most typical, commercially available containers used for reforestation have design features to prevent root circling. Some containers are treated with copper to prevent root spiraling, which also prevents lateral roots from growing downward on the exterior of the plug and forming a "birdcage," and this treatment was associated with changes in root system morphology, shoot and root biomass (Barnett and McGilvray 2002), and root growth potential (South and others 2005). In general, these seedlings are easier to extract from containers, especially those made of Styrofoam™, and fresh copper on container walls decreases the level of potential disease inoculum (Dumroese and others 2002). Copper-coated containers yield seedlings with better, more uniform root distribution higher on the initial root plug, which is believed to improve resistance to windthrow (Burdett 1978; Burdett and others 1986). Neither South and others (2005) nor Sung and others (forthcoming) noted any short-term benefit, in terms of survival or growth, from growing seedlings in copper-treated containers.

Tinus and others (2002) determined that exposing longleaf roots to temperatures below –4 °C (25 °F) caused significant damage. South (2006) reports damage is more severe if that temperature is achieved before seedlings have acclimated to cold temperatures (early winter), or the frost is preceded by warm temperatures that cause deacclimation of seedling tissues to cold.

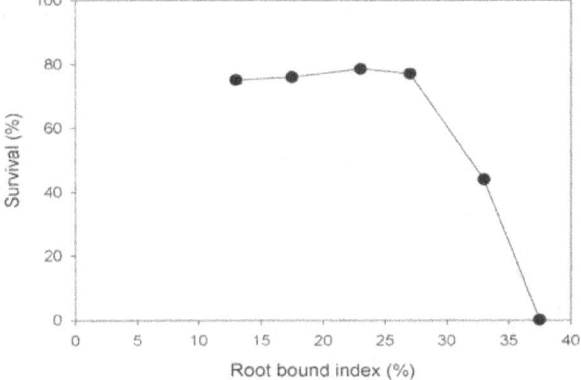

Figure 1. Effect of the root bound index (RCD/cell diameter) on second-year survival of container longleaf pine seedlings (South and others 2005).

Buds

2002 Interim Guideline—Buds should be present on 90% of the crop. Seedlings outplanted in late October or early November are more likely to have green buds, whereas seedlings outplanted in late December or January are more likely to have brown buds. Brown buds are thought to be more mature, but outplanting should not be delayed to obtain better bud development.

Rationale—Personal observations of quality seedling crops grown during a variety of research projects indicated that seedlings at the end of the growing cycle in late fall had a cessation of needle growth, hardening of tissue, and formation of notable, green, terminal buds, which then became brown during winter.

2008 Update—Early researchers noted that longleaf pine seedlings in the grass stage exhibit a progression of bud types (Pessin 1939; Wahlenberg 1946). Wakeley (1954) noted that bud status during a single growing season changed as terminal buds formed, opened, re-formed, and re-opened. We have observed development of the apex during several studies and have attempted some quantification. Attempting to use the bud descriptions (pincushion, round, and elongated) of Pessin (1939), Wahlenberg (1946), and Wakeley (1954) during nursery production has been problematic, as nursery stock shows a wide variation in apex characters not necessarily meeting those descriptions. Jackson (2006) found that increasing rates of fertilizer resulted in larger, more robust buds. At deficient nitrogen rates, buds were small and brownish, whereas seedlings given high doses of nitrogen had larger, green buds. In another trial, we observed that frequency of terminal buds varied by month, generally increasing from September through December and then decreasing dramatically in January (fig. 2). In another study, more than 90% of the crop still had firm terminal buds in January. Larson (2002) points out that dormant buds may be difficult to see. Therefore, additional quantification, and perhaps a new framework for describing/measuring bud development during nursery culture, would help identify if, and what, the effect of differing bud/apex condition on longleaf pine seedling quality might be. Because we have outplanted groups of longleaf pine seedlings with wide variation in the presence of terminal buds (ranging from 20% [Jackson and others 2007] to 100% [fig. 2]), and survival and growth have been similar, it appears that the bud criteria in the 2002 guidelines does not appear to be useful.

Container Size

2002 Interim Guideline—Container diameter should be no less than 25 mm (1 in), with 38 mm (1.5 in) or greater desired. Container depth should be no less than 9 cm (3.5 in), with 11.5 cm (4.5 in) or more preferred. Container volume should be no less than 90 cm³ (5.5 in³), with 100 cm³ (6 in³) or more recommended.

Rationale—The guidelines were based on observations from a variety of studies (Barnett 1974, 1984, 1988, 1991; Amidon and others 1982; Barnett and McGilvray 1997).

2008 Update—Since the interim guidelines were published, most of our work has focused on seedlings grown in

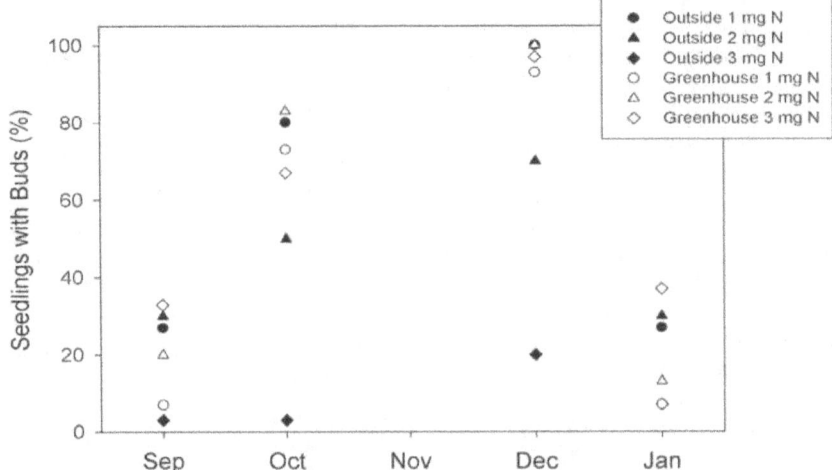

Figure 2. Bud occurrence from September through January for longleaf pine seedlings in a recent fertilizer trial completed by the authors. Although no pattern was observed between seedlings grown in a greenhouse or outside, or among three levels of nitrogen fertilizer, pooled data showed that buds formed from September, with most of the crop having discernable terminal buds in December, followed by an opening of terminal buds in January.

Ropak® Multipot #3-96® (Jackson 2006; Jackson and others 2007, forthcoming) or Ropak® Multipot #6-45® (Dumroese and others 2005) containers. The Multipot #6-45® is the same as the Multipot #3-96® described above except seedlings are grown at a higher density (581 per m² [54 per ft²]). Seedlings grown in Ropak® Multipot #3-96® containers have been evaluated up to 3 years in the field; preliminary data shows excellent survival and growth (Jackson and others 2007, forthcoming). South and others (2005) evaluated six different container types of various materials, ranging in depth from 6.5 to 15 cm (2.6 to 6 in) and volume from 60 to 120 cm³ (4 to 6 in³), outplanted on four field sites. They concluded that container type (Styrofoam™, hard plastic, or mesh) may not affect survival on easy-to-regenerate sites, but mesh-type containers (such as Jiffy pellets) performed poorer than Styrofoam™ and hard plastic containers, which had characteristics consistent with the original guidelines. Sung and others (forthcoming) found reduced survival, height growth, and exit from the grass stage for seedlings grown in small volume (54 cm³ [4 in³]) containers compared to larger cohorts. A study examining a wider range of container sizes (60 to 340 cm³ [4 to 20 in³]) was outplanted on the USDA Forest Service Palustris Experimental Forest (Louisiana) in December 2008.

Other Important Attributes

2002 Interim Guideline—Root plugs should remain intact (no loss of medium) when extracted and during handling, and they should always be moist. Seedlings should lack competing weeds and insect pests. The nursery manager and the buyer should agree whether to cull sonderegger seedlings.

Rationale—Firm root plugs indicate good root development and seedlings with firm plugs and appropriate RCD

for the container diameter are not "floppy," as described in the "roots" section. Furthermore, firm plugs facilitate handling in the nursery and outplanting because they do not fall apart, and losing a portion of the root plug during the process of extraction through outplanting was associated with a decrease in survival and subsequent growth in a conifer species (Tinus 1974). Moisture held in the growing medium prevents root desiccation. A seedling sharing its container with a competing weed has less access to nutrients and water, resulting in reduced growth (Pessin and Chapman 1944). Seedlings that begin height growth during nursery production are usually sonderegger pines (*Pinus* X *sondereggeri*), a naturally occurring hybrid of longleaf and loblolly (*P. taeda*) pines (Little 1979). These seedlings produce poorly formed trees in plantations and are less desirable than longleaf pine.

2008 Update—Many growers irrigate their seedlings just prior to extraction (Dumroese and Barnett 2004). Seedlings may be hot-planted (no or very limited storage) or cooler stored for a week to a few months (Dumroese and Barnett 2004). Regardless, having moist plugs when shipped to the field is important. This may be especially true for seedlings hot-planted during the April through October planting window because these seedlings likely have more exposure to greater vapor pressure deficits than seedlings hot-planted, or outplanted after cooler storage, during the relatively mild "winter" season. Luoranen and others (2004) found that mortality of silver birch (*Betula pendula*) increased with decreasing plug moisture content; rate of mortality with decreasing plug moisture was greatest on dry sites. More detailed observations by Hainds and Barnett (2006) suggest that seedlings with as much as 10 cm (4 in) of height growth in the nursery may not necessarily be sonderegger pines. This may complicate identification of hybrid seedlings in the nursery; as always, the best solution is for the grower and the buyer to communicate about this beforehand.

Not discussed in the original guidelines were "double seedlings," two seedlings growing in a single container. During nursery production, a "single" seedling can have twice the dry weight of a "double" seedling (Brissette and Barnett 1989), which affects outplanting performance. After outplanting, Brissette and Barnett (1989) showed that survival was greatly reduced when two or three seedlings occupied the same container (fig. 3A), and Hainds and Barnett (2006) report that height growth was also diminished (fig. 3B).

Summary

Results from recent studies confirm that most of the recommendations made when the 2002 interim guidelines were developed are still sound (table 1). The main exception is related to the presence of terminal buds and its effect on outplanting performance. Additional information regarding "floppy" seedlings, double seedlings, and classification of sonderegger pines has also been included.

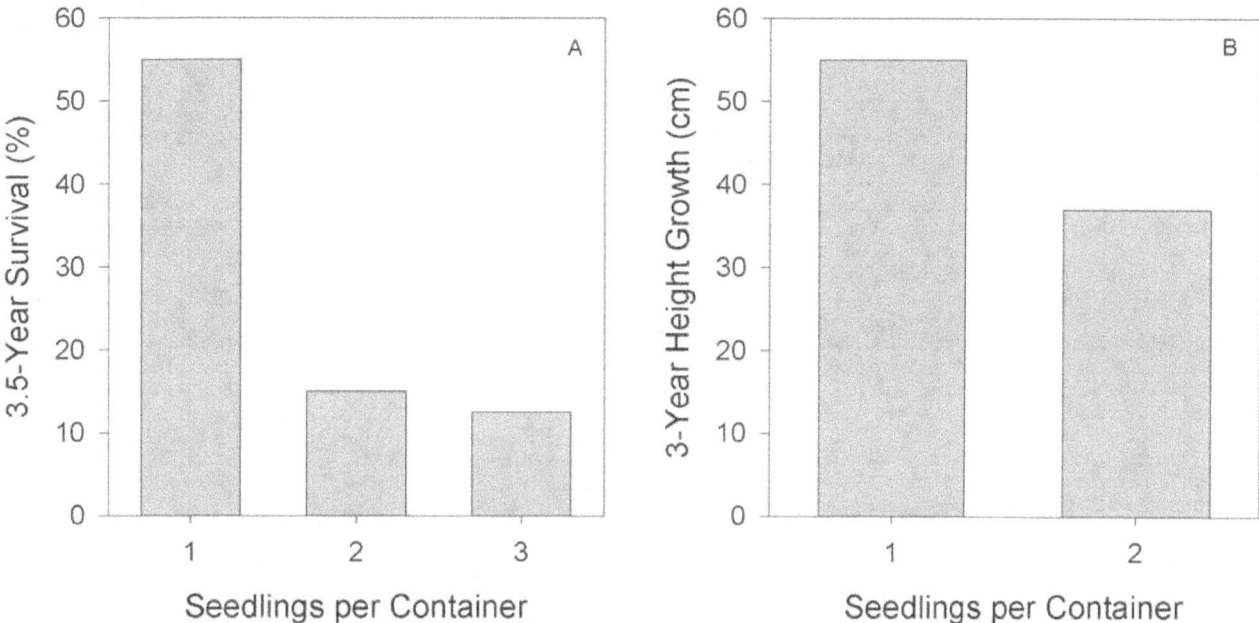

Figure 3. (A) Survival of longleaf pine seedlings decreases when multiple seedlings exist within a single container (Brissette and Barnett 1989). (B) Height growth of seedlings at Samson Site Alabama (see Hainds and Barnett 2006 for more details). "Double" had 2 seedlings growing within the same container. Note: This figure was presented incorrectly in Hainds and Barnett (2006).

Table 1. The 2008 interim guidelines for nursery production of longleaf pine seedlings.

Needles	Needles should be 15 to 30 cm (6 to 12 in) long, and not less than 10 cm (4 in). Needles should have a "medium to dark" green color. Avoid yellow or brown seedlings.
Roots	Root-collar diameter, measured at the base of the needles, should be no less than 4.75 mm (0.19 in). Larger RCDs are encouraged as long as the ratio of seedling RCD to container diameter is less than 27% to avoid root binding. Roots should be light brown in color with white root tips, free of disease symptoms, and without circling. Cambium at or near the root-collar should be whitish or greenish, never orange or brown. Plugs should be firm and moist and stay intact during extraction and outplanting. Avoid "floppy" seedlings—these seedlings, when held by the terminal horizontally, bend or flop, unable to maintain a straight horizontal alignment.
Buds	May or may not be present.
Container size	Diameter ≥ 25 mm (1 in), with 38 mm (1.5 in) or greater desired. Depth ≥ 9 cm (3.5 in), with 11.5 cm (4.5 in) or more preferred. Volume ≥ 90 cm³ (5.5 in³), with 100 cm³ (6 in³) or more recommended.
Other important attributes	Seedlings should be free of weeds and insects. Avoid multiple seedlings within a single container. Sonderegger pines retained or removed pending decision by grower and buyer in agreement.

Acknowledgments_____

We appreciate the comments and suggestions provided by Dr. David South on earlier drafts.

References _____

Amidon TE, Barnett JP, Gallagher HP, McGilvray JM. 1982. A field test of containerized seedlings under drought conditions. In: Guilin RW, Barnett JP, editors. Proceedings of the southern containerized forest tree seedling conference. New Orleans (LA): USDA Forest Service, Southern Forest Experiment Station. General Technical Report SO-37. p 139-144.

Barnett JP. 1974. Tube lengths, site treatments, and seedling ages affect survival and growth of containerized southern pine seedlings. New Orleans (LA): USDA Forest Service, Southern Forest Experiment Station. Research Note SO-174. 3 p.

Barnett JP. 1980. Density and age affect performance of containerized loblolly pine seedlings. New Orleans (LA): USDA Forest Service, Southern Forest Experiment Station. Research Note SO-256. 5 p.

Barnett JP. 1984. Top pruning and needle clipping of container-grown southern pine seedlings. In: Lantz C, compiler. Proceedings: southern nursery conferences. Atlanta (GA): USDA Forest Service, State and Private Forestry, Southern Region. p 39-45.

Barnett JP. 1988. Site preparation, containers, and soil types affect field performance of loblolly and longleaf pine seedlings. In: Proceedings, 5th biennial southern silvicultural research conference. New Orleans (LA): USDA Forest Service, Southern Forest Experiment Station. General Technical Report SO-74. p 155-158.

Barnett JP. 1989. Shading reduces growth of longleaf and loblolly pine seedlings in containers. Tree Planters' Notes 40(1):23-26.

Barnett JP. 1991. Effects of morphological grade on field performance of container-grown southern pine seedings. In: Coleman SS, Neary DG, editors. In: Proceedings, 5th biennial southern silvicultural research conference. New Orleans (LA): USDA Forest Service, Southern Forest Experiment Station. General Technical Report SE-70. p 94-99.

Barnett JP. 2002. Longleaf pine: Why plant it? Why use containers? In: Barnett JP, Dumroese RK, Moorhead DJ, editors. Proceedings of workshops on growing longleaf pine in containers—1999 and 2001. Asheville (NC): USDA Forest Service, Southern Research Station. General Technical Report SRS-56. p 5-7.

Barnett JP, Brissette JC. 1986. Producing southern pine seedlings in containers. New Orleans (LA): USDA Forest Service, Southern Forest Experiment Station. General Technical Report SO-59. 71 p.

Barnett JP, McGilvary JM. 1997. Practical guidelines for producing longleaf pine seedlings in containers. Asheville (NC): USDA Forest Service, Southern Research Station. General Technical Report SO-14. 28 p.

Barnett JP, McGilvary JM. 2002. Copper-treated containers influence root development of longleaf pine seedlings. In: Barnett JP, Dumroese RK, Moorhead DJ, editors. Proceedings of workshops on growing longleaf pine in containers—1999 and 2001. Asheville (NC): USDA Forest Service, Southern Research Station. General Technical Report SRS-56. p 24-26.

Barnett JP, Hainds MJ, Hernandez GA. 2002a. Interim guidelines for growing longleaf seedlings in containers. In: Barnett JP, Dumroese RK, Moorhead DJ, editors. Proceedings of workshops on growing longleaf pine in containers—1999 and 2001. Asheville (NC): USDA Forest Service, Southern Research Station. General Technical Report SRS-56. p 27-29.

Barnett JP, Hainds MJ, Hernandez GA. 2002b. Interim guidelines for growing longleaf seedlings in containers. Asheville (NC): USDA Forest Service, Southern Research Station. General Technical Report SRS-60. 3 p.

Boyer WD. 1989. Response of planted longleaf pine bare-root and container stock to site preparation and release: fifth year results. In: Proceedings, 5th biennial southern silvicultural research conference. New Orleans (LA): USDA Forest Service, Southern Forest Experiment Station. General Technical Report SO-74. p 165-168.

Brissette JC, Barnett JP. 1989. Comparing first-year growth in bare-root and container planting of shortleaf pine half-sib families. In: Proceedings, 20th southern forest tree improvement conference; 1989 June 26-30; Charleston, SC. Atlanta (GA): Southern Forest Tree Improvement Committee. Publication 42. p 354-361.

Burdett AN. 1978. Control of root morphogenesis for improved mechanical stability in container-grown lodgepole pine. Canadian Journal of Forest Research 8:483-486.

Burdett AN, Coates H, Eremko R, Martin PAF. 1986. Toppling in British Columbia's lodgepole pine plantations: significance, cause and prevention. Forestry Chronicle 62:433-439.

Dumroese RK. 2003. Hardening fertilization and nutrient loading of conifer seedlings. In: Riley LE, Dumroese RK, Landis TD, technical coordinators. National proceedings, forest and conservation nursery associations—2002. Ogden (UT): USDA Forest Service, Rocky Mountain Research Station. Proceedings RMRS-P-28. p 31-36.

Dumroese RK, Barnett JP. 2004. Container seedling handling and storage in the southeastern states. In: Riley LE, Dumroese RK, Landis TD, technical coordinators. National proceedings, forest and conservation nursery associations—2003. Ogden (UT): USDA Forest Service, Rocky Mountain Research Station. Proceedings RMRS-P-33. p 22-25.

Dumroese RK, James RL, Wenny DL. 2002. Hot water and copper coatings in reused containers decrease inoculum of *Fusarium* and *Cylindrocarpon* and increase Douglas-fir seedling growth. HortScience 37:943-947.

Dumroese RK, Parkhurst J, Barnett JP. 2005. Controlled release fertilizer improves quality of container longleaf pine seedlings. In: Dumroese RK, Riley LE, Landis TD, technical coordinators. National proceedings, forest and conservation nursery associations—2004. Fort Collins (CO): USDA Forest Service, Rocky Mountain Research Station. Proceedings RMRS-P-35. p 3-8.

Enebak S, Carey B. 2002. Pest control for container-grown longleaf pine. In: Barnett JP, Dumroese RK, Moorhead DJ, editors. Proceedings of workshops on growing longleaf pine in containers—1999 and 2001. Asheville (NC): USDA Forest Service, Southern Research Station. General Technical Report SRS-56. p 43-46.

Hainds MJ. 2002. Longleaf seedling trends. In: Barnett JP, Dumroese RK, Moorhead DJ, editors. Proceedings of workshops on growing longleaf pine in containers—1999 and 2001. Asheville (NC): USDA Forest Service, Southern Research Station. General Technical Report SRS-56. p 3-4.

Hainds MJ. 2004. Establishing longleaf pine seedlings on agricultural fields and pastures. In: Connor KF, editor. Proceedings of the 12th biennial southern silvicultural research conference. Asheville (NC): USDA Forest Service, Southern Research Station. General Technical Report SRS-71. p 309-313.

Hainds MJ, Barnett JP. 2004. Container grown longleaf pine seedling quality. In: Connor KF, editor. Proceedings of the 12th biennial southern silvicultural research conference. Asheville (NC): USDA Forest Service, Southern Research Station. General Technical Report SRS-71. p 319-320.

Hainds MJ, Barnett JP. 2006. Container grown longleaf pine seedling quality. In: Connor KF, editor. Proceedings of the 13th biennial southern silvicultural research conference. Asheville (NC): USDA Forest Service, Southern Research Station. General Technical Report SRS-92. p 102-104.

Hinesley LE, Maki TE. 1980. Fall fertilization helps longleaf pine nursery stock. Southern Journal of Applied Forestry 4:132–135.

Jackson DP. 2006. Relating morphology, nutrition, and bud development to liquid fertilizer application of containerized longleaf pine [MSc thesis]. Ruston (LA): Louisiana Tech University, College of Applied and Natural Resources. 62 p.

Jackson DP, Dumroese RK, Barnett JP, Patterson WB. 2007. Container longleaf pine seedling morphology in response to varying rates of nitrogen fertilization in the nursery and subsequent growth after outplanting. In: Riley LE, Dumroese RK, Landis TD, technical coordinators. National proceedings, forest and conservation nursery associations—2006. Fort Collins (CO): USDA Forest Service, Rocky Mountain Research Station. Proceedings RMRS-P-50. p 114-119.

Jackson DP, Dumroese RK, Barnett JP, Patterson WB. Effects of liquid fertilizer application on the morphological and outplanting success of container longleaf pine seedlings. In: Proceedings of the 14th biennial southern silvicultural research conference. Asheville (NC): USDA Forest Service, Southern Research Station. General Technical Report. Forthcoming.

Landis TD, Dumroese RK. 2006. Applying the target plant concept to nursery stock quality. In: MacLennan L, Fennessy J, editors. Plant quality: a key to success in forest establishment. Proceedings of the COFORD Conference. Dublin (Ireland): National Council for Forest Research and Development. p 1-10.

Larson DR. 2002. Field planting containerized longleaf pine seedlings. In: Barnett JP, Dumroese RK, Moorhead DJ, editors. Proceedings of workshops on growing longleaf pine in containers—1999 and 2001. Asheville (NC): USDA Forest Service, Southern Research Station. General Technical Report SRS-56. p 62-63.

Little EL Jr. 1979. Checklist of United States trees (native and naturalized). Washington (DC): USDA Forest Service. Agriculture Handbook 541. 375 p.

Luoranen J, Rikala R, Smolander H. 2004. Summer planting of hot-lifted silver birch container seedlings. In: Ciccarese L, Lucci S, Mattsson A, editors. Nursery production and stand establishment of broadleaves to promote sustainable forest management; 7-10 May 2001; Rome, Italy. Rome (Italy): Agency for the Protection of the Environment and Technical Services. p 207-218. URL: http://www.iufro.org/publications/proceedings/ (accessed 23 Jan 2009).

Noss RF, LaRoe TE III, Scott JM. 1995. Endangered ecosystems of the United States: a preliminary assessment of loss and degradation. Washington (DC): USDI National Biological Service. Biological Report 128. 58 p.

Outcalt KW. 2000. The longleaf pine ecosystem of the South. Native Plants Journal 1:42-44, 47-53.

Pessin LJ. 1939. Density of stocking and character of ground cover as factors in longleaf pine reproduction. Journal of Forestry 37:255-258.

Pessin LJ, Chapman RA. 1944. The effect of living grass on the growth of longleaf pine seedlings in pots. Ecology 25:85-90.

Salonius P, Hallett R, Beaton K, French C. 2002. Extended nursery rearing compromises field performance of container-reared conifer seedlings. Fredericton (NB): Canadian Forest Service. Information Report M-X-214E. 20 p.

Shibu J, Jokela EJ, Miller DL, editors. 2006. The longleaf pine ecosystem-ecology, silviculture, and restoration. New York (NY): Springer. 438 p.

South DB. 1998. Needle-clipping longleaf pine and top-pruning loblolly pine in bareroot nurseries. Southern Journal of Applied Forestry 22:235-240.

South DB. 2006. Freeze injury to southern pine seedlings. In: Connor KF, editor. Proceedings of the 13th biennial southern silvicultural research conference. Asheville (NC): USDA Forest Service, Southern Research Station. General Technical Report SRS-92. p 441-447.

South DB. 2008. Personal communication. Auburn (AL): Auburn University, School of Forestry and Wildlife Sciences, Alabama Agricultural Experiment Station, Professor.

South DB, Mitchell RG. 2006. A root-bound index for evaluating planting stock quality of container-grown pines. Southern African Forestry Journal 207:47-54.

South DB, Harris SW, Barnett JP, Hainds MJ, Gjerstad DH. 2005. Effect of container type and seedling size on survival and early height growth of *Pinus palustris* seedlings in Alabama, U.S A. Forest Ecology and Management 204:385-398.

Sung S S-J, Haywood JD, Sword-Sayer MA, Connor KF, Scott AD. Effects of container cavity size and copper coating on field performance of container-grown longleaf pine seedlings. In: Proceedings of the 14th biennial southern silvicultural research conference. Asheville (NC): USDA Forest Service, Southern Research Station. General Technical Report. Forthcoming.

Tinus RW. 1974. Characteristics of seedlings with high survival potential. In: Proceedings of the North American containerized forest tree seedling symposium. Great Plains Agricultural Council Publication 68:276-282.

Tinus RW, Sword MA, Barnett JP. 2002. Prevention of cold damage to container-grown longleaf pine roots. In: Barnett JP, Dumroese RK, Moorhead DJ, editors. Proceedings of workshops on growing longleaf pine in containers—1999 and 2001. Asheville (NC): USDA Forest Service, Southern Research Station. General Technical Report SRS-56. p 55-57.

Wahlenberg WG. 1946. Longleaf pine: its use, ecology, regeneration, protection, growth and management. Washington (DC): Charles Lathrop Pack Foundation in cooperation with the USDA Forest Service. 429 p.

Wakeley PC. 1954. Planting the southern pines. Washington (DC): USDA Forest Service. Agriculture Monograph 18. 233 p.

White JB. 1981. The influence of seedling size and length of storage on longleaf pine survival. Tree Planters' Notes 32(4):3-4.

Acorn Storage: Can You Really Fool Mother Nature?

Kristina Connor

Kristina Connor is Project Leader, Restoring and Managing Longleaf Pine Ecosystems, USDA Forest Service, Southern Research Station, 520 Devall Drive, Auburn, AL 36830; Tel: 334.826.8700; E-mail: kconnor@fs.fed.us.

Connor, K. 2009. Acorn storage: Can you really fool Mother Nature? In: Dumroese, R.K.; Riley, L.E., tech. coords. 2009. National Proceedings: Forest and Conservation Nursery Associations—2008. Proc. RMRS-P-58. Fort Collins, CO: U.S. Department of Agriculture, Forest Service, Rocky Mountain Research Station: 108–113. Online: http://www.fs.fed.us/rm/pubs/rmrs_p058.html.

Abstract: Moisture levels in acorns before storage are critical. Two years after being dried before storage, water oak (*Quercus nigra*) acorns had 17% to 25% germination, while cherrybark oak (*Q. pagoda*) acorns were dead. Acorns stored fully hydrated faired far better after 2 years in storage, with germination ranging from 48% to 53% in water oak acorns, and from 67% to 76% in cherrybark oak acorns. Survival of acorns in the field was also dependent on moisture. The moderating effects of high relative humidity and rainfall throughout the collection period of the second experiment led to higher viability of white oak acorns left in the field for up to 15 days. We also observed a higher sucrose concentration in desiccating white oak acorns. While this increase may serve to initially protect cellular membranes in the acorn tissues, the mechanism is obviously not successful in preserving viability, which dropped rapidly after day 5 of the experiment.

Keywords: acorn storage, moisture content, insect damage, sucrose content

Introduction

Orthodox seeds are easily stored. When dried to moisture contents (MCs) of 12% or less, they become metabolically quiescent and can be stored at temperatures ranging from 4 to 18 °C (39 to 64 °F) or cryostored in liquid nitrogen at –196 °C (–321 °F) (Roberts 1973). However, some seeds are desiccation-sensitive, or recalcitrant. These seeds are sensitive to moisture loss and/or to low temperatures, and must be stored fully hydrated (Roberts 1973; Ellis and others 1990). In this state, they are not only metabolically active, but are also subject to deterioration through fungal and insect attacks. These are the seeds that cannot be stored for long periods of time and that pose great difficulties for seed buyers and sellers.

Attempts to improve storage longevity of recalcitrant seeds have produced mixed results. Generally, enhanced storage is the result of technical manipulation. For instance, Withers and King (1980) used 2-step freezing to enhance storage of cell cultures. Some researchers have successfully preserved embryonic axes and somatic and zygotic embryos (Shibli and Al-Juboory 2000; Towill and Bajaj 2002; Fang and others 2004). Dereuddre and others (1991) and Shibli and Al-Juboory (2000) used encapsulation-dehydration and Mycock and others (1995) used rapid cooling in storing somatic embryos. Flash-drying (Berjak and others 1989; Wesley-Smith and others 1992) and vitrification (Touchell and others 2002) have also been utilized. Other researchers have cryopreserved shoot tips, buds, and apical meristems (Towill and others 2004). In general, these are labor-intensive processes, and primarily used to store germplasm of valuable agricultural species, fruit trees, or economically important forest tree species.

While such studies hold promise for future advancements and provide avenues of preservation for threatened germplasm, our studies focused on storing entire seeds rather than seed tissues. Here, we examined seed storage at different temperatures and MCs and how our laboratory desiccation experiments compared to field longevity. The objectives of these studies were: (1) to study storage of cherrybark oak (*Quercus pagoda*) and water oak (*Q. nigra*) acorns at two temperatures and two MCs; (2) to determine changes in MC and germination in acorns left exposed to natural conditions and track the percentage of collected acorns that had insect damage through the shedding season; and (3) to give a brief overview of changes that occurred in the sucrose content of drying white oak (*Q. alba*) acorns.

Methods

Experiment 1

Acorns of cherrybark oak and water oak were collected and soaked overnight in tap water to ensure full hydration. Floaters were discarded. Half of the acorns were stored fully hydrated and the others half dried on a lab bench for 48 hours prior to storage. Acorns were stored in 4-mil polyethylene bags in lots of 110 to 120 acorns. Storage was at either 4 °C (39 °F) in a Lab-Line Ambi-Hi-Low Chamber (Lab-Line Instruments Incorporated, Melrose Park, IL) or at –2 °C (28 °F) in a modified chest freezer. Original germination percentages and MCs were determined and then tested at yearly intervals for up to 3 years. For germination tests, acorns were cut in half horizontally and the seed coat removed from the half containing the embryo. These sections were placed, cut side down, on moist Kimpac® and put in a Stultz germinator (Stultz Scientific Engineering Corporation, Springfield, IL) set at an alternating temperature regime of 20 °C (68 °F) for 16 hours in the dark and 30 °C (86 °F) for 8 hours with light (Bonner and Vozzo 1987). Acorns were germinated as two replications of 50 seeds per sampling period and were soaked overnight in tap water prior to germination testing. Counts were conducted weekly for 4 weeks. MCs of these fresh acorns were determined by drying two to four samples at 105 °C (221 °F) for 16 to 17 hours (ISTA 1993).

Experiment 2

Two large, open-grown white oak trees, less than 100 m (330 ft) apart, were selected for this study at Starkville, MS. Acorn collections began when the daily number of acorns shed reached at least 500, and ended when acorn fall dropped below 500. Collected acorns were marked with Uni-Paint® PX-21 Opaque oil-base paint-marking pens (Mitsubishi Pencil Company, Tokyo, Japan), a different color or color combination for each day of collection. Remaining acorns were raked aside so that only freshly shed acorns were collected each day. Marked acorns were placed under the canopy of a non-oak tree. On the last day of collection, all marked acorns were brought to the lab. Germination tests and MC determinations were performed as in experiment 1. Germination was tallied weekly for up to 4 weeks on 6 replications of 50 acorns from each day's collection. The number of acorns that germinated while acorns were still in the field was also recorded. MC was measured using five replications of three acorns each. Insect damage was recorded for each acorn cut open and used in the above two measurements and for all other acorns collected. Damage was recorded as either present or absent. Minimum and maximum temperatures, relative humidity, and rainfall data were obtained from the Mississippi State University weather site for the length of the collection period.

Experiment 3

We collected 2,000 white oak acorns, soaked them overnight in tap water, and spread them evenly on four trays lined with blotter paper. Acorns were divided into two subsets, wet and dry. The wet subset consisted of two trays of acorns that were covered with Kimpac®, kept at room temperature, and moistened throughout the 9-day experiment. The remaining two trays of acorns that were kept at room temperature and allowed to dehydrate were the dry subset. At intervals of 0, 1, 3, 5, 7, and 9 days, acorns were randomly selected from each subset and tested for germination, MC (as in experiment 1), and sucrose content via gas chromatography.

Sugars were extracted for the gas chromatography analyses as follows: at each sampling time, embryonic axes of white oak with immediately adjacent cotyledon tissue were dissected from the surrounding cotyledon tissue of 50 wet and 50 dry acorns; tissues were immediately frozen in liquid nitrogen and freeze-dried. The freeze-dried cotyledons were finely ground in a Wiley mill using a 20-mesh screen, while embryonic axis tissue was ground by hand with a mortar and pestle. A 0.3 to 0.5 g dry tissue sample was used for each carbohydrate extraction. The tissue sample was placed in 10 ml (0.3 oz) of an 80% ethanol solution and heated in a water bath at 75 °C (167 °F) for 1 hour. The sample was then filtered, rinsed with more of the ethanol solution, and rotoevaporated to dryness. The evaporation flask was rinsed with more of the ethanol solution and rotoevaported to dryness. The evaporation flask was rinsed with 10 ml (0.3 oz) of distilled water, and the water plus contents stirred with 1 g of Amberlite® MB-3 resin for 1 hour. This sample was then filtered, rinsed, and freeze-dried overnight. The dried sample was dissolved in 1 ml of trimethylsilylimidazole, heated in a water bath at 75 °C (167 °F) for 30 minutes, blown to dryness, and then redissolved in 1 ml chloroform and stored until analysis. Analyses were performed on an HP® 5890 gas chromatograph using a Supelco® SPB-5 capillary column (30 m x 0.25 mm ID x 0.25 film thickness). A minimum of three extractions were made from each cotyledon sample, and one or more from the embryonic axis sample, depending on amount of tissue available. Sucrose was identified by comparing it with a standard of the pure sugar prepared in a similar manner and injected onto the gas chromatograph.

Results

Experiment 1

Initial MC for water oak acorns was 30.5% and, after drying for 48 hours on the lab bench, 25.6%. Germination of the fresh acorns was 93%, while germination of acorns that were dried for 48 hours dropped to 84 % (fig. 1A). After 1 year of storage, we found that the temperature at which acorns were stored was significant, but acorn MC was not. Seeds stored at –2 °C (28 °F) had higher viability than those stored at 4 °C (39 °F). However, after 2 years of storage, the situation was reversed; MC of the stored acorns was significant, not temperature of storage. Acorns that had been dried prior to storage had lower viability than those that had not been dried; this pattern continued into year 3. Germination of dried acorns dropped to 25% or less by year 2, while acorns that were fully hydrated before storage germinated at about 50%. By year 3, hydrated acorns were still maintaining about 25% germination, while those dried before storage were dead.

Drying reduced the MC of cherrybark oak acorns by about 10%, from 29.6% to 19.9%, but had little effect on initial acorn viability, reducing it only 2%, from 100% to 98% (fig. 1B). Unlike water oak, temperature of storage was not significant.

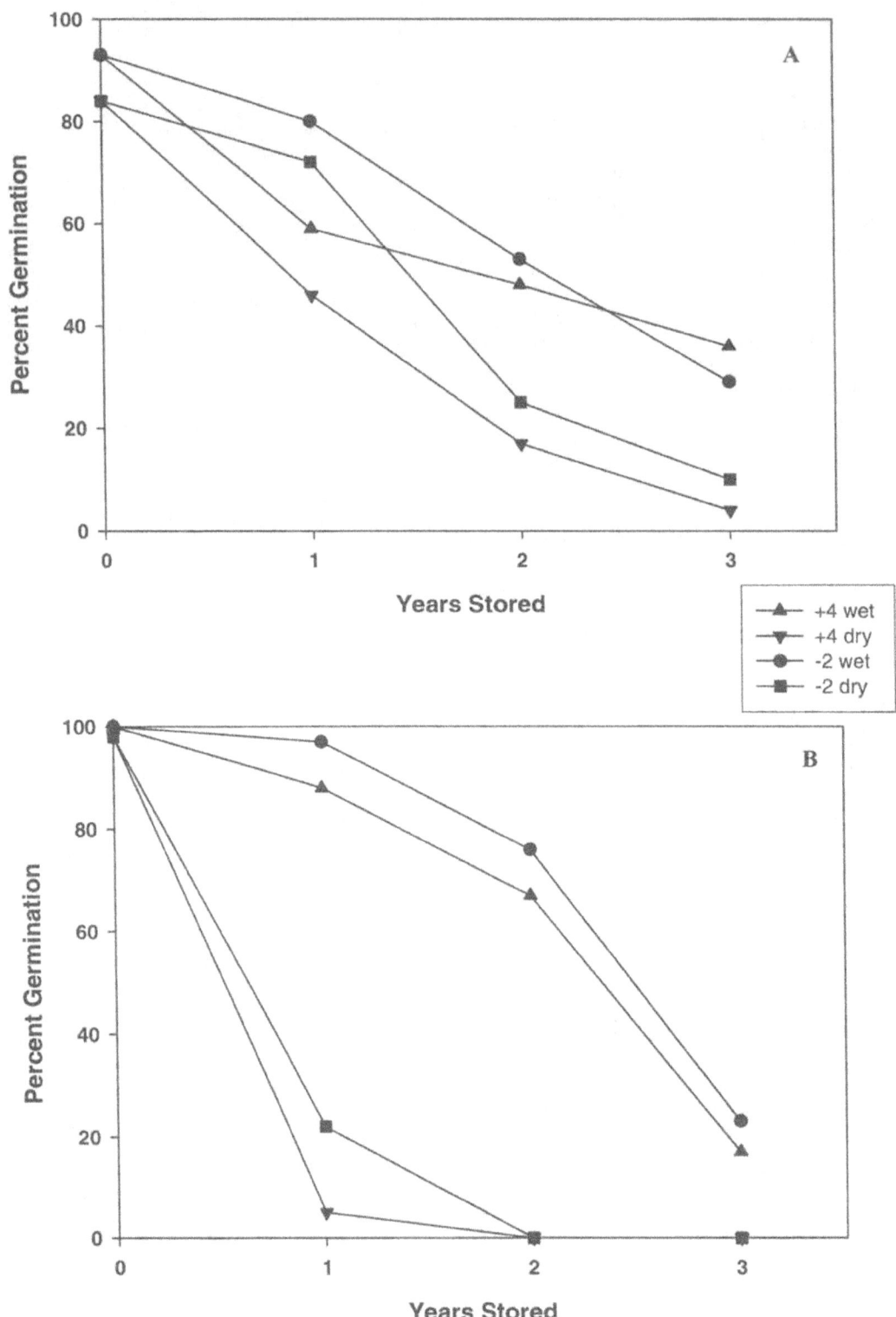

Figure 1. Germination percentage of water oak (A) and cherrybark oak (B) acorns stored at two different temperatures and two different moisture contents for 3 years.

MC, however, was highly significant, and acorns stored fully hydrated for 1 year retained viability over 88%, while germination of cherrybark oak acorns dried before storage dropped to 22% or less. After 2 years, germination of stored hydrated acorns remained a respectable 67% and 76% for acorns stored at 4 and 2 °C (39 and 36 °F), respectively.

Experiment 2

Acorn fall on Tree 1 began 7 days earlier than on Tree 2; the experiment on Tree 1 ran from 12 October through 26 October; the experiment on Tree 2 ran from 19 October through 1 November. Unlike the laboratory experiments, germination tests on acorns left in the field gave variable results, and no distinct pattern of decreasing viability was observed. Although some acorns remained in the field for 11 days, acorn MCs remained relatively high, never dropping below 37% on Tree 1 and 35% on Tree 2. In our laboratory experiments, white oak acorns dried to 22% MC in only 9 days.

The moderating effects of the rainfall that occurred throughout the experiment helped keep MC high in the acorns from both trees. Each tree's collection period had 8 days where some precipitation occurred. The higher germination percentage results from the field-collected acorns are probably a result of this higher MC.

We believe that the random declines in acorn viability we observed are more a reflection of problems in the germination cabinets than of physiological changes. The number of acorns being tested filled every tray in the four germination cabinets used for this experiment. We experienced some difficulty with moisture accumulation on the trays and resulting mold growth. It is our opinion that germination would have been uniformly high if the moisture wicking problems could have been controlled and mold growth reduced.

Although the two trees were separated by no more than 100 m (330 ft), the insect damage on Tree 1 was significantly higher than that on Tree 2 (fig. 2). On average, 66% of the acorns collected from Tree 1 in the first 4 days of the experiment were damaged, and this percentage did not drop below 40% throughout the experiment. Damage was much lower on Tree 2, averaging 19% over the first 4 days. Damage on this tree also peaked early in the experiment, supporting the claim that damaged acorns are the first to fall. Because we did not begin collecting acorns until 500 per day were available, damage may very well have been even higher in the early drop.

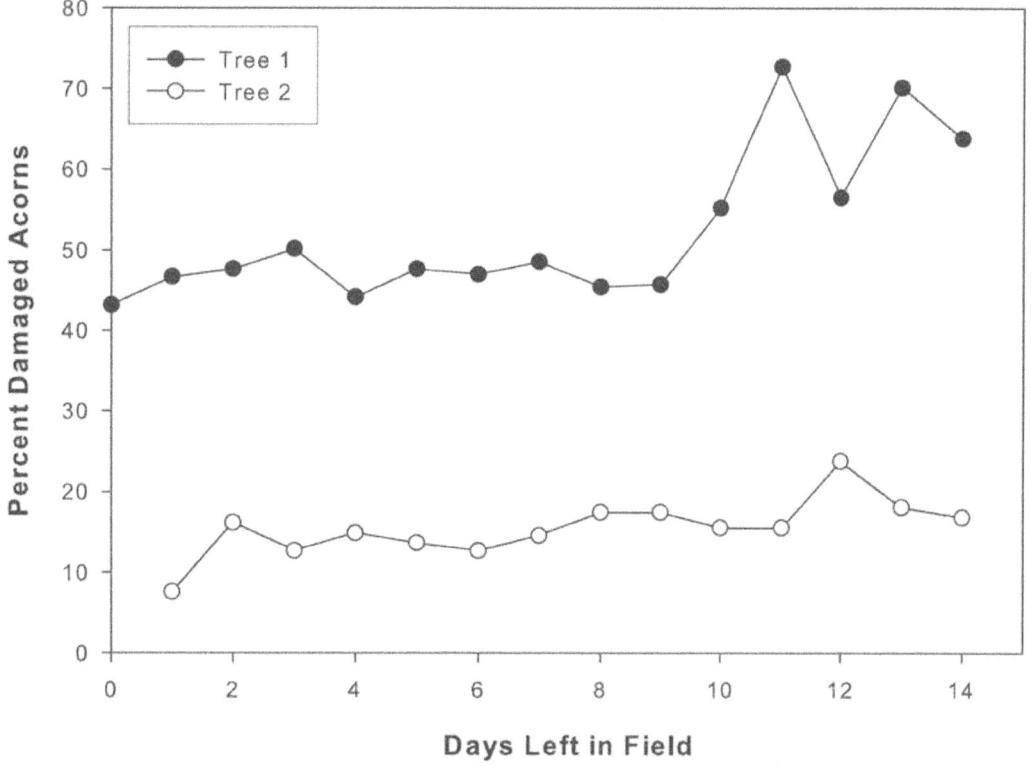

Figure 2. Percentage of insect-damaged acorns collected from trees 1 and 2. Data points to the left of the graph represent acorns that remained on the ground the least amount of time (shed last) before being brought into the laboratory for analyses.

Experiment 3

Initial acorn germination for the freshly collected white oak acorns was 80% (fig. 3). Drying acorns were dead after 9 days on the laboratory bench, while wet acorns had over 90% germination throughout the experiment. MC in the wet acorns remained high and fairly constant; moisture in the drying acorns fell from 44.6% to 22.2%.

Sucrose concentrations of the dry acorn embryonic axes and cotyledons were higher than those of the wet acorns throughout the experiment. Differences became significantly higher on day 5 of the experiment and remained so thereafter. Sucrose concentrations of the embryonic axes and cotyledon tissue were similar at the start of the experiment, but sucrose of the embryonic axes became significantly higher than that of the cotyledon tissue in both wet and dry acorns as the experiment progressed.

Discussion

Collecting and handling protocols for acorns are critical. If acorns are not collected for immediate use and MC falls before storing, seed quality can be negatively affected. Cherrybark and water oak acorns retained high viability for 2 years if stored fully hydrated (fig. 1). However, while the initial 48-hour drying period before storage reduced germination of water oak and cherrybark oak acorns only by 9% and 2%, respectively, dried water oak acorns stored at 4 °C (39 °F) and dried cherrybark acorns stored at either temperature had significant losses in viability after 1 year. After 2 years, germination of water oak acorns dried before storing was 25% or less, and dried cherrybark oak acorns were dead. Although losses of acorns stored fully hydrated to insects and fungi may be significant, drying acorns before storing results in critical quality reduction.

Interesting differences were observed between the two white oak trees used in experiment 2. Acorn shed began a full week earlier on Tree 1 than on Tree 2. Because the two trees are separated by less than 100 m (330 ft), and thus exposed to the same meteorological conditions, we attribute this to either significant morphological differences between the two trees in flowering times and acorn development, or to the high incidence of bug damage on Tree 1 (fig. 2).

MC was high in acorns from both trees throughout the experiment, primarily due to the amount of rainfall that occurred over the entire collection period, keeping the ground moist and relative humidity high. We believe because of this, and mild temperatures throughout the collection period, acorn germination also remained high. We still suggest that time and frequency of acorn collections should reflect weather conditions throughout the collection period. If temperatures are hot and drought conditions prevail, frequent collections should be the order of the day. While the results from this experiment have provided some interesting information, the tests obviously need to be repeated before definite conclusions can be drawn.

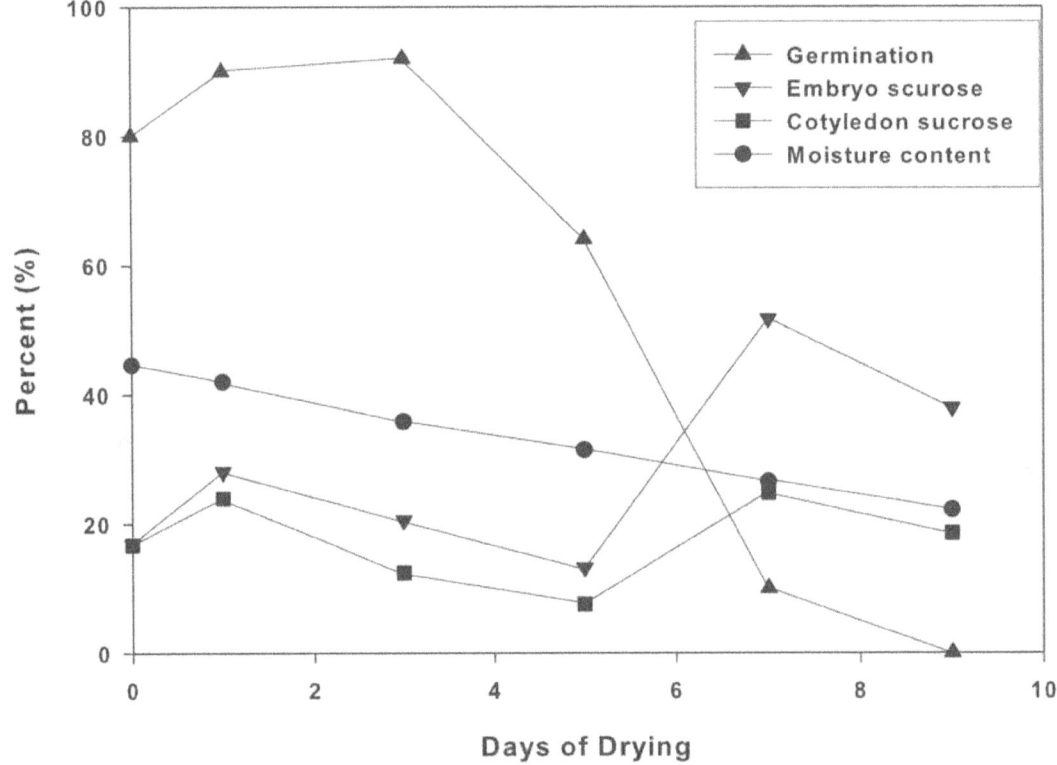

Figure 3. Germination, moisture content, and sucrose content of white oak embryonic axis and cotyledon tissues. Half of the acorns were allowed to dry out, while the remaining half were kept hydrated (wet) throughout the 9-day experiment.

We found a clear effect of desiccation on the sucrose contents of the embryonic axes and cotyledons in white oak acorns. The dry acorns overall had higher sucrose contents than the wet acorns throughout the experiment (fig. 3). Additionally, sucrose content in both the wet and dry embryonic axes was always higher than that of the cotyledon tissue. We suggest that, while this increase did not prevent loss of acorn viability, it did serve to initially protect against cellular collapse in the acorn tissues. Li and Sun (1999) reported that desiccation sensitivity of *Theobroma cacao* embryonic axes might be due to a decrease of enzymatic protection against oxidative stresses rather than a lack of sugar-related protective mechanisms during desiccation. They did not, however, find significant shifts in carbohydrate content during desiccation of axes.

Electron micrographs taken of desiccating embryonic axis and cotyledon tissue of white oak acorns (Connor and others 1996) show that cell membranes of the embryo and cotyledon tissues remain intact despite the stress imposed by lowering moisture contents. However, while the combination of high sucrose content and high axis moisture content may protect membranes in white oak acorn tissues, the mechanism is obviously not successful in preserving viability, which dropped rapidly after day 5 of the experiment.

References _____

Berjak P, Farrant JM, Mycock DJ, Pammenter NW. 1989. Homoiohydrous (recalcitrant) seeds: the enigma of their desiccation sensitivity and the state of water in axes of *Landolphia kirkii* Dyer. Planta 186:249-261.

Bonner FT, Vozzo JA. 1987. Seed biology and technology of Quercus. New Orleans (LA): USDA Forest Service, Southern Forest Experiment Station. General Technical Report SO-66. 21 p.

Connor KF, Bonner FT, Vozzo JA. 1996. Effects of desiccation on temperate recalcitrant seeds: differential scanning calorimetry, gas chromatography, electron microscopy, and moisture studies on *Quercus nigra* and *Quercus alba*. Canadian Journal of Forest Research 26:1813-1820.

Dereuddre J, Hassen M, Blandin S, Kaminski M. 1991. Resistance of alginate-coated somatic embryos of carrot (*Daucus carota* L.) to desiccation and freezing in liquid nitrogen: 2. thermal analysis. CryoLetters 12:135-148.

Ellis RH, Hong TD, Roberts EH. 1990. An intermediate category of seed storage behaviour? I. Coffee. Journal of Experimental Botany 41:1167-1174.

Fang J-Y, Wetten A, Hadley P. 2004. Cryopreservation of cocoa (*Theobroma cacao* L.) somatic embryos for long-term germplasm storage. Plant Science 166:669-675.

[ISTA] International Seed Testing Association. 1993. International rules for seed testing. Seed Science and Technology 21 (supplement, rules). 258 p.

Li C, Sun WQ. 1999. Desiccation sensitivity and activities of free-radical scavenging enzymes in recalcitrant *Theobroma cacao* seeds. Seed Science Research 9:209-217.

Mycock D, Wesley-Smith J, Berjak P. 1995. Cryopreservation of somatic embryos of 4 species with and without cryoprotectant pretreatment. Annals of Botany 75:331-336.

Roberts EH. 1973. Predicting the storage life of seeds. Seed Science and Technology 1:499-514.

Shibli RA, Al-Juboory KH. 2000. Cryopreservation of 'nabali' olive (*Olea europea* L.) somatic embryos by encapsulation-dehydration and encapsulation-vitrification. CryoLetters 21(6):357-366.

Touchell DH, Chiang VL, Tsai C-J. 2002. Cryopreservation of embryogenic cultures of *Picea mariana* (black spruce) using vitrification. Plant Cell Reports 21:118-124.

Towill LE, Bajaj YPS, editors. 2002. Cryopreservation of plant germplasm II. Biotechnology in agriculture and forestry series, volume 50. London (United Kingdom): Springer. 390 p.

Towill LE, Forsline P, Walters C, Waddell J, Laufmann J. 2004. Cryopreservation of Malus germplasm using a winter vegetative bud method: results from 1915 accessions. CryoLetters 25:323-334.

Wesley-Smith J, Vertucci CW, Berjak P, Pammenter NW, Crane J. 1992. Cryopreservation of desiccation-sensitive axes of *Camellia sinensis* in relation to dehydration, freezing rate and the thermal properties of tissue water. Journal of Plant Physiology 140:596-604.

Withers LA, King PJ. 1980. A simple freezing unit and routine cryopreservation method for plant cell cultures. CryoLetters 1:213-220.

Participants:

Western Forest and Conservation Nursery Association Meeting

Southern Forest Nursery Association Biennial Meeting

Ponderosa pine drawing by Lorraine Ashland, College of Natural Resources, University of Idaho.

Western Forest and Conservation
Nursery Association Meeting
Missoula, Montana (June 23 to 25, 2008)

Abbie Acuff
Potlatch Forest Holdings, Inc.
PO Box 1388
Lewiston, ID 83501
Tel: 208.799.1103
E-mail: Abbie.Acuff@potlatchcorp.com

Ronald Best
Colville Tribe Greenhouse
PO Box 72
Nespelem, WA 99155
Tel: 509.634.2321
E-mail: cctgreenhouse@cuonline.com

Brian Block
Montana Conservation Seedling
  Nursery
2705 Spurgin Road
Missoula, MT 59808
Tel: 406.549.3778

John Bruna
Idaho Department of Lands
3780 Industrial Avenue S
Coeur d'Alene, ID 83815
Tel: 208.666.8616
E-mail: jbruna@idl.idaho.gov

Maria Gabriela Buamscha
USDA Forest Service
Portland, OR 97204

Brian Cayson
Antal/Cayson Equipment
7474 SE Johnson Creek Boulevard
Portland, OR 97206
Tel: 503.775.5610
E-mail: plugpopper@aol.com

Rico Cruz
Confederated Tribes of the Umatilla
  Indian Reservation
Eastern Oregon University
PO Box 638
Pendleton, OR 97801
Tel: 541.966.2803
E-mail: ricocruz@ctuir.com

Jay Cushman
Sun-Gro Horticulture Inc.
11332 Karen Scott Drive
Oregon City, OR 97045
Tel: 503.655.0313
E-mail: jayc@sungro.com

Jude Danielson
USDA Forest Service
Dorena Genetic Resource Center
34963 Shoreview Road
Cottage Grove, OR 97424
Tel: 541.767.5711
E-mail: jdanielson@fs.fed.us

Anthony Davis
University of Idaho
Department of Forest Resources
PO Box 441133
Moscow, ID 83844
Tel: 208.885.7211
E-mail: asdavis@uidaho.edu

Kas Dumroese
USDA Forest Service
1221 South Main Street
Moscow, ID 83843
Tel: 208.883.2324
E-mail: kdumroese@fs.fed.us

Kent Eggleston
USDA Forest Service
Coeur d'Alene Nursery
3600 Nursery Road
Coeur d'Alene, ID 83815
Tel: 208.765.7391
E-mail: keggleston@fs.fed.us

Aram Eramian
USDA Forest Service
Coeur D'Alene Nursery
3600 Nursery Road
Coeur d'Alene, ID 83815
Tel: 208.765.7372
E-mail: aeramian@fs.fed.us

Glenn Fain
Auburn University
School of Forestry and Wildlife
  Sciences
Auburn, AL 36849
E-mail: gbf0002@auburn.edu

Richard Faltonson
41 Midnight Canyon Road
Nye, MT 59061
Tel: 406.328.6459
E-mail: faltonson@nemont.net

Meghan Fenoglio
OASIS Environmental Native
  Nursery
PO Box 582
Livingston, MT 59047
Tel: 406.222.7600
E-mail: m.fenoglio@oasisenviro.com

Clark Fleege
USDA Forest Service
Lucky Peak Nursery
15169 E Highway 21
Boise, ID 83716
Tel: 208.336.8232
E-mail: cfleege@fs.fed.us

Jacky Friedman
IFA Nurseries
1205 S Spring Street
Klamath Falls, OR 97601
Tel: 541.850.0952
E-mail: jfriedman@ifanurseries.com

Dave Grantz
Montana Conservation Seedling
  Nursery
1734 Missoula Avenue
Missoula, MT 59802
Tel: 406.493.0106

Nancy Heater
Weyerhaeuser Company
16014 Pletzer Road
Turner, OR 97392
Tel: 541.327.2212 ext 16
E-mail:
nancy.heater@weyerhaeuser.com

George Hernandez
USDA Forest Service
1720 Peachtree Road NW
Atlanta, GA 30309
Tel: 404.347.3554
E-mail: ghernandez@fs.fed.us

Kayla Herriman
University of Idaho
Department of Forest Resources
PO Box 441133
Moscow, ID 83844
E-mail:
kayla.traver@vandals.uidaho.edu

Jol Hodgson
Beaver Plastics Limited
7-23618-TWP Road 531A
Acheson, AB T7X 5A3 CANADA
Tel: 888.453.5961
E-mail: tjhodgson@shaw.ca

Matt Howell
University of Georgia Extension
Forest Resources 4-433
Athens, GA 30602
Tel: 706.614.0103
E-mail: mhowell@sref.info

Amber Jackson
Montana Conservation Seedling
  Nursery
2705 Spurgin Road
Missoula, MT 59804
Tel: 406.542.4244
E-mail: ajackson@mt.gov

Scott Jensen
USDA Forest Service
735 N 500 E
Provo, UT 84606
Tel: 801.356.5128
E-mail: sljensen@fs.fed.us

Tom Jopson
Cal Forest Nurseries
PO Box 719
Etna, CA 96027
Tel: 530.467.5211
E-mail: calforest@sisqtel.net

John Justin
Montana Conservation Seedling
  Nursery
2705 Spurgin Road
Missoula, MT 59804
Tel: 406.542.4327
E-mail: jjustin@mt.gov

Robert Karrfalt
National Seed Laboratory
5675 Riggins Mill Road
Dry Branch, GA 31020
Tel: 478.751.3551
E-mail: rkarrfalt@fs.fed.us

Rob Keefe
University of Idaho
Department of Forest Resources
PO Box 441133
Moscow, ID 83844
E-mail: rkeefe@vandals.uidaho.edu

Gary Kees
USDA Forest Service
5785 Highway 10 West
Missoula, MT 59808
Tel: 406.829.6752
E-mail: gkees@fs.fed.us

Nabil Khadduri
Washington State Department of
  Natural Resources
Webster Nursery
PO Box 47017
Olympia, WA 98504
Tel: 360.586.4117
E-mail: nabil.khadduri@dnr.wa.gov

Charlie Krebs
USDA Forest Service
PO Box 3623
Portland, OR 97208
Tel: 503.808.2729
E-mail: ckrebs@fs.fed.us

Tom Landis
Native Plant Nursery Consulting
3248 Sycamore Way
Medford, OR 97504
Tel: 541.245.6892
E-mail: nurseries@aol.com

Tim Lichatowich
Natural Industries, Inc.
6223 Theall Road
Houston, TX 77066
Tel: 281.580.1643
E-mail: timl@naturalindustries.com

Doug McCreary
University of California
8279 Scott Forbes Road
Browns Valley, CA 95918
Tel: 530.639.8807
E-mail:
mccreary@nature.berkeley.edu

Deborah McLean
Washington State Department of
  Natural Resources
Webster Nursery
PO Box 47017
Olympia, WA 98504
Tel: 360.386.4117
E-mail: deborah.mclean@dnr.wa.gov

Robert McNitt
Forest Seedling Network
1740 Shaff Road #306
Stayton, OR 97383
Tel: 503.769.2520
E-mail:
bob@forestseedlingnetwork.com

Joe Myers
USDA Forest Service
Coeur d'Alene Nursery
3600 Nursery Road
Coeur d'Alene, ID 83815
Tel: 208.765.7387
E-mail: jfmyers@fs.fed.us

Celia Ochoa
Rancho San Agustin
Km 32,5 Autopista Tenango
  Ixtapan de la
Villa Guerrero, Mexico
Tel: 52 714 140 7676
E-mail:
celia@ranchosanagustin.com.mx

Ronald Overton
USDA Forest Service
Purdue University
PFEN, 715 West State Street
West Lafayette, IN 47907
Tel: 765.496.6417
E-mail: overtonr@purdue.edu

Barbara Peterson
Lava Nursery
PO Box 370
Parkdale, OR 97041
Tel: 541.352.7303
E-mail: lavanursery@aol.com

Jeremy Pinto
USDA Forest Service
1221 S Main Street
Moscow, ID 83843
Tel: 208.883.2352
E-mail: jpinto@fs.fed.us

Brian Quilter
Montana Conservation Seedling
  Nursery
2705 Spurgin Road
Missoula, MT 59801
Tel: 406.542.4334
E-mail: bquilter@mt.gov

Nita Rauch
USDA Forest Service
Bend Seed Extractory
63095 Deschutes Market Road
Bend, OR 97701
Tel: 541.383.5646
E-mail: nrauch@fs.fed.us

Lee Riley
USDA Forest Service
Dorena Genetic Resource Center
34963 Shoreview Drive
Cottage Grove, OR 97424
Tel: 541.767.5723
E-mail: leriley@fs.fed.us

Susan Rinehart
USDA Forest Service
200 E Broadway
Missoula, MT 59802
Tel: 406.329.3669
E-mail: srinehart@fs.fed.us

Amanda Roberson
Montana Conservation Seedling
 Nursery
2705 Spurgin Road
Missoula, MT 59801

Bill Sayward
Itasca Greehouse, Inc.
PO Box 273
Cohasset, MN 55721
Tel: 218.328.6261
E-mail: info@itascagreenhouse.com

Janice Schaefer
Western Forest Systems, Inc.
3731 15th Street
Lewiston, ID 83501
Tel: 208.743.0147
E-mail:
scahaeferj@valley.internet.net

Marla Schwartz
North Woods Nursery
PO Box 149
Elk River, ID 83827
Tel: 208.826.3408
E-mail: idahoice@tds.net

Glenda Scott
USDA Forest Service
PO Box 7669
Missoula, MT 59807
Tel: 406.329.3122
E-mail: glscott@fs.fed.us

Hunter Smith
Portco Packaging
3601 SE Columbia Way, Suite 260
Vancouver, WA 98661
Tel: 360.696.1641 ext 5239
E-mail: hsmith@portco.com

Paul Michael Stormo
Champoeg Nursery Inc.
9661 Yergen Road NE
Aurora, OR 97002
Tel: 503.678.6348
E-mail: info@champoegnursery.com

Kent Stralbiski
K&C Silviculture Limited
Box 459
Oliver, BC V0H 1T0 Canada
Tel: 250.498.4974
E-mail: kent@silviculture.com

Eric Stuewe
Stuewe and Sons Inc.
2290 SE Kiger Island Drive
Corvallis, OR 97333
Tel: 541.757.7798
E-mail: eric@stuewe.com

Seth Swanson
Lawyer Nursery
7515 Meridian Road SE
Olympia, WA 98513
Tel: 360.456.1839
E-mail: seths@lawyernursery.com

Gale Thompson
Weyerhaeuser Rochester Greenhouse
7935 Highway 12 SW
Rochester, WA 98579
Tel: 360.273.5527 ext 113
E-mail:
gale.thompson@weyerhaeuser.com

Eric van Steenis
TerraLink Horticulture Inc.
464 Riverside Road
Abbotsford, BC V2S 7M1 Canada
Tel: 604.864.9044
E-mail:
eric@terralink-horticulture.com

Ron Webb
Arbutus Grove Nursery Limited
9721 West Saanich Road
Sidney, BC V8C 5T5 Canada
Tel: 250.656.4162
E-mail: info@arbutusgrove.com

Gloria Whitefeather-Spears
Redlake Department of Natural
 Resources
PO Box 279
Red Lake, MN 56671
Tel: 218.679.3310
E-mail: gspears@paulbunyan.net

Heather Whiteley
Montana Conservation Seedling
 Nursery
2705 Spurgin Road
Missoula, MT 59801
Tel: 406.542.4244
E-mail: hwhiteley@mt.gov

Don Willis
Jiffy Products
5401 Baumhart Road Suite B
Lorain, OH 44053
Tel: 800.323.1047
E-mail: dewjif@aol.com

Richard Zabel
Western Forestry and Conservation
 Association
4033 SW Canyon Road
Portland, OR 97221
Tel: 503.226.4562

Southern Forest Nursery
Association Biennial Meeting
Asheville, North Carolina (July 12 to 24, 2008)

Doug Akin
Arkansas Forestry Commission
3821 W Roosevelt Road
Little Rock, AR 72204
Tel: 501.296.1861
E-mail: doug.akin@arkansas.gov

Tom Anderson
Plum Creek Timber
1444 Shubuta Eucutta Road
Shubuta, MS 39360
Tel: 601.687.5766
E-mail:
tom.anderson@plumcreek.com

Dave Andres
North Carolina Division of Forest
  Resources
1616 Mail Service Center
Raleigh, NC 27699
Tel: 919.857.4811
E-mail: dave.andres@ncmail.net

Mike Arnette
South Carolina SuperTree Nursery
5594 Highway 38 S
Blenheim, SC 29516
Tel: 800.222.1290
E-mail: dmarnet@arborgen.com

Wayne Bagwell
Sun-Gro Horticulture Inc.
3011 Quarles Drive
Canton, GA 30115
Tel: 770.479.0232
E-mail: wayneb@sungro.com

Jill Barbour
USDA Forest Service
5675 Riggins Mill Road
Dry Branch, GA 31020
Tel: 478.751.3551
E-mail: jbarbour@fs.fed.us

Richard Barham
International Paper
3659 Castle Pointe Drive
Southaven, MS 38672
Tel: 912.655.7946
E-mail: barhamjm@yahoo.com

James Barnett
USDA Forest Service—Emeritus
2500 Shreveport Highway
Pineville, LA 71360
Tel: 318.473.7214
E-mail: jpbarnett@fs.fed.us

Wayne Bell
International Forest Company
1265 Georgia Highway 133 N
Moultrie, GA 31768
Tel: 800.633.4506
E-mail: wbell@interforestry.com

Aaron Bodenhamer
Bodenhamer Farms and Nursery
6392 Kitchen Street
Rowland, NC 28383
Tel: 910.422.8588
E-mail: bodie@carolina.net

Louie Bodenhamer
Bodenhamer Farms and Nursery
6547 Kitchen Street
Rowland, NC 28383
Tel: 910.422.8118
E-mail: bodenhamer@carolina.net

Ralph Bower
Weyerhaeuser Company
3890 Highway 28 W
Camden, AL 36726
Tel: 334.682.9882 ext 21
E-mail:
ralph.bower@weyerhaeuser.com

Dave Bowling
Arkansas Forestry Commission
3821 W Roosevelt Road
Little Rock, AR 72204
Tel: 501.296.1859
E-mail: david.bowling@arkansas.gov

Josh Bronson
USDA Forest Service
1579 Brevard Road
Asheville, NC 28806
E-mail: jjbronson@fs.fed.us

Allen Brown
Louisiana Department of Agriculture
  and Forestry
PO Box 1388
Columbia, LA 71418
Tel: 318.649.7501

Sam Campbell
Molpus Timberlands Management
29650 Comstock Road
Elberta, AL 36530
Tel: 251.986.5210
E-mail: scampbell@molpus.com

Stephen Cantrell
South Carolina Forestry Commission
PO Box 219
Trenton, SC 29847
Tel: 803.275.3578
E-mail: taylortree@pbtcomm.net

Kristina Connor
USDA Forest Service
520 Devall Drive
Auburn, AL 36849
Tel: 334.826.8700
E-mail: kconnor@fs.fed.us

Michael Cornett
Temperature Control Solutions
6463 Flowers Road
Wilson, NC 27893
Tel: 252.291.5045
E-mail: mcornett@tcstk.com

Roger Cornett
Temperature Control Solutions
6463 Flowers Road
Wilson, NC 27893
Tel: 252.291.5045

Kelly Coyle
International Forest Company
1265 Georgia Highway 133 N
Moultrie, GA 31768
Tel: 229.985.5959

Mike Coyle
International Paper Company
1265 Georgia Highway 133N
Moultrie, GA 31768
Tel: 229.985.5959
E-mail: mcoyle@interforestry.com

Michelle Cram
USDA Forest Service
320 Green Street
Athens, GA 30605
Tel: 706.559.4233
E-mail: mcram@fs.fed.us

Barbara Crane
USDA Forest Service
1720 Peachtree Road NW
Atlanta, GA 30309
Tel: 404.347.4039
E-mail: barbaracrane@fs.fed.us

Ronnie Creech
North Carolina Division of Forest
 Resources
762 Claridge Nursery Road
Goldsboro, NC 27530
Tel: 919.731.7988
E-mail: ronnie.creech@ncmail.net

Robert Cross
Georgia SuperTree Nursery/ArborGen
#78 SuperTree Lane
Shellman, GA 39886
Tel: 229.679.5640
E-mail: recross@arborgen.com

Jude Danielson
USDA Forest Service
Dorena Genetic Resource Center
34963 Shoreview Road
Cottage Grove, OR 97424
Tel: 541.767.5711
E-mail: jdanielson@fs.fed.us

Charles Bingham Davey
North Carolina State University—
 Emeritus
5219 Melbourne Road
Raleigh, NC 27606
Tel: 919.851.1168
E-mail: char1168@bellsouth.net

Gary Delaney
Louisiana Forest Seed Company
303 Forestry Road
Lecompte, LA 71346
Tel: 318.443.5026
E-mail: gdelaney@lfsco.com

Eddie Denny
Hendrix and Dail, Inc.
PO Box 648
Greenville, NC 27835
Tel: 252.758.4263

Kelly Dougherty
Rayonier
PO Box 456
Glennville, GA 30427
Tel: 912.654.4065
E-mail: kelly.dougherty@rayonier.com

Kas Dumroese
USDA Forest Service
1221 South Main Street
Moscow, ID 83843
Tel: 208.883.2324
E-mail: kdumroese@fs.fed.us

Scott Enebak
Auburn University
602 Duncan Drive
Auburn University, AL 36849
Tel: 334.844.1028
E-mail: enebasa@auburn.edu

Jim Engel
Engel's Nursery
2080 64th Street
Fennville, MI 49408
Tel: 269.543.4123
E-mail: info@engelsnursery.com

Mary Engel
Engel's Nursery
2080 64th Street
Fennville, MI 49408
Tel: 269.543.4123
E-mail: info@engelsnursery.com

Larry Estes
Virginia Department of Forestry
PO Box 160
Crimora, VA 24431
Tel: 540.363.7000
E-mail: larry.estes@dof.virginia.gov

Larry Foster
ArborGen LLC
264 Country Road 888
Selma, AL 36703
Tel: 334.872.5452
E-mail: lhfoste@arborgen.com

Michelle Frank
USDA Forest Service
Northeastern Research Station
11 Campus Boulevard—Suite 200
Newtown Square, PA 19073
Tel: 610.557.4113
E-mail: mfrank@fs.fed.us

Emile Gardiner
USDA Forest Service
PO Box 227
Stoneville, MS 38776
Tel: 662.686.3184
E-mail: egardiner@fs.fed.us

Richard Garrett
Maryland State Department of
 Natural Resources
Ayton Tree Nursery
3424 Gallagher Road
Preston, MD 21655
Tel: 410.673.2467
E-mail: rgarrett@dnr.state.md.us

Steven Gilly
Florida Division of Forestry
Andrews Nursery
PO Box 849
Chiefland, FL 32544
Tel: 352.493.6096
E-mail: gillys@doacs.state.fl.us

Tony Ginn
North Carolina Division of Forest
 Resources
762 Claridge Nursery Road
Goldsboro, NC 27530
Tel: 919.731.7988
E-mail: tony.ginn@ncmail.net

Steve Godbehere
Hendrix and Dail, Inc.
186 Deer Hill Drive
Ochlockonee, GA 31773
Tel: 229.387.4256
E-mail: stevegodbehere@usa.net

Laura Gurley
North Carolina Division of Forest
 Resources
762 Claridge Nursery Road
Goldsboro, NC 27530
Tel: 919.731.7988
E-mail: laura.gurley@ncmail.net

Kinney Hanchey
Louisiana Department of Agriculture
 and Forestry
PO Box 935
DeRidder, LA 70634
Tel: 337.463.5509

Beat Hauenstein
Bartschi-FOBRO, LLC
1715 Airpark Drive
Grand Haven, MI 49417
Tel: 616.847.0300
E-mail: beat.hauenstein@fobro.com

Selby Hawk
North Carolina Division of Forest
 Resources
2572 Mountain Home Road
Morgantown, NC 28655
Tel: 828.413.3195
E-mail: selbyhawk@charter.net

George Hernandez
USDA Forest Service
1720 Peachtree Road NW
Atlanta, GA 30309
Tel: 404.347.3554
E-mail: ghernandez@fs.fed.us

Drew Hinnant
North Carolina Division of Forest
 Resources
762 Claridge Nursery Road
Goldsboro, NC 27530
Tel: 919.222.4168
E-mail: drew.hinnant@ncmail.net

Stanley Hinson
Southern Seed Company
PO Box 340
Baldwin, GA 30511
Tel: 706.968.9284

Jol Hodgson
Beaver Plastics Limited
7-23618-TWP Road 531A
Acheson, AB T7X 5A3 Canada
Tel: 888.453.5961
E-mail: tjhodgson@shaw.ca

Anna Hollifield
North Carolina Division of Forest
 Resources
6321 Linville Falls Highway
Newland, NC 28657
Tel: 828.733.5236
E-mail: anna.hollifield@ncmail.net

David Horvath
Illinois State Department of Natural
 Resources
17885 N County Road 2400E
Topeka, IL 61567
Tel: 309.535.2185
E-mail: dave.horvath@illinois.gov

Gregory Hoss
Missouri Department of Conservation
14027 Shafer Road
Licking, MO 65542
Tel: 573.674.3229
E-mail: greg.hoss@mdc.mo.gov

Matt Howell
University of Georgia Extension
Forest Resources 4-433
Athens, GA 30602
Tel: 706.614.0103
E-mail: mhowell@sref.info

Bill Hubbard
Southern Regional Extension Forestry
Room 433, Forestry Building 4
University of Georgia
Athens, GA 30602-2152
Tel: 706.542.7813
E-mail: whubbard@uga.edu

Scott Huff
Oklahoma Department of Agriculture,
 Food, and Forestry
830 NE 12th Avenue
Goldsby, OK 73093
Tel: 405.288.2385
E-mail: scott.huff@oda.state.ok.us

Jason Huffman
West Virginia Division of Forestry
Clements State Tree Nursery
PO Box 8
West Columbia, WV 25287
Tel: 304.675.1820
E-mail:
clements.state.treenursery@wv.gov

Paul Jackson
Auburn University
3301 School of Forestry Building
Auburn, AL 36849
Tel: 334.844.8071
E-mail: dpj0001@auburn.edu

Roger Jacob
Iowa Department of Natural
 Resources
2404 S Duff
Ames, IA 50201
Tel: 515.233.1161
E-mail: roger.jacob@dnr.iowa.gov

Carolyn Jernigan
North Carolina Division of Forest
 Resources
762 Claridge Nursery Road
Goldsboro, NC 27530
Tel: 919.731.7988
E-mail:
carolyn.g.jernigan@ncmail.net

Robert Karrfalt
National Seed Laboratory
5675 Riggins Mill Road
Dry Branch, GA 31020
Tel: 478.751.3551
E-mail: rkarrfalt@fs.fed.us

Jeff Kozar
Department of Conservation and
 Natural Resources/Bureau of Forestry
Penn Nursery
137 Penn Nursery Road
Spring Mills, PA 16875
Tel: 814.364.5150
E-mail: jekozar@state.pa.us

Clyde Leggins
North Carolina Division of Forest
 Resources
220 Old Colony Road
Morgantown, NC 28655
Tel: 828.438.3793
E-mail: clyde.leggins@ncmail.net

Jimmy Lisenby
South Carolina Forestry Commission
PO Box 219
Trenton, SC 29847
Tel: 803.275.3578
E-mail: jlisenby@starband.net

Rob Lovelace
Lovelace Seeds Inc.
1187 Brownsmill Road
Elsberry, MO 63343
Tel: 573.898.2103
E-mail: judy.lovelace@sbcglobal.com

George Lowerts
ArborGen LLC
PO Box 56
Bellville, GA 30414
Tel: 912.739.4721
E-mail: galower@arborgen.com

Monty Maldonado
USDA Forest Service
201 14th Street SW
Washington, DC 20250

Maxie Maynor
North Carolina Division of Forest
 Resources
762 Claridge Nursery Road
Goldsboro, NC 27530
Tel: 919.731.7988
E-mail: maxie.maynor@ncmail.net

Steve McKeand
Department of Forestry and
 Environmental Resources
North Carolina State University
PO Box 8008
Raleigh, NC 27695
Tel: 919.515.6073
E-mail: steve_mckeand@ncsu.edu

Andy Meeks
Meeks' Farms and Nursery, Inc.
187 Flanders Road
Kite, GA 31049
Tel: 478.299.2999

John Mexal
New Mexico State University
Box 3Q Skeen Hall 127
Las Cruces, NM 88003
Tel: 505.646.3335
E-mail: jmexal@nmsu.edu

Brad Miller
Weyerhaeuser Company
169 Weyerhaeuser Road
Aiken, SC 29801
Tel: 803.649.0489 ext 22
E-mail:
brad.miller2@weyerhaeuser.com

Allan Murray
Arkansas Forestry Commission
1402 Highway 391N
North Little Rock, AR 72117
Tel: 501.907.2485
E-mail:
baucumnursery@arkansas.gov

Kim Mushrush
ArborGen LLC
PO Box 56
Bellville, GA 30414
Tel: 912.739.4721
E-mail: kamushr@arborgen.com

Al Myatt
Oklahoma Department of Agriculture
and Forestry
830 NE 12th Avenue
Goldsby, OK 73093
Tel: 405.288.2385
E-mail: amyatt@oda.state.ok.us

Gary Lee Nelson
Arborgen, LLC
5594 Highway 38 S
Blenheim, SC 29516
Tel: 843.528.3203
E-mail: glnelso@arborgen.com

Ronald Overton
USDA Forest Service
Purdue University
PFEN, 715 West State Street
West Lafayette, IN 47907
Tel: 765.496.6417
E-mail: overtonr@purdue.edu

Greg Pate
North Carolina Forest Service
762 Claridge Nursery Road
Goldsboro, NC 27530
Tel: 919.731.7988 ext 216
E-mail: greg.pate@ncmail.net

Ed Peele
Jiffy
Lorain, OH

Beverly Peoples
Texas SuperTree Nursery
1235 FM 3198 West
Bullard, TX 75757
Tel: 903.825.6101 ext 24
E-mail:
beverly.peoples@arborgen.com

Jeremy Pinto
USDA Forest Service
1221 S Main Street
Moscow, ID 83843
Tel: 208.883.2352
E-mail: jpinto@fs.fed.us

Archie Poppell
Rayonier
PO Box 456
Glennville, GA 30427
Tel: 912.654.4065
E-mail: archie.poppell@rayonier.com

Randy Rentz
Louisiana Department of Agriculture
and Forestry
PO Box 1388
Columbia, LA 71418
Tel: 318.649.7501

Jim Rideout
North Carolina Division of Forest
Resources
6321 Linville Falls Highway
Newland, NC 28657
Tel: 828.733.5236
E-mail: jim.rideout@ncmail.net

Lee Riley
USDA Forest Service
Dorena Genetic Resource Center
34963 Shoreview Drive
Cottage Grove, OR 97424
Tel: 541.767.5723
E-mail: leriley@fs.fed.us

Ken Roeder
North Carolina Division of Forest
Resources
762 Claridge Nursery Road
Goldsboro, NC 27530
Tel: 919.731.7988
E-mail: ken.roeder@ncmail.net

Tommy Rogers
Florida Division of Forestry
Andrews Nursery
PO Box 849
Chiefland, FL 32544-0849
Tel: 352.493.6096
E-mail: rogerst@doacs.state.fl.us

Robin Rose
Oregon State University
College of Forestry
Corvallis, OR 97331
Tel: 541.737.6580
E-mail: robin.rose@orst.edu

Christopher Rosier
CellFor
13 Ballastone Court
Savannah, GA 31410
Tel: 904.753.3713
E-mail: crosier@cellfor.com

Ed Saksa
West Virginia Division of Forestry
Clements Nursery
624 Forestry Drive
West Columbia, WV 25287
Tel: 304.675.1820
E-mail:
clements.state.treenursery@wv.gov

Jerry Scott
Georgia Forestry Commission/Flat
River Nursery
9850 River Road
Byronville, GA 31007
Tel: 229.268.7308
E-mail: jscott@gfc.state.ga.us

Greg Seabolt
Georgia Forestry Commission/Flat
River Nursery
9850 River Road
Byronville, GA 31007
Tel: 229.268.7308

Doug Sharp
Plum Creek
161 N Macon Street
Jesup, GA 31545
Tel: 912.588.9798 ext 13
E-mail: doug.sharp@plumcreek.com

Doug Shelburne
Smurfit-Stone Rock Creek Nursery
4346 Parker Springs Road
Brewton, AL 36426
Tel: 251.867.9480
E-mail: dshelburne@smurfit.com

James Shelton
Arkansas Forestry Commission
1402 Highway 391N
North Little Rock, AR 72117
Tel: 501.907.2485
E-mail: baucumnursery@arkansas.gov

Jill Sidebottom
North Carolina State University
455 Research Drive
Mills River, NC 28732-9244
Tel: 828.684.3562
E-mail: jill_sidebottom@ncsu.edu

Paul Sisco
Southern Appalachian Regional Office
The American Chestnut Foundation
One Oak Plaza, Suite 308
Asheville, NC 28801
E-mail: paul@acf.org

Hunter Smith
Portco Packaging
3601 SE Columbia Way, Suite 260
Vancouver, WA 98661
Tel: 360.696.1641 ext 5239
E-mail: hsmith@portco.com

David South
Auburn University Nursery Cooperative
495 Lee Road 14
Auburn, AL 36830
Tel: 334.844.1022
E-mail: southdb@auburn.edu

David Sparkman
105 South Wilkinson Drive
St Pauls, NC 28384
Tel: 910.865.1075

Dwight Stallard
Virginia Department of Forestry
19127 Sandy Hill Road
Courtland, VA 23837
Tel: 804.834.2855
E-mail:
dwight.stallard@dof.virginia.gov

Tom Starkey
Auburn University
School of Forestry and Wildlife Sciences
602 Duncan Drive
Auburn, AL 36849
Tel: 334.844.8069
E-mail: starkte@auburn.edu

Bradley Stevens
North Carolina Division of Forest
  Resources
762 Claridge Nursery Road
Goldsboro, NC 27530
Tel: 919.731.7988
E-mail: bradley.stevens@ncmail.net

Shannon Stewart
ArborGen LLC
3535 Nursery Road
Livingston, TX 77351
Tel: 936.563.2302
E-mail: smstewa@arborgen.com

Tim Stewart
Campbell Timberland Management
2027 CR 101
Jasper, TX 75951
Tel: 409.384.6164
E-mail: tstewart@campbellgroup.com

Eric Stuewe
Stuewe and Sons Inc.
2290 SE Kiger Island Drive
Corvallis, OR 97333
Tel: 541.757.7798
E-mail: eric@stuewe.com

Larry Such
North Carolina Forest Service
1616 Mail Service Center
Raleigh, NC 27699
Tel: 919.857.4854
E-mail: larry.such@ncmail.net

Don Thompson
NE Mississippi Community College
20 CR 84
Golden, MS 38847
Tel: 662.676.2980
E-mail: dhthompson@nemcc.edu

William Upchurch
Hendrix and Dail, Inc.
PO Box 648
Greenville, NC 27835
Tel: 252.758.4263

Craig VanSickle
Minnesota State Department of
  Natural Resources
Badoura Nursery
13885 State 64
Akeley, MN 56433
Tel: 218.732.5107
E-mail:
craig.vansickle@dnr.state.mn.us

Victor Vankus
USDA Forest Service
5675 Riggins Mill Road
Dry Branch, GA 31020
Tel: 478.751.3551
E-mail: vvankus@fs.fed.us

Ron Walden
Sun-Gro Horticulture Inc.
3011 Quarles Drive
Canton, GA 30115
Tel: 770.479.0232
E-mail: wayneb@sungro.com

Lucy Walker
Weyerhaueser Company
1123 Dinah's Landing Road
Washington, NC 27889
Tel: 252.948.2720
E-mail:
lucy.walker@weyerhaeuser.com

James West
North Carolina Division of Forest
  Resources
762 Claridge Nursery Road
Goldsboro, NC 27530
Tel: 919.731.7988
E-mail: james.west@ncmail.net

Sam Wiggins
Knud Nielsen Company Inc.
PO Box 746
Evergreen, AL 36401
Tel: 251.227.0641
E-mail: sam@knudnielsen.com

Rick Williams
Williams Forestry and Associates
PO Box 1543
Calhoun, GA 30703
Tel: 706.629.0353
E-mail: rjwfa@mindspring.com

Don Willis
Jiffy Products
5401 Baumhart Road Suite B
Lorain, OH 44053
Tel: 800.323.1047
E-mail: dewjif@aol.com

Ken Woody
Plum Creek
1689 Nursery Road
Jesup, GA 31546
Tel: 912.427.4571
E-mail: ken.woody@plumcreek.com

www.ingramcontent.com/pod-product-compliance
Lightning Source LLC
Chambersburg PA
CBHW081219280526
45787CB00006B/2450